The New Latin America

The New Latin America

Fernando Calderón and Manuel Castells

Translated by Ramsey McGlazer

polity

First published in Spanish as *La nueva América Latina* by Fondo de Cultura Económica 2019

This English edition © Polity Press 2020

Polity Press
65 Bridge Street
Cambridge CB2 1UR, UK

Polity Press
101 Station Landing
Suite 300
Medford, MA 02155, USA

ISBN-13: 978-1-5095-4001-3 – hardback
ISBN-13: 978-1-5095-4002-0 – paperback

A catalogue record for this book is available from the British Library.

Library of Congress Cataloging-in-Publication Data
Names: Calderón G., Fernando, author.
Title: The new Latin America / Fernando Calderón and Manuel Castells ;
    translated by Ramsey McGlazer.
Other titles: Nueva America Latina.
Description: Cambridge ; Medford, MA : Polity Press, 2020. | Includes
    bibliographical references and index. | Translated from Spanish. |
    Summary: "A comprehensive and up-to-date analysis of Latin America
    today"-- Provided by publisher.
Identifiers: LCCN 2019057548 (print) | LCCN 2019057549 (ebook) | ISBN
    9781509540013 (hardback) | ISBN 9781509540020 (paperback) | ISBN
    9781509540037 (epub)
Subjects: LCSH: Latin America--Economic conditions--21st century. | Latin
    America--Social conditions--21st century.
Classification: LCC HC125 .C243313 2020 (print) | LCC HC125 (ebook) | DDC
    330.98--dc23
LC record available at https://lccn.loc.gov/2019057548
LC ebook record available at https://lccn.loc.gov/2019057549

Typeset in 10.5 on 12 pt Sabon by
Servis Filmsetting Ltd, Stockport, Cheshire
Printed and bound in Great Britain by TJ International Limited

For further information on Polity, visit our website: politybooks.com

CONTENTS

v

CONTENTS

FIGURES AND TABLES

Figures

Tables

ACKNOWLEDGMENTS

This book has had a peculiar trajectory. It began as a shared intellectual project, one that developed during a seven-year period, drawing on the empirical research of a group of scholars from 11 Latin American countries who studied the region's transformation during the first decades of the twenty-first century. But each of us also traveled along separate paths through various countries, gathering information and reflecting on our findings, together with a broad range of colleagues and friends who helped us to understand the complex context that is Latin America. For this reason, we wish to thank everyone who worked on the book *Navegar contra el viento: América Latina en la era de la información* [Sailing against the Wind: Latin America in the Information Age], edited by Fernando Calderón. For joining us on this thrilling adventure, thanks to: Martin Puchet, Isadora Chacón, Diego Escobar, Isabel Licha, Haydee Ochoa, Miguel Ángel Contreras, Rodrigo Márquez, Fernando Mayorga, Solange Novelle, Juan Pablo Deluca, Ignacio Cretini, Ana Rivoir, Santiago Escuder, Gonzalo Vásquez, Deborah Pragier, and Juan Wahren. Special thanks to the Universidad Nacional de San Martín (UNSAM) in Argentina for supporting this project.

We have made numerous friends and met many colleagues during the last few years. Many thanks to them as well. For their intellectual contributions to the analyses offered in this book, we thank Fernando Henrique Cardoso, Francisco Delich, Ernesto Ottone, Isidora Chacón, Alejandra Moreno Toscano, Alicia Ziccardi, Manuel Perló, Carmen Rodríguez Armesta, Helena Useche, Tarso Genro, and Marcelo Branco.

We also had the privilege to discuss our progress and our research in several academic contexts. Fernando Calderón benefited from a year of reflection spent at the University of Cambridge, where he held the Simón Bolívar Chair. He would especially like to thank the Center for Latin American Studies and the Department of Sociology at the University of Cambridge, as well as Clare Hall College and his colleagues and friends in Cambridge: John Thompson, Jeff Milley, Johanna Page, and especially Julie Coimbra.

In addition, we would like to highlight the contributions made by all of our friends and collaborators in the Programa de Innovación Desarrollo y Multiculturalismo at the UNSAM in Buenos Aires.

Several other academic institutions provided organizational and/ or financial support for the research on which this book is based, among them: the UNSAM in Argentina, the Annenberg School of Communication at the University of Southern California, and the Universitat Oberta de Catalunya. We would like to extend our sincerest thanks to these institutions. The book's final composition benefitted from opportunities to discuss and present our analyses in several academic contexts, in particular at the UNSAM, the Center for Latin American Studies at the University of Cambridge, and the Center for Latin American Studies at the University of California, Berkeley.

Most especially, we would also like to express our gratitude to the people who offered us technical assistance during the last stages of production: Caterina Colombo, for her crucial statistical and documentary support; Noelia Díaz López of the Universitat Oberta de Catalunya, for her excellent preparation and organization of the book's manuscript; and Pauline Martinez of the University of Southern California, for logistical support during the final phase of the project.

This work is the product of a complex Socratic journey, through which we sought to understand recent changes in Latin America. We have had the good fortune to rely, as always, on our loved ones. Many thanks to them for their support and their patience: to Alicia, Manuel, Coral, and Daniel from Fernando; and to Nuria, Irene, and José from Manuel.

As always, our friend and teacher Alain Touraine is a presence in this book.

Finally, we acknowledge the Editorial Fondo de Cultura Económica and especially Julio Sau Aguayo, our editor and friend, with thanks for the support for this book's publication and for inspiring other, past books as well.

PREFACE TO THE ENGLISH EDITION

At the time when this translation went into production (January 2020), Latin America had exploded. The streets of Ecuador, Chile, Bolivia, and Colombia filled with people protesting against government policies and ruling elites. Argentina elected a progressive president after a wave of social protests against the neoliberal policies of the administration of Mauricio Macri, policies that reduced social benefits, increased poverty, and ultimately led to hyper-inflation, placing the country once again under the fiscal control of the International Monetary Fund. Peru was still reeling from a constitutional conflict between the provisional president (replacing a dismissed president) and congress. Brazil was painfully waking up to the reality of Jair Bolsonaro's authoritarianism. Venezuela persisted in a political stalemate, a conflict between the president and congress resulting in frequent and violent street confrontations. Uruguay, the most stable country in South America, suddenly turned to the right thanks to popular support for an ultra-conservative force led by a retired general defending the country's military dictatorship. And Mexico was facing a new round of assaults by violent *narcos*, who went so far as to occupy the city of Culiacán, capital of Sinaloa, for a day, after defeating the army unit sent to arrest their leader at the request of the US Drug Enforcement Administration. In each of these cases, the causes of the protests and of the ensuing political instability were specific to the individual countries. However, a number of common threads can help to explain the conflicts and confrontations that emerged from beneath a misleading calm. This book identifies and investigates the processes that led to the emergence of simultaneous social and political crises in most of Latin America. Indeed, when a decade ago we sought to understand Latin America's transformation in the twenty-first century, we did not intend to study each country in isolation. Instead, we explored a few trends that, taken together, explained the transformations that we observed in every country, although these changes had different degrees of relevance to and intensity in each of the societies we studied.

There are connections between the key developments identified in this book and the events that took place in the second half of 2019 and shocked South America's elites. In fact, these events did not surprise us. We did not predict them, as prediction is not the task of social scientists like us. We simply detected and explained traits and trends in the social structure and social dynamics whose unfolding has resulted in the social disruption and political change that we are witnessing.

We started our investigation, and this book, by studying the contradictory processes through which Latin America was incorporated into the global economy at the turn of the millennium. For the sake of simplicity, we identified two successive economic models that guided the globalization of Latin America. We named these neoliberalism and neo-developmentalism. Under neoliberalism, market forces provided the template for restructuring both the economy and society, for implementing the mantra of the so-called "Washington Consensus". In most cases, these policies induced export-oriented economic growth, increased competitiveness, and improved technological infrastructures, particularly in telecommunications, digitization, and transportation.

Yet full-scale privatization and reductions in social spending resulted in poverty, rampant inequality, low wages, a lack of social benefits, particularly in pensions, and an expansion of the informal economy, as economic growth was not matched by growth in employment. Key services such as education and healthcare were left to self-financing by families, creating unbearable debt burdens. Erratic fiscal policies in several countries, in the absence of effective taxation of elites and corporations, prompted bursts of inflation that were controlled by sharp policy turns to austerity, destabilizing the economy and social life. The social inequity of this model triggered a wave of protests that shook up political order, although the timing of these protests, and their political impact varied from country to country. The neoliberal model ultimately collapsed in all countries under the pressure of social protests and political alternatives.

The emergence of left-wing governments with different ideological orientations, particularly in Venezuela, Argentina, Brazil, Uruguay, Bolivia, Ecuador, and Mexico, changed the political map of Latin

America. Government policies shifted to a new model, one that we call neo-developmentalism. This model was characterized by active state intervention, an emphasis on the development of productive infrastructure, and an export-oriented model of what we call informational extractivism, guided by the state, together with substantial efforts at social redistribution and anti-poverty policies. Neo-developmentalism triggered new forms of social opposition that ultimately led to its political demise. The sources of this opposition were, on the one hand, the hostility of business elites who found their privileges threatened, particularly in terms of taxation, and, on the other hand, the growing corruption of state bureaucracies, largely to support the parties in government, in a context of rapid state expansion. Paradoxically, a segment of the new middle classes created by the redistribution of incomes and opportunities opposed left-wing governments, as these middle classes also came to defend their newly acquired privileges.

Thus the neo-developmental model, like the neoliberal one, crumbled under the pressure of socio-political opposition from large sectors of society. After two decades of successive rise and fall of the two models, entire Latin American economies and societies were in disarray, and this opened the path to a potentially chaotic situation. However, the timing of the rise and fall of the two models varied, and this complicates our interpretation of the situations in various countries. Venezuela exploded first to counter a corrupt elite that had sent the majority of the population in a rich country into poverty. The country collapsed as a corrupt military elite took over, replacing the old conservative elites and resisting new demands for democracy, inducing a systemic crisis whose denouement is perhaps still to come in Caracas. Chile exploded last, in part because of the inclusionary social orientation of the neoliberalism introduced by the Concertación, which gave way to a completely free market system under Sebastián Piñera, ultimately provoking a groundswell of opposition in the entire region. Colombia, a case of economic neoliberalism with extreme inequality, lived through a long period of institutional uncertainty under the effects of the longest-lasting guerrilla war in Latin America, made crueler by drug cartels and the paramilitary forces created by the US-designed "Plan Colombia." As soon as the country started to live in relative peace, its citizens joined the movement of street protests, which included new political actors at the local level. Mexico emerged from a deadly combination of neoliberalism and narco-terrorism with a last call for survival under the presidency of Andrés Manuel Lopez Obrador. The new president, elected by a large majority, went in search of policies that would have learned from the mistakes of both preceding models in Latin America.

The crises of both neoliberalism and neo-developmentalism must be seen in a historical perspective. The understanding of the new Latin America should start from the premise that looking at history is a requirement for the recovery of social meaning in a context of dramatic changes like those discussed in this book.

In a moment of multidimensional global restructuring, multinational companies are being substantially reorganized at the productive, financial, and commercial levels. Latin America has always been defined by global powers and companies as a territory for the extraction of commodities and natural resources; currently this mainly means lithium, copper, iron, rare and precious minerals, agricultural products, forestry, oil, gas, and coca leaves, among others. However, the networks of economic power that connect extractive territories to global developments driven by companies in sharp competition (as in the Chinese, German, Australian, and Japanese companies caught in disputes over lithium) are still in flux. These conflicts have an increasing influence on the dynamics of crisis and political confrontation in the region. This can be seen in the breaking of the agreement between the Bolivian government and German companies, meant to allow the latter to extract lithium, a break that resulted from the criticisms and protests that took place in the second half of 2019 in the Potosí Department in Bolivia.

In political terms, threats to liberal democracy are also related to profound changes in the international arena, particularly given the United States' aggressive policy toward Latin America under the Trump administration. This policy appears to represent a return to the Cold War era, when conspiracies and misinformation were the norm and contributed to the deterioration of democracy in the region. Thus, new crises and conflicts lead to fragmentation, with military forces once again taking center stage. The more socio-institutional processes and agreements fail, the greater the power and influence of the military will become. This phenomenon is furthered by the resurgence of hyper-ideologization, which has found a perfect vehicle for expression in social media.

The crisis has resulted in various social outcomes. On the one hand, in Chile, citizens have demanded democratic participation in local governments as well as a new constitution and a more inclusive economic model. On the other hand, in Bolivia, a process of social polarization has taken place, despite all the positive changes made by the government led by the Movimiento al Socialismo (MAS). After the November 2019 electoral mess, an authoritarian regime, with significant representation of the military and police forces, seized power. This democratic regression in Bolivia was facilitated by the territorial polarization that, once again, split the country, dividing Amazonian from Andean regions and rural from urban. At the time of writing, we observe a breakdown in the social fabric, which will be difficult to reconstitute in the future.

The crises of the neoliberal and neo-developmental models are part of a multidimensional global crisis. This is leading to the rise of a new set of social conflicts, which are modifying daily life as well as the social bond itself. The outcomes of these crises are uncertain not least because of the frailty of institutions and their incapacity to provide social support. Hostility permeates inter-personal relations and cultures.

What kind of new model could be implemented given the region's now irreversible integration in the global economy? The answers to this question ultimately depend on the social conflicts and political arrangements in each country. But to understand both the region's recent past and its future prospects, we have to consider other factors that are distinct from class interests and economic policies, which are only windows that open onto a much more complex reality.

This is particularly the case with the political awakening of indigenous peoples, and the social-racist reaction of elites against these peoples' coming to power through democratic elections, as in Ecuador and, more significantly, in Bolivia. The latter country enjoyed steady economic growth and modernization for over a decade, together with a substantial improvement in living conditions and reduction of poverty. Yet the charismatic leadership of Evo Morales – an indigenous, peasant trade unionist – and the election of indigenous people, particularly "cholas," to key state positions were not tolerated by the white elite, especially in the pro-business province of Santa Cruz. This hostility ultimately led to a military coup that took advantage of the mistakes made by Morales, including his attempt to stay in power by bureaucratic maneuvers that may (or may not) have included electoral fraud. A similar socio-cultural conflict underlies the social explosion in Ecuador, where the rural indigenous populations have been suffering under the austerity policies imposed by the traditional oligarchy with the support of the armed forces and foreign powers. We should note as well the tensions surging in Chile among the Mapuche and among the Indian minorities in Mexico. Guatemala is constantly shaken by white elites' violent attempts to subdue the marginalized 70 percent of the population of indigenous descent.

However, to understand processes of social and political change like the ones we are now witnessing in Latin America, we need to move beyond the study of social structures and institutions. We need to identify the actors responsible for social change. We have spent considerable time and effort studying social movements and forms of social protest. And in this book we have identified the main social actors involved in these processes, actors who are at the forefront of the protests that have shaken multiple countries in the last wave of street mobilizations. They are made up of youth first and foremost, usually student movements, including secondary education students, but more broadly young people in all social conditions, whether they are students or not. In this volume, we explain the profound transformations that have shaped new generations in Latin American, generations that are more educated, better informed, and empowered by their communicative autonomy in digital networks. In every instance, youth have initiated protests, and they have been those who sustain it when harsh repression comes. They are fearless, having overcome the terror that their parents experienced under bloody dictatorships. Moreover, they often revolt on behalf of their grandparents, as was explicitly the case in Chile when they tried repeatedly to attack the high-rise building of the Costanera Center in Providencia, because it was the symbol of the distress of the elderly without pensions, who frequently used that building to commit suicide. A vivid notion of intergenerational solidarity informed the protests, as when protestors demanded access to free decent education because their parents had gone into debt to pay for it.

Women were also powerful actors who sought to overthrow patriarchy and end violence against women, defending their rights over their own bodies and their personal freedom. The intensity of women's mobilizations in Argentina, for instance, was a decisive factor in political change in that country, but it was also present in other countries, particularly in Brazil, Bolivia, Chile, and Mexico.

While workers' demands and unions were significant in the mobilizations, particularly in Argentina where Peronist trade unions are a major force, the new social movements brought together very different actors, including urban social movements, environmentalists, animal rights defenders, ethnic minorities, LGBT activists, human rights advocates, and artists. A common banner united these disparate actors: dignity.

Dignity was the word used as the rallying cry in most of these movements, as it has been in the majority of networked social movements taking place around the world during the last decade, from

Spain to Hong Kong and from New York to Chile. In this context, dignity means something other than claiming the right to a decent livelihood. It is a demand for the right to be treated as dignified human beings, with respect from elites who despise what they see as an ignorant populace and refuse to be accountable to those who elect and pay them.

The new social movements in Latin America, like those emerging elsewhere, can only be understood in the context of a widespread crisis of legitimacy affecting social institutions, a crisis that we document and analyze in this book. Political parties, parliaments, governments, courts of justice, police forces, financial institutions, mainstream media outlets: all are distrusted by a large majority of citizens (83 percent in Latin America as a whole in 2019, according to the United Nations Development Program). Implicated in this collapse of moral authority is the Catholic Church, whose demise we study in this book. This demise has left an empty space in the lives of many in Latin America, depriving people of a place of psychological refuge that helped them to endure the harsh reality of existence. This space is now being filled by a myriad of unscrupulous Evangelical churches that generally are the main support for reactionary demands for "law and order" that can pave the way for authoritarian rule.

At the heart of this widespread crisis of legitimacy is state corruption, a decisive feature of almost all Latin American countries. Denunciations of corruption recur and even predominate in all recent mobilizations in the region, indicating a deep distrust of the institutions responsible for managing people's lives. A factor in the increasing state corruption is the relentless expansion of the criminal economy, whose causes and consequences are covered in detail in chapter 3. But the corruption extends beyond the pervasive presence of criminal elements. It is rooted in the systemic illegal financing of political parties; it derives from the role of the Latin American states in connecting global networks with local networks in the new economy. And it is related to the importance of public markets as sources of capital accumulation for oligopolistic companies ready to buy presidents and other politicians, because of profitable investments in infrastructure linked to modernization projects, and to the chaotic urbanization of Latin America. A paradigmatic case concerns the Brazilian multinational Odebrecht, responsible for corruption of political leaders in Brazil, Peru, Ecuador, Chile, and Mexico, among other countries. The causes and effects of state corruption are the themes of the penultimate chapter of our book. This corruption underlies the collapse of public institutions and ultimately the social explosions taking place throughout the region.

There was, however, one development that we did not foresee: the return of the military as a political actor. Because of our empirical knowledge of the new make-up of the armed forces in different countries, we thought that the military had learned the lessons of past criminal adventures and had surrendered power to the political authorities in exchange for legitimacy, as well as, in some cases, favorable treatment in shady deals. The case of the military coup or conspiracy against Evo Morales in Bolivia shows that we were wrong. Something similar may also happen in Venezuela, itself a military dictatorship. Probably our naïve belief in the stability of elected governments was based on the waning of US interventionism during the Obama administration, something that was reversed by Trump. Moreover, "Brazilian sub-imperialism" is now at work, with Bolsonaro playing the role of chief conspirator on behalf of the Latin American elites who feel threatened in their domination. If this dark hypothesis is verified, this will add another sinister touch to our already gloomy conclusion in this volume, where we discuss the spread of the *kamanchaka* in most of Latin America. (On the meaning of the word, consult our final chapter in this volume.) However, our last word in the book refers to "the color of hope," to the social movements, mainly supported by youth, women, environmentalists, and indigenous peoples, that might reconstruct life from the ground up. This process has indeed started, as we foresaw it would. But if social explosions overtake social movements, then such outrage may or may not open the path to hope. Saying "enough" to violence, and to repression entails understanding that social life – regardless of political, ideological, cultural, or economic affiliations – can only be balanced through the acknowledgment of social pluralism and the unequivocal defense of human rights, dignity, and diversity. The elements for understanding future developments in Latin America are the subject of this volume, which is rooted in the observation of the recent past.

F.C. and M.C.
January 2020

INTRODUCTION:
THE NEW LATIN AMERICA

At the dawn of the third millennium of the Common Era, Latin America and its people have experienced a profound transformation. The region has been fully integrated into globalization, which dominates both the world economy and world culture. This does not mean, however, that everything or everyone in Latin America has been integrated into this global process, because globalization, operating at a planetary scale, is both inclusive and exclusive. It simultaneously involves selective incorporation and structural marginalization, as we have argued elsewhere (Calderón, 2003). In a context of technological and informational revolution, the restructuring of Latin America has entailed a profound modernization of the processes of production and corporate management necessary to compete in global markets for goods, services, and capital. A new model of production – informational extractivism – has become central to many Latin American economies and to the largest of these economies in particular. Technological modernization has rapidly expanded into the realms of communication and culture, globalizing the media and leading to the diffusion of internet networks, which have become vectors for the transformation of culture and everyday life for new generations. At the same time, and as in the rest of the world, globalization and digitization have not produced a homogeneous global culture or relegated the diverse cultures produced by human experience to the dustbin of history, where they would await gradual destruction. The ideology that defines modernization as a vector of cultural domination has thus been disproven again. In fact, the opposite has occurred. From the depths of the souls of Latin American people, a constellation of identities has forcefully reemerged. These were created in the context of an everyday life that has never been

1

fully subjugated and that retains a character of its own, allowing for the survival of an oral tradition and giving rise to a specific form of life. This form of life is human, to be sure – more human, even, than the standards of behavior implicit in the market as a form of life and not only an economy. But it is made up of practices rooted in secular sharing, fraught with sufferings and hopes. Indigenous peoples have thus asserted themselves except in those lands where genocide has led to their extermination. But so, too, have other identities, regional, local, and religious, except in the case of the dominant religion of the region, Catholicism, whose crisis we will consider in this book, investigating both its causes and its consequences.

New identities have likewise emerged as result of a complex process of transformation that has challenged the patriarchy, which is at the root of an institutional domination that has lasted for millennia. Women, feminists, lesbians, gays, transgender people, and bisexuals have all affirmed their right to love and to be loved by anyone they want, setting aside the dictates of sexual repression. And alongside these personal identities, new ways of relating nature and culture have emerged, giving rise to the recognition of animals as our companion species. A systematic questioning of the dark side of institutionally imposed culture has also taken place.

Moreover, in a globalized world, national identity has forcefully reemerged as a means by which to resist the force of history and to reassert the rights of those who live in delimited territories, and who cannot become "citizens of the world" because they do not have the resources to do so. At the same time, however, these people feel themselves to be in solidarity with the planet and their fellow human beings, without thereby wanting to lose the protection of the national institutions that remain available to them.

Caught between globalization and identities, the nation-state is beset by the onslaughts of history. In general, the nation-state seeks to integrate itself into globalization in order to maximize its access to wealth and power, forming transnational networks. In the process, the distance between the state and the nation grows, as does the distance between global imperatives and local representation. Hence the repeated emergence of a longing and ultimately a politics that seek to regain control of the nation. These register the people's responses to the flight of their elites, after the latter become members of a club run by the owners of the world, by networks of power and capital that operate in a space of flows that have become increasingly abstracted from those who seek to maintain control over their restless subjects.

In this conjuncture, the mechanism by which the state relates to its citizens – that is, the political system – has also been beset by the onslaughts of recent history. On the one hand, the institutions of liberal democracy, which were constantly subverted in the twentieth century by military coups generally supported by the United States, became the rule in Latin America during the last decade of that century. We note the possible exception of Cuba (which was not a liberal democracy, but whose government enjoyed a certain kind of popular support) as well as the range of opinions about other regimes in the region, such as those in Venezuela, Nicaragua, Guatemala, and Honduras (which were formally liberal democracies but with diminishing levels of support from their citizens). In any case, at the turn of the millennium, Latin America appeared to have reached a phase of democratic stability after centuries of blood, sweat, and tears shed in order to reach this point. But the current crisis of political legitimacy and state corruption in the vast majority of Latin American countries has, in just a few years, destroyed the minimal confidence that formerly bound those who govern to the governed, leading to a fragmentation of society and calling into question both neo-populist leaders and the deceptive facades of electoral democracies. The why and how of these processes are the objects of our investigation in this book.

In the end, however, beyond the economy, technology, and institutions, there are people's lives. And for the vast majority of the population, the new Latin America, even with a considerable improvement in basic indicators of human development – including education, health, and (mainly informal) employment – is marked by damage to the natural habitat caused by destructive metropolises. This Latin America is also marked by an urbanization driven by speculation, a process that affects 80 percent of the population. It is marked, moreover, by a toxic environment, by the destruction of the region's marvelous ecology, and by violence and fear as forms of life, while criminal gangs teem everywhere, killing, destroying, and intimidating millions of people, often enabled by the passivity or the complicity of those charged with providing protection.

This new Latin America is made up of light and shadows, but the light has increasingly faded, and the shadows already envelop the lives of countless people. This leads to the emergence of new kinds of individual awareness, prompting a search for collective alternatives that might yet make another Latin America possible. Hence our determination to observe and acknowledge the new historical territory in this book – because it is only by acknowledging where we are that we can know how we might get to where we want to be.

3

— 1 —

THE GLOBALIZATION OF LATIN AMERICA

From the Crisis of Neoliberalism to the Crisis of
Neo-developmentalism

Since the end of the twentieth century, Latin America has experienced a process of profound transformation. In order to understand this process, it is necessary to attend to different levels of human development and to local contexts of growth, while also bearing in mind the considerable internal differences that result from the specific situations of various countries, that is, from their different social structures, cultures, and institutions as well as from their different relationships to the global system. Latin America's transformation is the result of two opposing socioeconomic models, their ascent, and their crises. By "neoliberalism," we mean a model of growth and distribution based essentially on the dynamics of the market, supported by the state. In what we call "neo-developmentalism," by contrast, the state is the motor of economic growth and the mechanism for the distribution of products; it actively intervenes in market processes and in the creation of infrastructures, though without fully nationalizing the economy.

Socioeconomic Changes

In terms of economic growth, in the first decades of the twenty-first century, the region as a whole has modernized its productive structure, increased its competitiveness in the global economy, and modified its traditional patterns of dependency on the United States. Growth in annual gross domestic product (GDP) (in constant prices) was 4.5 percent on average between 2003 and 2008. This growth did slow to 3.0 percent between 2009 and 2011, due to the impact of the economic crisis of 2008 in the United States and Europe. Between 2012 and 2013, growth slowed again to 2.3 percent. During the period between 2014 and 2015, the real rate of growth in the region was just 0.5 percent, and in 2016 it was negative (–1.1 percent). Still, for the first time, despite its thorough integration into the global economy, Latin America was more successful than the United States or Europe in combating the effects of an economic crisis, the crisis of 2008; it effectively disengaged itself from the crisis that unfolded in these other world regions.

Obsessed with oil production and considered by many to exemplify bad economic management, Venezuela grew at an average rate of 7.5 percent between 2003 and 2008. Then, during the years between 2009 and 2011, the country had a negative rate of growth (–0.2 percent), only to recover between 2012 and 2013 (when growth reached 3.5 percent). In 2014, the last year for which information was available at the time of writing, Venezuela's GDP fell by 3.9 percent in real terms. For its part, Argentina grew at an average rate of 8 percent between 2003 and 2008, and at a rate of 3.4 percent between 2009 and 2011, whereas between 2012 and 2013 growth was just 0.7 percent, and between 2014 and 2015, it fell to 0.1 percent. The country's economy then contracted another 1.8 percent in 2016 (ECLAC, 2018).

In Brazil, as in Argentina and Venezuela, the period between 2003 and 2008 was the period of greatest real growth (4.2 percent on average), followed by the years from 2009 to 2011 (3.8 percent). From this point, the rate of growth slowed to 2.5 percent between 2012 and 2013, and it then fell again to 1.5 percent and 3.5 percent in 2014–15 and 2016, respectively. Mexico's economy grew by an average of 2.6 percent between 2003 and 2008 before then seeing its rate of real growth slow to 1.2 percent between 2009 and 2011, only to recover to reach 2.5 percent between 2012 and 2013. In 2014–15, the rate of growth of Mexico's GDP rose to 3.0 percent, and it slowed slightly to 2.9 percent in 2016 (ECLAC, 2018). The economies of Bolivia and Peru grew by around 6 percent between 2012 and 2013. To sum up, then, between 2003 and 2013, Latin America lived through more than a decade of sustained economic growth and increased competitiveness.

Countries in the region managed to contain the effects of the global financial crisis and to ensure continued economic growth between 2002 and 2013 on account of two main factors. The first was the regulatory role of the state, which was stronger in Latin America than in the United States and Europe, especially regulating financial markets after the crisis of the 1990s (or the "Tequila Effect"), the crisis of the *real* in Brazil in 1999, and the collapse of the banking system in Argentina in 2001. The Cardoso and Kirchner administrations

Table 1.1: Rates of Year-to-Year Change in Gross Domestic Product, 2003–2016
In percentages and in descending order according to the 2003–8 averages

Country	Average 2003–8	Average 2009–11	Average 2014–15	2016
Argentina	8.0%	3.4%	0.1%	−1.8%
Venezuela	7.5%	−0.2%	−3.9%	n.a.
Peru	6.8%	5.3%	2.8%	4.0%
Uruguay	6.4%	5.7%	1.8%	1.7%
Costa Rica	5.4%	2.8%	3.6%	4.2%
Colombia	5.1%	4.3%	3.8%	2.0%
Ecuador	4.9%	4.0%	1.9%	−1.6%
Chile	4.7%	3.5%	2.0%	1.3%
Paraguay	4.5%	5.0%	4.0%	4.3%
Latin America	**4.5%**	**3.0%**	**0.5%**	**−1.1%**
Bolivia	4.5%	4.2%	5.2%	4.3%
Brazil	4.2%	3.8%	−1.5%	−3.5%
Mexico	2.6%	1.2%	3.0%	2.9%

Note: n.a. = not available

Source: The authors' own calculations, based on data in ECLAC (2018)

introduced regulatory measures into the financial systems of Brazil and Argentina, respectively, that seem to have been more effective than those in the United States or Europe. These administrations thus adapted more efficiently to the systemic volatility of global financial markets. Secondly, there was a transformation in patterns of world trade, and South–South trade partnerships (both with Asia and within Latin America) became more significant than the classic dependency on the United States and Europe.

At the same time, however, although democracy, a key issue in Latin American history, has been stabilized throughout Central and South America, its legitimacy has been weakened recently. In 1976, there were only three democracies in the region. Now democracy is generalized throughout Latin America (with the case of Cuba remaining debatable), at least if we apply the standards of democracy used in Florida during the United States presidential election in 2000, and if we set aside the 16 recent presidential ousters in the region, including two coups, both quickly reversed. According to Latinobarómetro, the rate of support for democracy as a form of government preferable to any other reached its highest level (61 percent) in 2010. But a series of experiences and events have worn away at confidence in democracy and especially in the political system that supports it. Support for democracy thus fell to 53 percent in 2017. By contrast, support for authoritarian regimes has increased under conditions of corruption and organized crime. This mainly affects parliaments and political parties whose legitimacy is very weak (Cohen et al., 2017). Today the crisis of the state and of the political system are central to the problems that Latin America is confronting.

Rates of poverty, the other "disease" from which Latin America has traditionally suffered, were reduced from 45.9 percent of the region's population in 2002 to 30.7 percent in 2017. Extreme poverty also decreased during the same period, from 12.4 percent to 10.2 percent (ECLAC, 2018b: 88). If we also factor in the improvement in one of the main indicators of health and the near universalization of primary school education (despite the poor quality of many schools in the region), we see a Latin America that differs markedly from its traditional image.

The Gini coefficient, which measures inequality, was 0.469 and 0.467 in 2015 and 2016, respectively, for 17 Latin American countries (ECLAC, 2017: 52 and ECLAC, 2018b: 44). According to the same source, this index for the region decreased by an average of 1.5 percent yearly between 2002 and 2008, but it only decreased by 0.4 percent yearly between 2014 and 2016 (ECLAC, 2018b). The reduction in levels of inequality was caused by an improvement in wages in key sectors and an increase in monetary transfers from governments to these sectors. This tendency has, however, begun to be reversed during the last few years. Figure 1.1 shows the evolution and slow decrease in inequality in selected Latin American countries between 2002 and 2016.

We suggest that these phenomena, particularly the decrease in poverty, were caused in large part by the greater presence of the state as a central player in processes of development, with a strategic orientation, a willingness to invest public funds in infrastructure, education, and healthcare, and a commitment to redistributive policies like the program known as Bolsa Família in Brazil.[1] In fact, the neoliberal model of unrestricted national participation in globalization, a model generated by the market, collapsed both economically and socially around the beginning of the twenty-first century in most Latin American countries. (The bank freeze in 2001 in Argentina is the clearest symbol of this collapse.) A new model then emerged, a model that proclaimed itself *neo-developmentalist*, and that was centered on the state but oriented toward competition in the global market. This model is apparently very similar to the model of development that prevailed in East Asia from 1960 to 1980, the period of East Asia's "economic takeoff."

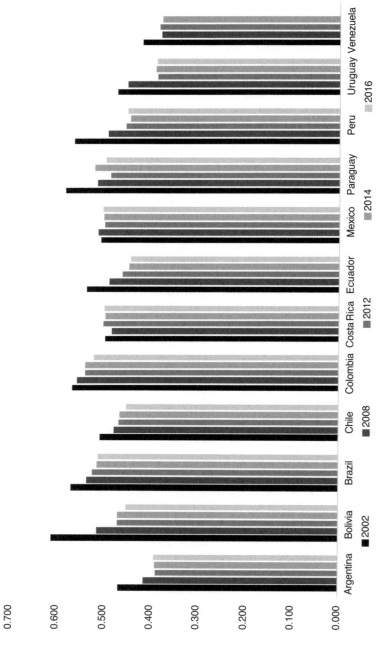

Figure 1.1: Gini Coefficient of Inequality: Selected Latin American Countries, 2002–2016

A more complex and internally differentiated picture emerges when we consider the Human Development Index (HDI). Table 1.2 shows tendencies in and differences between countries according to their levels of human development. Overall, the region has a high level of human development. Chile and Argentina are the only countries with a very high level of human development, and only Paraguay and Bolivia have average levels of human development. All countries witnessed increases in HDI, except Venezuela, where the HDI began to decrease in 2013.

In terms of the factors that the HDI takes into account (education, health, and incomes), Chile has the highest rates of income measured as a factor of HDI (0.812 in 2015), followed by Argentina and Uruguay (0.807 and 0.794, respectively, in 2015). Argentina leads the region in rates of education measured as a factor of HDI (0.808 in 2015), while Chile and Uruguay occupy second and third place in the region. Finally, in rates of health measured as a factor of HDI, Chile is in first place, followed by Costa Rica and Uruguay, with Argentina in fifth place, after Mexico, in 2015.

The transformation in approaches to development, from neoliberalism to neo-developmentalism, was caused in large part by the resistance mounted by vast swathes of the population against the exclusionary policies that sought to force Latin America to incorporate itself into the global economy, policies that benefitted old and new elites. Another key factor leading to the emergence of a new set of policies and politics was the demand for the recognition of oppressed cultural identities. This demand was made especially in Bolivia, Ecuador, and Peru, but members of other ethnic groups also sought recognition in Chile, Mexico, and Colombia. A combination of social movements opposing exclusion and identitarian movements opposing institutionalized racism led to the emergence of a new constellation of political actors, including Bolivarian regimes (in Venezuela, Ecuador, and Nicaragua), nationalist and indigenous regimes (in Bolivia), neo-Peronism or Kirchnerism (in Argentina), and progressive governments like those of the Partido dos Trabalhadores or PT (in Brazil) and the Frente Amplio (in Uruguay). A process of widespread social change accompanied these political transformations, leading to the affirmation of human rights, the growth of feminist movements and improvements in living conditions for women, and increased multicultural awareness in society and politics. Moreover, the emergence of new political actors opposing the United States' control of the region led to a new geopolitical role for Latin America in the world. The region has diversified its economic and political relationships

Table 1.2: Changes in the Human Development Index, 1990–2015

HDI Ranking	Country	Human Development Index (HDI)								Change in HD Ranking	Average Growth in HDI			
		1990	2000	2010	2011	2012	2013	2014	2015	2010–2015	1990–2000	2000–2010	2010–2015	1990–2015
Very High Human Development														
38	Chile	0.700	0.761	0.820	0.826	0.831	0.841	0.845	0.847	2	0.84%	0.75%	0.65%	0.76%
45	Argentina	0.705	0.771	0.816	0.822	0.823	0.825	0.826	0.827	-2	0.90%	0.57%	0.28%	0.64%
High Human Development														
54	Uruguay	0.692	0.742	0.780	0.784	0.788	0.791	0.794	0.795	2	0.70%	0.50%	0.37%	0.55%
66	Costa Rica	0.653	0.708	0.752	0.758	0.762	0.768	0.775	0.776	3	0.82%	0.61%	0.64%	0.70%
71	Venezuela	0.634	0.672	0.756	0.767	0.770	0.771	0.769	0.767	-4	0.58%	1.18%	0.29%	0.76%
77	Mexico	0.648	0.700	0.745	0.748	0.753	0.754	0.758	0.762	-5	0.77%	0.63%	0.44%	0.65%
79	Brazil	0.611	0.685	0.724	0.730	0.734	0.747	0.754	0.754	7	1.15%	0.55%	0.83%	0.85%
87	Peru	0.613	0.677	0.721	0.725	0.731	0.735	0.737	0.740	3	1.01%	0.63%	0.53%	0.76%
89	Ecuador	0.643	0.670	0.710	0.717	0.725	0.737	0.739	0.739	7	0.41%	0.58%	0.83%	0.56%
95	Colombia	0.592	0.653	0.700	0.707	0.712	0.720	0.724	0.727	6	0.99%	0.70%	0.76%	0.83%
Average Human Development														
110	Paraguay	0.580	0.624	0.675	0.679	0.679	0.688	0.692	0.693	-4	0.73%	0.79%	0.54%	0.71%
118	Bolivia	0.535	0.607	0.649	0.655	0.661	0.666	0.671	0.674	0	1.26%	0.66%	0.77%	0.92%

Source: Authors' own calculations, based on the Human Development Report, 2016 (UNDP, 2016)

10

with countries including China, Japan, South Africa, and, to a lesser extent, Russia, while also encouraging closer ties with the countries of the European Union. Nevertheless, the presence of the United States remains significant, especially in Mexico, Central America, and Colombia.

Furthermore, the new hegemony of the state was built on weak political institutions, especially weak political parties. These quickly became vulnerable to creeping corruption and clientelism in a context of democratic freedoms in which civil society could be mobilized and the media and social networks used as instruments of denunciation. In the middle of the 2010s, the state's hegemony entered a period of crisis, caused by a combination of national and regional political factors as well as by the crisis in, and contraction of, the global market. This has led to a new historical turning point for politics and development in the region. Both the economic model centered on the market and the model of development centered on the state seem to have been weakened, and both seem to be undergoing a process of further weakening. It is still not clear what will result or where we should look for political alternatives. What new politics of development might allow us to envision a new democratic order?

The Rise and Fall of Neoliberalism

After a lost decade, Latin America's socioeconomic development in the 1980s and 1990s was characterized by accelerated integration into the global economy. This process led to dependency and was unsustainable. It entailed the liberalization of markets and the privatization of formerly public industries and of natural resources. For both businesses and states, this process led to the formation of strategic alliances with multinational corporations, particularly in banking, communications, and technology. This meant decreased dependency on the United States, and it allowed for technological modernization, especially in the use of communications technologies and the expansion of digital media. However, during these years, Latin America witnessed spreading corruption, was subjected to the interests of multinational corporations, and suffered from the lack of a model of informational development that would allow its economies to become truly competitive in a global information age. Massive increases in poverty, inequality, and vulnerability to economic crises (including the Tequila crisis of 1995, the crisis in Brazil in 1999, and the Argentinean collapse that led to the bank freeze in 2001) marked

11

the limits of the region's integration into the global economy. It was clear that Fernando Fajnzylber's strategy, which called for productive transformation "with equity," was the only one that might have made Latin America into a modernized region that was competitive in its own right (1990). But the political conditions for implementing this strategy did not exist in any Latin American country in the last decades of the twentieth century.

According to a study undertaken by the United Nations Development Programme (2004), there were increases throughout the region in economic reforms implemented between 1981 and 1990 and again between 1988 and 2003, accompanied by an increase in rates of electoral democracy. Nevertheless, these increases did not translate into significant reductions in rates of poverty, indigence, inequality, or unemployment. The average rate of poverty fell from 46 percent in the period between 1981 and 1990 to 41.3 percent in the period between 1998 and 2003. And, in fact, in the Southern Cone (the sub-region with the highest rate of economic reforms), unemployment actually increased by three percentage points during this time. Rates of poverty and indigence also increased in this period, from 25.6 percent to 26 percent and from 7.1 percent to 8.7 percent, respectively.

We can identify an unfortunate lack of change in the rate of participation of the region's GDP in global GDP. According to the World Bank, since the 1980s, this has remained around 8 percent. By contrast, China's relative participation in global GDP went from 2 percent to 11 percent between the 1980s and the second decade of the twenty-first century (World Bank, 2018).

Social protests and political challenges attending neoliberal glo-balization led to openings in the political systems of many countries (Calderón, 2008). In Venezuela, this resulted in the taking of insti-tutional power by new political actors through elections. These new actors launched the Bolivarian Revolution after the election of 1998, and they were then strengthened by a series of electoral victories for Hugo Chávez and his followers. Nicaragua, Ecuador, and Bolivia elected governments that challenged the Washington Consensus with left-wing strategies for autonomous nationalist development. Costa Rica continued its policies of social democratic pacifism and moderni-zation and preserved its tropical welfare state. Brazil, Argentina, and Uruguay clearly positioned themselves against global financial capi-talism even while they were integrated into global competition. On the other hand, in Colombia, the civil war and the paramilitary state led by Álvaro Uribe prevented political change for a time, although this type of change did take place at the municipal level, especially in Medellín and Bogotá. Peru maintained the neoliberal model promoted by Alberto Fujimori in partnership with various political coalitions. And in Mexico, the infiltration of the state by drug cartels created a context of particularly violent confrontation both within and between the cartels and the state apparatuses; estimates suggest that more than 235,000 lives were lost between 2006 and 2016, leading to a dire situation in one of Latin America's major countries.[2]

The Chilean model of neoliberalism was a special case. We note that, importantly, there were two models of development in Chile, whose democratic model was neoliberal at the level of the economy but not at the level of the state. In his book about development in Chile, Castells (2005) draws an empirical distinction between these two models of development in Chile: the neoliberal, authoritarian, and exclusionary model that prevailed under Pinochet's dictatorship (1973–89), and the liberal, democratic, and inclusive model that first took effect in 1990 under the transitional governments of the Concertación and reached its fullest expression during the administration of Ricardo Lagos between 2000 and 2006. The data and analyses presented in Castells (2005) demonstrate that, when one compares the two periods, the democratic model was much more efficient in terms of economic growth, limited inflation, indicators of human development, macroeconomic stability, productivity, and international competitiveness. At the same time, human rights were affirmed, and democracy was reinstated, though with some limitations inherited from the dictatorship. Poverty and extreme poverty were significantly reduced. Although inequality in the distribution of incomes remains high in Chile when the country's economy is compared with that of Argentina or Uruguay, for example, a decrease in this tendency can also be observed. In 2016, the Gini coefficient for Chile was 0.453, whereas at the beginning of the 1990s it was over 0.500.

On the other hand, free market policies, at both the domestic and the international levels, were central to Chile's strategy for development, and widespread liberalization continued, in keeping with a forceful strategy that prioritized exports. Thus, copper mines (the source of "Chile's salary"), which had been nationalized by Allende, remained in the public sector, since Pinochet did not reverse Allende's nationalization, choosing instead to retain direct control over Chile's main source of wealth and to use this control for the predatory accumulation of a personal fortune. In general, it seems to us demonstrably true that the strictly neoliberal model in Chile ended in 1990, but some of its economic traits continued to mark Chile's successful development, because businesses, a democratically controlled state, and a legitimate government defused social resistance and the kind of political challenges that the neoliberal model faced in other countries. This was because Chile was able to sustain economic growth and to increase its productivity and competitiveness during the post-dictatorship years. The process of modernization nevertheless generated a certain discontent in the population, which, as the report on human development released by the United Nations Development Programme in 1998 noted, even began to question the value of modernization itself. This discontent also had political and subjective effects associated with inefficiency and widespread political corruption.

Another *sui generis* case is the Peruvian one. Here the neoliberal model was consistent and lasting, and it has prevailed economically throughout the first decades of the twenty-first century. It was based on an economic policy initiated by Fujimori, which coexisted with various other political projects, like the neo-developmentalist project of Alan García or the indigenist projects of Ollanta Humala. Here, as in Chile, poverty was reduced, in the Peruvian case from 55 percent in 2001 to 31 percent in 2010. But chronic social inequality persisted (Araníbar et al., 2013: 293). Real salaries rose from $101 (in US dollars) in 2001 to $110 in 2010, that is, at a rate much lower than the Latin American average, which went from $101 to $158 in the same period (Araníbar et al., 2013: 302). Moreover, the Peruvian context remains characterized by social conflict, especially in the south of the county. Interestingly, according to public opinion polls, citizens express widespread dissatisfaction with the functioning of the economy as well as with the state of Peruvian democracy (Araníbar et al., 2013).

Social Resistance and Political Change as Sources of Neo-Developmentalism

Revolts against social exclusion and demands for multiculturalism and dignity are at the root of the political processes that took place in Venezuela, led by Chávez, in Ecuador led by Rafael Correa, and in Bolivia led by Evo Morales. Moreover, the four consecutive electoral victories won by the Partido dos Trabalhadores (PT, or Workers' Party) in Brazil, under the charismatic leadership of Luiz Inácio Lula da Silva changed the balance of political power in the region. Building on the stability of the macroeconomic and modernizing policies of Fernando Henrique Cardoso (despite profound differences between Lula and Cardoso), the PT was in the vanguard of the process as it sought to further stabilize a new developmentalist state. The Brazilian emphasis on investment in productive infrastructure, together with an increase in public spending and a set of redistributive policies, was at the origin of neo-developmentalism in Latin America.

Argentina underwent a similar process under Kirchnerism, combining socio-political mobilization from the Peronist movement with a state that played a dominant role, which came to prevail over multinational corporations and to exercise control over financial markets as well as over Argentina's economy more generally. Uruguay joined this effort under the leadership of President Mujica, a former Tupamaro militant who fully embraced democracy, affirming dignity and welfare and becoming one of the most respected political figures on the international stage.

Thus, Latin America laid the political foundations for a strategy of development organized by the state, based on the extraction of natural resources for export and the creation of productive infrastructures that would generate funds for the sort of public social spending that could improve living conditions for the population. Statism, productivism, and social welfare were expanded in a process of combined interaction that lent support to neo-populist movements and parties on the left and gave rise to a twenty-first century version of left politics. The success of this strategy, however, depended in large part on charismatic leaders and on the favorable new conditions of the world economy. In this way, a system of corporate patronage and domination was established that would later undergo a general crisis.

Charismatic Leaders, State, and Society

The idea of a return to the people, defined as the subject of history and identified with the nation and the state, was fundamental for the construction of the neo-developmentalist strategies that arose in new global and regional contexts. The state and the charismatic leader combine in the popular imagination, becoming fundamental referents for policies that seek both social integration and development, as well as for confrontations with traditional powers and national conservative elites. At the same time, there was widespread and realistic political resistance to negotiations and agreements with transnational corporations and neoliberal states, especially developed countries and China.

As Cardoso and Enzo Faletto argued, considering the role of leaders in politics: "We know that the course of history depends largely on the daring of those who propose to act in terms of historically viable goals" (Cardoso and Faletto, 1979: 176; translation slightly modified). Even more than other leaders, charismatic neo-developmentalist leaders vary according to the particular psycho-social and cultural characteristics of various Latin American societies. Their "daring" is born from their own political mystique, but it is not unrelated to the possibilities and problems in these countries.

Around 2000, a historical turning point began, one that marked a shift in both democracy and development. This was a moment in which the political stage was reconstituted, neoliberal projects broke down, and neo-developmentalist projects with populist characteristics became widespread throughout the region. This led to the taking of power by more than fifteen neo-developmentalist governments in Latin America and the Caribbean. Each of these governments had different traits and confronted different national problems and challenges that varied in intensity.

At the center of these changes, charismatic leaders stood out, even in their absence. These leaders oversaw the processes of change, and their behavior decisively informed the crises that these countries experienced and are experiencing. As we have mentioned, the Chilean case was exceptional in that it combined the application of a relatively heterodox model of neoliberalism with political reforms overseen by the Concertación. Nevertheless, the parties involved in the Concertación dealt with clientelist practices every day.

Neoliberalism was associated with meager economic outcomes, with increases in social inequality, and especially with rising levels of poverty. Thus the result of neoliberal policies was a severe crisis of legitimacy for neoliberal institutions and political projects. Neo-developmentalist projects were more porous and variable than neoliberal ones. Notably, these projects resulted from looking back and reflecting on past national popular movements, especially those led by the first generation of populist social and political leaders after the Mexican Revolution. The ghosts of Emiliano Zapata, Juan Lechín, Juan Perón, Getúlio Vargas, Fidel Castro, and even indigenous leaders like Túpac Katari, among others, presided over the construction of charismatic neo-developmentalist forms of leadership.

It is worth mentioning some key points of reference in this context. On the one hand, a critical social vision emerged, one that was

16

dissenting but widespread and that expressed dissatisfaction with increases in social inequality. For example, in 2010 only 21 percent of Latin Americans considered the distribution of wealth in the region fair (Latinobarómetro, 2010: 19). On the other hand, we can easily recognize these movements as continuous with a long history of popular demands that the state play a leading role in the economy and in society, that it promote both social integration and the creation of jobs and social benefits, including the expansion of access to the systems of consumption that characterize societies centered on information and communication.

The rates of support for statism by country, calculated by the Latin American Public Opinion Project (see figure 1.2), reflect average

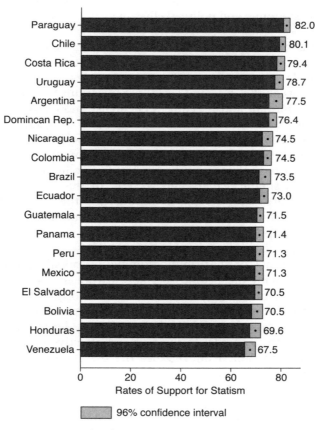

Figure 1.2: Average Levels of Support for Statism: Selected Latin American Countries, 2010

levels of citizens' support for a state that plays a leading role in four economic areas: ownership of the most important industries, social welfare protections, job creation, and the reduction of inequality. The conclusion is clear: the demand that the state play a fundamental role in the economy and society was prevalent. Similarly, in a study of social protest in 17 Latin American countries, the state was found to be the main target in the majority of social conflicts in the region between 2009 and 2010 (Calderón, 2012). These data show the importance of the state for Latin Americans.

Paradoxically, it seems that one of the reasons for the demand that the state play such a key role is clearly related to the *weakness* of the state as it seeks to confront and resolve demands for social integration and development. But this demand also follows from a profound distrust of economic and political elites in virtually all Latin American countries.

In this context, para-institutional mechanisms come to the fore, with their ability to mediate between society and the state, thus helping to enhance leaders' charisma. Given the weakness of institutions, the relation between the state and social organizations becomes informal rather than formal, and it acquires clientelist and charismatic traits, which then inform everyday relationships and introduce anomalies into formal institutions, further enabling corruption. The availability of informal alternatives, caused by failed socioeconomic policies in the past, favors the emergence of a fertile but limited relationship between charismatic leaders and society. In this way, an inability to generate satisfactory living conditions for the people decisively contributes to the demand for, and the installation of, charismatic leaders with populist traits.

We can conclude that, in this context, these kinds of processes make the presence of charismatic domination possible. The leader's identification with the people is a key feature in the phenomenon of Latin American charismatic politics. In his origins as well as his image and his dramatic and complicated trajectory, the leader must identify as one more member of the people in order to recast himself as a symbol of the people. In this way, an affective unity is created, one that is inseparable from the idea of "the people." The leader is one with the people because he is part of the people; he himself *is* the people. He lives for, and can sacrifice himself for, the people. In this sense, the people are reified, materialized in the image of the leader. The process of political change is motivating, a reason for living. But charismatic reason, as Weber said, is an epiphany in and of itself.

In this sense, in order to understand neo-populist movements in Latin America, it is crucial to understand the relationship between charismatic leaders and society in the region. These movements arise when institutions are structurally weakened, when processes of social integration and national cohesion are limited, when public insecurity is widespread, and when citizens' expectations are frustrated. But in addition to noting their commitment to social democracy, it is important to mention that none of these charismatic leaders disavowed or questioned electoral democracy either. The latter was, in fact, fundamental to their legitimacy.

On the other hand, today's society of information and communication has transformed the kinds of action in which charismatic leaders engage. The new demands made by communities, like the new forms of action taken by leaders, are increasingly expressed through the internet and through the multiple forms of communication that tend to proliferate online. The leader is no longer on his own in the public square, but rather in a mediated public sphere, in multiple and diverse public spaces of communication.

It is worth mentioning that the crisis of neo-developmentalism is inseparable not only from national and global socioeconomic conditions, but also, more specifically, from the fate of charismatic leaders, from what they have experienced and are experiencing. They disappeared for various reasons (the deaths of Chávez and Néstor Kirchner, the electoral defeats of others like Correa or Lula, and illnesses, among others), and their disappearance affected the unfolding of neo-developmentalist processes. They are among the fundamental factors that explain the current crisis of these political orientations toward development and democracy (Calderón and Moreno, 2017 [2013]).

The Neo-Developmentalist Model and the New Globalization: China and the Global South

China's rise to a prominent position in the new world economy created an enormous market for the kinds of exports that still characterize most Latin American economies: agricultural products, raw materials, and energy. The more China imports from and invests in Latin America and the rest of the Global South, the more it spurs economic growth in the Global South, which becomes an expanding market in its own right. Latin America took advantage of the boom in commodity prices linked to the explosion of demand from China, India, and other large markets; it modernized its primary sector, using

19

new technologies of information and genetically modified agriculture as well as new business strategies. A new model arose, one that we have called *informational extractivism*. Although information technologies did not completely transform the productive system, they did transform the production of soy, the production of meat, the creation of energy and gas, and the mining of precious metals (like lithium in Chile, Argentina, and most recently Bolivia), raising both quality and productivity in a virtuous circle of economic growth. Nevertheless, the success of neo-developmentalism followed from two premises that were soon shown to be fragile: first, that global demand for commodities would continue to increase; and, second, that the prices of these commodities would remain high. Reclaiming its redistributive role through new policies, the state could avoid opposition thanks to the fact that society remained active, was increasingly informed, and significantly increased its participation in consumption.

The Crisis of Neo-Developmentalism

Almost all countries in Latin America were unable to engage in a complete informational transformation of their economies and societies, one that would have led, for example, to the transformation of research, higher education, and policies for the promotion of innovation. This inability meant that the growth of the region's economies remained almost entirely dependent on exports from the extractive sector. As soon as China's growth slowed and the prices of commodities fell, Latin American economies revealed their vulnerability to the fluctuations of the global economy. Even Brazil, the region's most diversified economy, did not have sufficient knowledge to change its export patterns and add value to goods and services. While Latin America largely learned to manage financial volatility, it has not been able to do the same with the volatility of trade. As a result, Argentina's economy, for example, fell 2.5 percent in real terms in 2014, and the same happened in Brazil in 2015 (–3.5 percent), while rates of growth slowed considerably throughout the region, except in Bolivia and Peru. 2015 was the first year of the twenty-first century in which the Latin American economy did not grow. While governments for a time continued to engage in high levels of public spending (something fundamental for social stability), the renewed threat of inflation, poised to exceed economic growth, forced these governments to impose austerity, especially the administration of Dilma Rousseff in Brazil in 2014. This undermined the popularity of governments in Brazil,

Venezuela, and, to some extent, Bolivia and Argentina. Neo-populist governments won electoral victories but by ever smaller margins and with decreasing legitimacy.

Moreover, the neo-developmentalist model of development was based on the maintenance of economic growth and redistribution at all costs; it focused on the development of productive forces and on the improvement of the material living conditions for populations, especially for their poorest members. This productivist model ignored the environmental and social costs that it entailed. Enormous metropolitan areas became barely hospitable for most of the population, with rates of urbanization above 75 percent in the majority of Latin American countries. The conditions of housing, transportation, urban recreation, pollution, and the environment all deteriorated rapidly. While traditional measures of human development (health, education, and salaries) improved, a model of "inhuman development" arose and negatively affected the quality of life of most of the population. The criminal economy, brutal violence, pervasive crime, and the terror caused by gangs became the most significant problems affecting everyday life in every Latin American country. The media contributed to public panic, covering atrocious threats to daily life for ordinary citizens. Political corruption contributed to a shared sense of defenselessness.

At the same time, the consolidation of statist regimes, controlled by powerful political parties, led to the formation of a patrimonial and corporate state in which access to public businesses became a source of wealth, influence, and power for neo-populist movements, leading to widespread corruption in the political systems of almost all Latin American countries. The tradition of transparency characteristic of democratic politics in Chile was questioned, as networks of corruption were exposed both among conservative politicians and among those of the Nueva Mayoría (or New Majority, formerly the Concertación). This scandal even reached the family of President Bachelet, undoubtedly a moral person.

In addition, the state's vast powers were shored up in several countries through the repressive strategies implemented by police forces (sometimes with help from foreign countries), which developed into bureaucratic actors whose presence could be felt throughout societies. New generations – raised in democracies, educated, informed, and used to communicating on the internet – resented the crushing presence of the patrimonial state. Statism could not stifle the ethical demands and demands for freedom put forward by young people participating in various social movements.

21

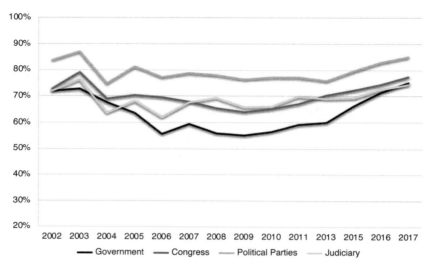

Figure 1.3: Distrust of Institutions: Totals for Latin America, 2002–2017 (%)

Note: Totals of responses expressing little + no trust

Indeed, public distrust of institutions is on the rise in almost all countries in the region (see figure 1.3). In 2016, the proportion of citizens who expressed distrust in both political institutions and the state was at least 63 percent, except in Uruguay, where the proportion drops to 51 percent (ECLAC, 2018a).

The convergence of the critique of inhuman development, the denunciation of state and political corruption, and the worsening of living conditions caused by economic stagnation and the politics of austerity triggered a rise in social movements in several countries, especially Brazil, Venezuela, Nicaragua, Chile, and Mexico. These movements directly challenged political regimes and their policies, and their demands focused on alternative forms of political representation.

Originally, these movements – in 2013 in Brazil, for example – were spontaneous and represented a younger population, which called for better societies. But they were soon joined by other middle-class sectors worried about the loss of their benefits, as in Venezuela or Brazil in 2015. Societies were broken apart, and the legitimacy of neo-developmentalism and its agent, the state, gradually dissipated.

In 2015, Latin America entered a period of economic uncertainty and political instability. The new social structure formed during

22

the period of growth during the 2000s ceased to correspond to the political agents who had reached positions of power thanks to their fight against neoliberalism. Latin America lived through conflicts and contradictions during the first decades of the twenty-first century, overcoming both neoliberalism and neo-developmentalism. In this way, the region was led into a multidimensional crisis. This consisted of three interrelated crises: a crisis of neoliberalism, a crisis of neo-developmentalism, and a crisis of political and institutional legitimacy resulting from the failure of both of these models.

Neoliberalism exacerbated inequality, which was not remedied by neo-developmentalism. For its part, neo-developmentalism exacerbated statism and thus corruption, because interests moved from the market to the state. The political system's crisis of legitimacy extended to institutions, causing lasting conflicts among groups wielding power, which enlisted judges and the media in their fights with one another. The absence of mechanisms for the aggregation and institutional negotiation of interests led to a complex crisis. This crisis is not essentially economic, given the region's dynamic integration into the global economy; nor is it essentially social, given that in the majority of countries poverty has been reduced, together with extreme poverty and even inequality. It is a crisis of values and a generalized crisis of confidence, one that has led to a sordid and lasting conflict between actors, to the breakdown of any kind of consensus, and to the absence of shared rules of engagement.

Moreover, a symbiotic relationship between the logic of institutions in crisis and the logic of the rampant criminal economy heightens uncertainty. The state's infiltration by drug traffickers emerges as a national problem, but even more so a regional and local one, not only in Mexico, Colombia, or Peru, but also in Brazil.

And thus, on this historical basis, various national situations intersect, in a set of multicultural transformations in public space and communications. It is, however, in the political system and in the state that the crisis is concentrated, and it is here that the limits of the new Latin American reality are becoming apparent.

— 2 —

A NEW SYSTEM OF PRODUCTION
Informational Extractivism and the Globalization of Markets

Extractivism is one of the main economic and cultural characteristics of Latin America and the Caribbean, one that has determined the place of our economies and societies in the world. We are, and we are seen as, countries with extractive economies and cultures, despite various efforts at industrialization, import substitution, and social integration.

Argentina's name comes from the silver mined in Potosí, and Brazil is named for a type of wood (*pau brazil*). Sergio Almaraz Paz's *El poder y la caída* (Power and the Fall from Power) is a magnificent book that recounts the political and economic drama of tin mining in Bolivia. Fernando Ortiz considers the economies and cultures that center on tobacco and sugar in Cuba. For his part, Gabriel García Márquez shows in *The Autumn of the Patriarch* how a tyrant ends up selling off the Caribbean Sea, leaving only sand. Manuel Ugarte's essays highlight the emancipatory hopes associated with the idea of the *Patria Grande* or Great Homeland, and in *Open Veins of Latin America*, Eduardo Galeano considers the frustrations, pains, and obstacles that the region has faced. All are associated with extraction.

A great deal of literature in sociology and economics hinges on the question of how to characterize extractivism, and how to leave it behind in order to industrialize Latin America. The works of Torcuato Di Tella, Alain Touraine, and others on coal and iron mining, or on the trade unions in Lota and Huachipato, Chile, are classics in the field. Fernando Fajnzylber's proposals for productive transformation "with equity," promoted by the Economic Commission for Latin America and the Caribbean, represent efforts to overcome a primarily extractive system.

Natural resources – land, mines, oil, and water – and the forms of social organization that first arose under colonialism to manage them

24

– including the *hacienda* system first and foremost – together created a prison, a place for the exercise of domination and the confinement of resistance. This is the history that weighs on all of Latin America, despite national differences.

Calderón's study *Navegar contra el viento: América Latina en la era de la información* (Sailing against the Wind: Latin America in the Information Age, 2018) suggests, among its main conclusions, that the region has witnessed the emergence of a new type of extractivism in recent decades, one that the author calls "informational." That study suggested that this constitutes the primary way in which Latin America's economies participate in globalization. In effect, the region was undergoing a sort of transition from industrial to informational extractivism, but to note that this was not to deny the importance of organized labor or of the world of informal work, statistically the most significant type of work in the region. For their part, communities of indigenous and African descent constituted a resource for, but also a source of resistance to, these new economies.

This new economic and techno-informational dynamic, built and dependent for its functioning on the web, became widespread in all Latin American countries. Countless corporations were established or reestablished along these lines, and as many forms of negotiation and resistance arose in response. These new extractive corporations are marked by particular characteristics, which vary according to the historical and cultural experience of various countries. They differ widely depending on the types of transnational business in which they participate and, of course, the types of activities they undertake, whether these relate to mining, oil, agriculture, or infrastructure. The types of organization that corporations, states, and regional and local societies adopt are another factor. The dynamics of informational extraction thus vary widely between and even within countries.

Our analysis in this book assumes that "informational extractivism" is inseparable from land. Indeed, the two are not only indissociable; together they produce a new field for historical conflicts that are also expressed in international social networks, given that the environmental impact of extractive forms of exploitation is as global as the corporations that engage in them.

Informational Extractivism

Essentially, "informational extractivism" is a new capitalist dynamic sustained by a techno-economy that operates both on the web and

25

in global centers for the production, marketing, and management of extracted products. We can therefore give these new products metaphorical names: informational copper, informational gas, informational soy, and even informational coca, since these products depend on multiple chains of value. Beyond the exploration and exploitation of natural resources, they incorporate advances in science and technology, dynamic and distinctive forms of specialization, and global corporate and financial networks.

A crucial feature of these new corporations is that, because of the international competition that they face, they are necessarily integrated into systems of innovation that depend on scientific and technological research and that rely on strategic networks and centers. In this sense, considering the scientific and technical capacities of a country, or a region, is crucial to understanding the dynamics and the power of negotiation and integration with these new corporations. As we will show below, the Grobocopatel group, based in the Humid Pampas of Argentina, represents one paradigmatic case, not least because of its links to the university system, which nurtures local systems of production.

Much of the power of these kinds of corporations derives from the dynamism of the market for their products and the international financial system, which also depends on informational networks, chains, and centers. Profits from computerized natural resources are thus the result of a combination of the natural resources themselves with technologies introduced at various stages in the production process to increase profits at greater scales.

In general, informational corporations extract, process, and generate assemblages of products. They are interconnected, moreover, with other corporations that allow them to refine and outsource their activities. From these corporations, they also receive the specialized goods and services necessary to maintain dynamism in business. This dynamism is indispensable to financing, especially external financing, and thus to the expansion of markets that ensures extraordinary rates of profitability. All of this means that corporations require networks and chains of productive, business, and financial exchange that are connected to systems of scientific and technological research, which in turn facilitate productive interaction and success in the market. In this way, extractive informational corporations are gradually positioned in, and integrated into, the global market. For its part, this market is increasingly constituted by competition and various systems of corporate power.

Finally, a crucial element in the functioning of this informational economy is its relationship to politics and communication, especially as a consequence of its environmental effects. Responding to these presupposes the construction of a complex matrix of strategies for negotiation both with nation-states and local governments and with the territorial organizations affected by economic activities. Hence the crucial importance of so-called "governance" for these corporations.

Territories

It is worth noting that extractive undertakings are shaped by the environmental characteristics of the territories on which they operate as well as by socio-cultural dynamics and, especially, by the environmental effects that they produce. In corporations located on such territories, there are two main groups of workers. One is made up of highly qualified workers, trained in extractive techniques, with specializations and the ability to handle a wide range of types of information, adapting to changes in information technologies. The other group includes workers who are less qualified and whose work is not central to the activities of computerized corporations. These are temporary workers or those included in a limited way, soon to be replaced by new machines. They are part of the territory and of the social and political relations that are developed on it.

This kind of relationship to territory presupposes a dynamic interaction between nature, which creates and reproduces biodiversity, and a matrix of socio-territorial relationships, often multicultural relationships, that depend on, and frequently destroy, the resilience of nature and its ecological systems. Informational corporations introduce innovations into the process of extractive exploitation, and very often the result is the degradation of the environment, or a reduction in ecological capacities for resilience.

Territories are also social, cultural, political, and institutional constructions. They are spaces connected to regional or local societies, with traditions and cultures that shape relationships with nature. Andean peoples, for example, cultivated a relationship with nature that centered on coexistence at various ecological levels. This is a good example of a fertile interaction between cultures and ecological territories (Murra, 2017 [1969]). Juan Wahren argues that we can "define a territory as a geographic space shot through with social, political, cultural, and economic relations, a space that is constantly resignified by the actors who live in and act on it, creating a territorial stage for conflicts through the appropriation and reterritorialization of space and of the natural resources that are found there" (Wahren, 2011: 12–13).

Various territorial actors tend to act not only on the territories that they inhabit, but also in networks. In such networks, they find support, solidarity, and even financing. Moreover, the effects of environmental degradation that can be directly experienced in a given territory can have global impacts, given their implications for climate change, which affects us all. The United Nations Development Programme's *Human Development Report* for 2007–2008 (UNDP, 2007) – like other reports, including the 2006 report on water by the same agency (UNDP, 2006) – noted that the countries that pollute most are those with the highest levels of human development, and those that suffer most from pollution are those that have the lowest levels of human development. Still, the consequences of pollution vary and are felt at a global scale. Every local territory is therefore "glocal," informational, and a new field for conflicts shaped by concrete experiences.

Let us consider some examples of the workings of informational extraction and its implications for territories.

Three Cases: Lithium in Jujuy, Soy in Carlos Casares in the Humid Pampa in Buenos Aires Province, and Unconventional Hydrocarbons in the Vaca Muerta

In Argentina, as in other countries,[1] we can find the coexistence of different types or models of corporate development and informational extraction. At least three such models coexist in this context.

In the province of Jujuy, in the new extractive market for lithium, productive, organizational, and informational processes are mainly linked to transnational corporations. This creates a dual dynamic. On the one hand, there are the simple extractive processes, which, especially during the early stages, rely on local manual labor. On the other hand, there are processes of complex reworking and mineral processing that turn raw materials into a series of technological and informational products, relying in large part on labor from abroad. According to information offered by the company Sales de Jujuy, in 2017 it created 270 jobs, of which around 120 were for workers who resided in local communities (Pragier and Deluca, forthcoming: 37).

Sales de Jujuy S. A. is a partnership that brings together the Japanese car manufacturer Toyota Tsusho, an Australian mining company called Orocobre Limited, and a company known as Jujuy Energía y Minería, Sociedad del Estado, based in the province of

28

Jujuy. Financing is mainly provided by the Mizuho Bank of Japan, which also underwrites the Japan Oil, Gas and Metals National Corporation. Of course, agreements between extractive corporations and the multinational corporations that require their products presuppose that the latter guarantee purchases in a given price range.

In the case of YPF, S. A., based in the Vaca Muerta formation in the province of Neuquén, we see a combination of industrial, oil-based extractivism and complex processing by technological and informational means, in networks that include systems for the importation and processing of gravel in China, wells for the extraction of gas and oil, digitally monitored through nodes installed by the corporation itself. In this context, new horizontal fracking technologies are also noteworthy, as are various commercial and financial systems, organized and managed through networks. This corporation is part of a global network of networks.

In the case of the soy produced by the company Los Grobo Agropecuaria, one of Gustavo Grobocopatel's companies, the systems of organization and management are totally computerized. They include broad networks of workers, divided into specializations according to the activities they perform; they range from young people processing algorithms to experts in finance at the global scale. From its headquarters in Carlos Casares, a range of activities are organized and completed, from the extraction of soy to the global promotion, marketing, and financial management of the company. It is worth pausing briefly to consider this company's workings.

The main business unit, based in Carlos Casares in the Province of Buenos Aires, is an informational corporation that is highly innovative and that is organized by a techno-informational division of labor, according to which various centers work on specific areas relevant to the different stages of production and circulation. These centers are interconnected as well as connected to other glocal networks. It is of particular interest that they are also associated with universities' systems for agricultural research, and in particular with the Instituto Nacional de Technology Agropecuaria and the Universidad de Buenos Aires.

The company's operational centers include sites for studying specific dynamics involved in technological production (at specific times of year) as well as for the processes of planting, harvesting, and storing crops in Carlos Casares. They also include sites for complex financial and commercial transactions, for the administration of trade, and for the development of production strategies. There are also sites for the study of business, sales, and projections for the price of soy on the various international stock exchanges. These, too, are, from the first, integrated into and connected with other sites in the country and the region where scientific and technological research takes place.

In cultural terms, this has generated a culture of informational work that valorizes innovation and the scientific and technological capabilities of workers. These qualities are seen to be pivotal for agricultural and land development, and this has influenced all other producers in the Humid Pampas as well as others in other regions and other countries in South America and the Caribbean.

In political terms, despite the partisan politics of the municipality and the region, the company's activities and its efforts at social integration and cultural participation (for example, in public schools) are highly valued by local citizens. Opposition to the company comes mainly from outside Carlos Casares.

In a report by Leila Guerrero for the magazine *Gatopardo*, Gustavo Grobocopatel is quoted as saying:

> Because of a flood, we learned to farm in fields other than our own, and I realized that it did not make sense to have land of your own. That you could grow enormously by planting crops in the ground with very little money and very quickly. After this, things got more sophisticated, but I think that this was the conceptual origin of our business model: the realization that you can farm without land, without capital, and without labor. Without land, because you rent; without labor, because you outsource it; and without capital, because they lend it to you. I don't know if we are the inventors, but we are the people who have gone farthest with this idea.

Nevertheless, as Wahren adds, all of this takes place in a very complex territorial context. In the late 1940s, Argentina used only 10,000 liters per year of agrochemicals, a figure that increased to 3.5 million by the 1970s. But beginning in 1996 (the year when the use of genetically modified soy seeds was approved), more than 200 billion liters of glyphosate were added to the 69 billion traditional agrochemicals already in use. According to some sources, the former figure should in fact be closer to 300 billion. In other words, this is an unprecedented situation, involving 19 million hectares of genetically modified soy and around 370 billion liters of agrochemicals that have not been proven to be harmless, since the precautionary principle has not been observed.

In terms of their relations with and ways of organizing their workers, these three companies differ widely from one another. In Jujuy, Salar de Olaroz interacts with Andean community organizations, made up mostly of young people who participate in the company's activities by performing both the hardest and the simplest tasks. It is also worth noting that there are communities that have refused to participate in the company's undertakings. In other cases, communities have been dominated and divided by relations of distrust across the local social spectrum.

In Vaca Muerta, at the highest level of the stratified workforce, there is a sort of "worker aristocracy" that is highly technologically skilled and well paid. These workers shore up a culture of oil-drilling that has a long history and has been privileged in the region and in Argentina. They have their own trade unions that take practical measures to advocate for their interests. On the other hand, there is also a set of part-time and temporary workers who sustain the extractive system in a different way. Another key factor in the company's success is the outsourcing of various activities both to other national companies and to international corporations.

Mapuche communities are key actors and significant territorial presences in this context, as are the labor organizing networks and non-governmental organizations to which Mapuche people belong. These networks are international in their reach, connecting them with Chilean Mapuches, for instance, and Sioux tribes in the United States. These communities' critique of Salar de Olaroz is primarily ecological in nature; it points to the possible contamination of groundwater on their territory. Other labor and business organizations in the region interact and participate in oil-drilling ventures. In this context, research units from the Universidad del Camagüey stand out, making significant contributions.

Environmental impacts, including water pollution and various other alterations to the ecosystem, are just some of the many frequent consequences of these corporate projects. Lithium mining requires considerable amounts of water, which tends to be scarce in fragile ecosystems like the salt flats (*salares*) for which Salar de Olaroz is named. Even a slight alteration to the conditions of these ecosystems can cause major disturbances in their equilibrium. For this reason, lithium mining worries local and surrounding communities, which see the mining company's use of nearby water sources as a threat, given that water is a scarce community resource, indispensable for both life and the maintenance of ancestral traditions including llama raising and mountain farming. In fact, in several interviews with local actors, we heard lithium mining called "water mining"; conflicts here are not over the extraction of lithium, but over the extraction of water.

The intensity of water use in lithium mining depends both on the

31

method of extraction and on the concentration of lithium in the brine involved in this process. In keeping with the concentration of lithium in Salar de Olaroz, according to a detailed feasibility study, every ton of lithium extracted requires around two million liters of water; in other words, the extraction of every gram of lithium takes two liters of water.[2]

In Vaca Muerta, we find differing expectations about the ecological or environmental consequences of fracking. Corporate leaders, the provincial government, civil society groups, trade unions, and Mapuche communities all have different worldviews, different understandings of the cosmos. The Mapuche question the logic of extraction as such; companies see it as the road to development; local citizens' views are somewhere in between, but suspicious. "Risk" is often argued over, as are the questions of whether risks are calculable and what the real costs of extraction are. People worry above all about the depletion of groundwater in the region. If the environmental effects of extraction could be mitigated and/or communities could ensure that these effects were no greater than those generated by traditional activities – that is, by the demands for energy, water, and materials for construction (steel, cement, and gravel, among others), within the limits determined by these activities – this would still entail territorial transformations at an unforeseen scale (Giuliani et al., 2016).

Pollution from farming is increasingly intense throughout the region. "Today, in Argentina there are 12 million people living in areas where more than 300 million liters of agrotoxins per year are disposed of" (Svampa and Viale, 2014: 150). High concentrations of genetically modified foods and agrochemicals, spread across so many hectares used for farming, have turned the country into a kind of open-air laboratory (Gras and Hernández, 2013).

According to Wahren's baseline study, no major critical voices have emerged in Carlos Casares to question Los Grobo Agropecuaria in particular or the extractive economy of mining more generally. Nevertheless, in the region more broadly, the last few years have witnessed the emergence of ever more forceful assemblies and local associations that have begun organizing to put an end to the spraying of chemicals near towns and rural schools, a practice that has led to increases in respiratory illnesses, skin diseases, and cancer. These groups associate such increases with the indiscriminate use of agrotoxins, including glyphosate the most widely used herbicide in the region. Rural communities, located in areas that are at the center of agribusiness in Argentina, have joined the struggles of peasants and indigenous people who have been denouncing corporate practices of despoliation and subjugation, as well as the corporate pollution of land and water, since the mid-1990s.

Until now, none of these collective actions seems to have reached Carlos Casares or to have directly affected Los Grobo, a corporation that takes pride in its own manual of agricultural "best practices," which has even been adopted by some local governments in the region, including that of Carlos Casares, of course.

As for conflicts in Salar de Olaroz, "broadly speaking, groups with opposing interests have been forming. In certain social sectors, we see the consolidation of an identity related to the universe of mining, with characteristics that follow from modernization, whereas in other social sectors people reject this model and seek to return to traditional activities or search for alternative approaches to local development" (Pragier and Deluca, forthcoming: 45).

"Even more complexity is introduced [into this situation] when we note that neither of these groups is homogenous in its meanings. Instead we can identify subtle differences, expressed in the juxtaposition of identities present in the territory" (Pragier and Deluca, forthcoming: 45). Within these communities, a first confrontation occurs between those who are in favor of and those who oppose the corporation's presence; at the most fundamental level, this entails arguments about the ways of life that each group advocates, and the latent conflict that emerges when these ways of life turn out to be incompatible. Here a clear generational division emerges, a division between young people in these communities (many of whom study in San Salvador de Jujuy, the provincial capital) and the older inhabitants of the region, for whom cattle farming and traditional agriculture remain primary economic and cultural commitments. These indigenous young people have gone to school, and they know how to articulate their demands elsewhere, but in most cases they no longer depend on the pastoral economy. Social divisions are characteristic of the region's society and of residents' relationships to Sales de Jujuy (Pragier and Deluca, forthcoming).

Meanwhile in Vaca Muerta, "increasing social differentiation in urban areas compounds the territorial, social, and environmental conflicts that lead to frustrated expectations for the future of oil mining. In this context, the Mapuche are key agents of resistance, questioning the model of informational extraction but disconnected from other agents engaged in the same sort of questioning" (Cretini, 2018: 83).[3]

Disputes over the meaning of land development ensue. The use of unconventional hydrocarbons has created various visions of such development, producing a range of opinions. There are those who question and oppose the logic of extraction (indigenous people and the union Central de los Trabajadores Argentinos, CTA) and those who consider this logic indispensable for long-term development (the state at various levels, business interests, and bureaucrats). There is of course a broad middle range of opinions as well. Public debates persistently center on the risk of extraction, the question of whether such a risk is calculable, and thus also the question of what the real costs of extraction are. But often accurate information is lacking or ambiguous when it comes to environmental impacts.[4]

In this context, neither spaces for dialogue nor public, institutional channels for communication have been created. Instead, each side has largely refused to acknowledge the other and ignored its demands. This leads to uncertainty about how the territorial dynamics will play out, and in particular about the fate of the territorial and environmental disputes that were reactivated in 2017, after a violent confrontation. Overall, given these recent conflicts and a contraction in channels for mediation and spaces for dialogue, it is likely that social, environmental, and territorial conflicts will all increase in their intensity in the medium term.

In the area around Carlos Casares, by contrast, "Los Grobo seems to have built a nearly 'perfect hegemony.' In a region where farming has been foundational and continues to organize the reproduction of everyday life, whether directly or indirectly, for the vast majority of residents, the environmentalist critique prompted by the model of agribusiness seems not to have made a dent in the corporation's legitimacy or the status of the Grobocopatel family" (Wahren, forthcoming: 149). Nevertheless, protests have begun to take place at a more general level, especially in cities responding to the consumption of agro-industrial products.

It is worth emphasizing that in the area surrounding Carlos Casares, in the humid pampa in Argentina, informational development and the culture of business are both essentially home-grown. The corporation and the "corporate culture of Grobo" form a particular productive system for marketing and corporate management at a global scale, one developed in concert with the scientific and technological research taking place in Argentina's universities (Wahren, forthcoming).

Unconventional oil and gas in Vaca Muerta is produced through a partnership between the state-owned company YPF and a pool of transnational corporations that use fracking technologies in ways that are already computerized, in keeping with the workings of the global market. Here there is also a space for exchange and negotiation with scientific and technological systems of innovation. The state-owned company engages in these exchanges and negotiations with its transnational partners, presided over by powerful and capable transnational companies like Chevron, from the United States (Cretini, 2018). From this perspective, these companies have been integrated into diverse territories and multicultural situations throughout Argentina in new ways, with implications that are especially important for the environment and politics.

The Environmental Limits of Informational Extractivism

The transition from industrial to informational extractivism has involved the formation of a new field of historical conflict between informational corporations, on the one hand, and, on the other, globalized – and networked – territorial actors. This involves a passage from the working class formed under industrial extractivism to a range of territorial actors operating under informational extractivism. This means a working class that is organized and integrated through functional differentiation; these workers form territorial organizations of various kinds: communitarian organizations, local associations, and organizations formed on the internet that bring together people with shared opinions.

We also see the emergence of various kinds of informational corporations with various internal structures and relationships to other companies. These corporations put information to different technological and economic uses, and they participate in different kinds of global networks. This leads to the emergence of institutions, subjectivities, and social organizations that play different roles in conflicts. That is, we also see the emergence of various social and territorial organizations, technological economies, and global networks.

All of this implies a new relationship between structural reality and subjectivity, or the possibilities and capacities of informational agents. The categories of isolated masses or modern, industrial unions, which were key to explaining industrial extractivism, are obsolete or have become subordinate to new forms created by the technological economy of information and new social networks of power.

On the ground, the effects on local societies vary, and the results range from integration to conflict, distrust, and the fragmentation of communities. In Carlos Casares, for example, we find an integrated society; in Vaca Muerta, we find a society that is somewhat integrated but also marked by conflicts; and in Salar de Olaroz, such conflicts have led to community fragmentation and distrust, in a social context with little integration and a great deal of potential for further conflict. A key factor in all of these contexts is the presence of a form of extractivism that degrades the environment but at the same time provides resources for policies that promote social integration and the diversification of production or the strengthening of the market. All of this leads to changes in and redefinitions of territorial boundaries in a new informational context. This also means economies and cultures that are altered by networks. Here both real and virtual borders of extraction change in different ways. The nation-state is insufficient in such a context and has increasing difficulty dealing with these kinds of changes.

The examples that we have considered in this chapter reflect the multicultural dynamics of Latin America, where a "new communitarianism" has emerged, one that is also ecological and that is marked by these basic traits: the defense of land, the recognition of various social and environmental demands, the critique of the model of development that we have called informational extractivism, and, above all, a communitarian cultural tendency that opposes environmental despoliation and seeks to valorize forms of life based on ecological thought.

— 3 —

THE GLOBAL CRIMINAL ECONOMY

A specter has been haunting Latin America for decades, with growing intensity, changing forms, and shifting geographies: the specter of the glocal criminal economy.[1] This economy is criminal because it is based on the addition of value to – and the production of and traffic in – goods or services that have been criminalized by the state. It is global because it is essentially an economy organized by the global market, one whose participants seek to accumulate capital in global financial markets. And it is local because its activities are rooted in local cultures and societies, which supply a labor force ready for anything and give meaning to the actions of its participants. This economy is also local because local and national markets have, during the last phases of this economy's development, gained force as the purchasing power of Latin America's urban middle classes has also increased. For this reason, we call the Latin American criminal economy "glocal."

This economy is extremely dynamic, divided into several sectors (although drug trafficking is still the most important of these), and highly profitable as long as we do not seek to quantify its enormous human cost. Its power is based on the ability to circumvent the regulatory and coercive capacities of the state. For this reason, it seeks to wield a greater coercive power than the state, and thus to infiltrate the state through corruption and intimidation at all levels. It generates volatile economic growth and short-term employment, even while it is the source of institutional disintegration and social demoralization. Its dynamics are at once local and global, and its networked forms are based on technology and information. It is a capitalist industry bound ultimately to global financial markets. Quantitatively speaking, it is worth hundreds of billions of dollars, if we factor in all criminal

activities, of which drug trafficking might represent around 80 percent. Jeremy Haken's estimate in 2011 put this figure at US$651
billion globally (Haken, 2011). For Latin America, the estimated
profits from drug trafficking were calculated at around US$320 bil-
lion in 2014, according to the United Nations Office on Drugs and
Crime (UNODC, 2018). But these figures were tentative, not only
because of the inherent difficulty of measuring such activities statistically, but also because they accounted mainly for financial flows from
money laundering (Organization of American States, 2014). These
did not include the transactions on the streets of cities throughout
the world or the payments in cash that never reach banking systems.
What we can confirm, in any case, is that the scope of this economy
is vast and that it introduces considerable volatility into financial
markets, given the opacity and speed of the transactions it involves.
All estimates agree that in the first decades of the twenty-first century,

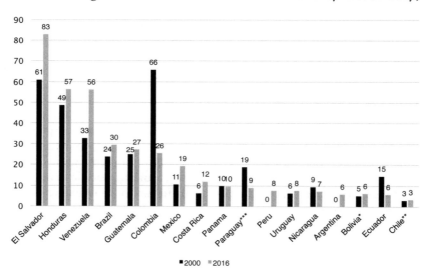

Figure 3.1: Victims of Intentional Homicides, Selected Latin American
Countries, 2000–2016 (rate per 100,000 residents)

Notes: "Intentional homicide" means illicit death intentionally inflicted on one
person by another person. Data on intentional homicide should also include serious
assaults that lead to death and deaths as a result of terrorist attacks. Such data
should exclude attempted murders, involuntary homicides, deaths caused by legal
interventions, deaths justifiable as self-defense, and deaths caused in armed conflicts
(UNODC, https://dataunodc.un.org/crime/intentional-homicide-victims)

*Data for the years 2000–15; ** data for the years 2003–16; *** data for the
years 2005–16

THE GLOBAL CRIMINAL ECONOMY

criminal activity has increased, although not all sectors in the criminal economy have developed in the same way.

A more meaningful indicator of this is the increase in violence and, in particular, in homicide rates in Latin America (see figure 3.1). Drug trafficking has been essential to this increase, as have other activities associated with the criminal economy, including the trafficking in women, children, and weapons as well as kidnappings, extortion, and all kinds of robbery (including, for example, fuel theft). Between 2005, when rates were already high, and 2014, homicides rates in Latin America increased by 12 percent. According to the UNODC's data (2018), in 2018, eight countries had more than ten homicides per 100,000 residents per year: El Salvador was at the top of this list, with 83 intentional homicides per 100,000 residents; Honduras followed with 57; Venezuela, with 56; and Brazil, with 30. In 2013, the UNODC's *Global Study on Homicide* noted that in Latin America around 30 percent of homicides were the result of confrontations between criminal groups, while in Asia and Europe this figure was less than 5 percent (UNODC, 2013: 43). In Ciudad Juárez, in Mexico, between 2006 and 2010, the murder rate increased by 1,000 percent. President Felipe Calderón's effort to tackle Mexican cartels directly led to more than 120,000 deaths and some 20,000 disappearances, without this slowing the growth of drug trafficking, though this trafficking now took new, less centralized forms.[2]

The Structure of the Criminal Economy

In order to situate the development of the criminal economy in the context of broader social dynamics in Latin America, we will begin by considering this economy's characteristics during the period of its formation, in the 1980s. Its nucleus was formed by drug trafficking, and in particular by the traffic in cocaine, although originally marijuana also played an important role in the constitution of drug trafficking networks, only to later disappear after marijuana's de facto legalization and its cultivation in the United States.

Originally, drug trafficking in Latin America was marked by six characteristics:

1 It was an industry driven by increasing demand for drugs at the global level and thus largely centered on exports, especially to wealthy markets like the United States and Europe, although the internal market in Latin America was also growing.

2 It was an internationalized industry, with a division of labor between different locations. The main producers of coca were Peru and Bolivia, although later Colombia also became a producer. The processing of cocaine took place in labs, especially in Colombia, with chemical precursors that were mostly imported from Argentina and Brazil. Transportation to and distribution in destination markets took place first in the Caribbean and Central America, especially Honduras, Guatemala, and Nicaragua. After increases in volume in the industry, transportation took place in Mexico, where Mexican cartels were able to control the market and ultimately the whole industry, using Colombian cartels as suppliers of raw materials. When regulations increased at the original sites of distribution, the use of other cities allowed for the diversification of the distribution process, especially through transport from Venezuela to Europe. As the market grew globally, both Colombian and Mexican cartels entered into partnerships for the purposes of distribution, joining criminal organizations from other areas, especially Russia after the fall of the Soviet Union.

3 It was an industry that depended on the coercive, intimidating, and corrupt power of state institutions. Hence the formation of veritable armies of hitmen (*sicarios*) working in the service of drug traffickers. These armies became essential to the expansion of the criminal economy. Violence in all its forms became consubstantial with organized crime. The capacity to use violence allowed for expansion into other kinds of criminal activity, including extortion, kidnapping, robbery, and sexual violence, breaking down state institutions and depriving citizens of protections. Enabled by this impunity, criminal gangs of traffickers proliferated, gangs that were independent but always ready to charge for their services.

4 The industry could not survive without the collusion or tolerance of state institutions. The infiltration of the state and corruption of the state's functionaries, the political system, and the police and armed forces became systematic factors that contributed to the gradual erosion of state institutions, both federal and local, in many countries in the region. These dynamics also created a generalized sense of suspicion and vulnerability among citizens. Intimidation and violence against the media and the journalists who were its representatives and against civil society as well were also part of a climate of terror through which the criminal industry imposed itself.

5 Given this capacity for violence, competition between different criminal groups, whether cartels or others, included forms

of extremely violent confrontation, at times even barbarism or sadism, used as techniques for frightening potential competitors. This raised the bar for entry into the industry.

6 Finally, the criminal economy's ultimate objective is the accumulation of capital to increase business and profits, both from the industry itself and especially from investments in legal enterprises. Hence money laundering and the infiltration of the financial world are of the utmost importance to the criminal industry. The mechanisms used to achieve these goals are varied, but they always include different phases, and they depend on the ability to deposit funds in welcoming banks, located in countries with little or no regulation; these locations are changed as the deposited funds are detected by international authorities. For example, for a time, Panama, the Cayman Islands, Turks and Caicos, Aruba, and the Bahamas, but also Luxemburg, Austria, and the Isle of Man were regularly used for these money laundering operations. Later, any transfer into financial systems in these places aroused suspicion, so that the locations for deposits were further diversified, as were the methods used (investments in property, Bitcoin, the purchasing of assets in cash, the purchasing of foreign currency through informal markets, casinos, and so on). There were also increases in the physical movement of funds in cash through the use of messengers who crossed borders in different ways in order to give payments to providers. But then this dirty money, after losing more than half of its nominal value as currency through the process of being laundered, still needs to end up in a financial institution in a financial haven, where such operations are sustained by businesses and embezzling politicians, as in Panama, for example. From here the funds can be invested in various consecutive kinds of activity until all trace of their origin has disappeared, and they can be used as investments throughout the globe. Respectable institutions like American Express and Citibank have been fined for failing to exercise control over the funds deposited into their Latin American branches. The ultimate goal of this process is to make capital available for use in financial institutions that are not suspicious, like those in the United States, Europe, or Japan, where they can be used for global investments.

Transformations in the Criminal Economy

Latin American drug trafficking was a successful business enterprise, native to the region. Begun by businessmen who came from nothing, like Pablo Escobar and the Ochoa brothers in Medellín, or by bourgeois elites, like the Rodríguez Orejuela brothers in Cali, who saved businesses that were in ruins, these enterprises grew into flexible networks as their production and export capacities increased. But the need to control capital, hitmen, access to the state, and means of transportation led to a process of concentration and to the formation of cartels. Something similar took place in Mexico, where local criminal groups, formed especially around traditional contraband networks operating along the northern border, competed and merged with one another, seeking protection in alliances around individual leaders. This was the origin of the famous Mexican cartels, whose structure and dynamics have been rigorously analyzed and brilliantly documented in John Sullivan's doctoral dissertation (2015). Although the drug cartels' mythology has often obscured their reality and exaggerated their power, it is true that they turned themselves into highly significant economic and, especially, political actors, with profound implications for several sectors, national and local. And this is true not only in Colombia or Mexico, whose histories have been so clearly marked by drug trafficking; it is also true in Central America (except in Costa Rica), in Bolivia, Peru, Ecuador, and Paraguay, and in many cities in Brazil, especially Rio. At the same time, the cartels' visibility and that of their leaders, the perception of their power and the proof of their brutality, has made them into privileged targets for states and for US intelligence agencies, which, under the pretext of the "war on drugs," infiltrated the military and intelligence apparatuses of most Latin American states. One by one, the cartels' leaders have been killed or incarcerated (preferably in the United States, so that what happened with Escobar, who was allowed his own prison in collaboration with the Colombian government, does not repeat itself). Some, like Escobar or El Chapo Guzmán, became mythical figures for some sectors of the population, who felt helped by them, rather than abandoned as they had been by governments. Other cartel leaders set aside their savings to keep their families comfortable. Many others, at other levels of the structure, broke away from the cartels to form autonomous organizations that simply worked with other organizations to complete local and specific criminal tasks. They specialized in different operations and different kinds of activity. Financial organizations became semi-legal, hiring teams of respectable lawyers; hitmen formed professional groups of assassins, working for the highest bidder; transport specialists adapted to new routes and means of transport as the US market decreased in value, while shipments to destinations in Europe and Asia increased. Still other organizations persisted in their original drug trafficking activity, but in much smaller and less visible units.

Thus the breakdown of the seven major Mexican cartels led to the formation of some 60 autonomous organizations rooted in different regions. Some of these were admittedly more notorious than others: La Familia in Michoacán, for example, or Jalisco Nueva Generación. It is important to note that at the same time, according to data gathered by Castells in 2018, some of the militarized cartels that absorbed parts of the Gulf Cartel, including Los Zetas in particular, also persisted. Meanwhile other new and powerful cartels appeared, especially Jalisco Nueva Generación, which used extreme and extraordinarily cruel violence to expand beyond its territory near Guadalajara and become the most powerful cartel in Mexico. In Colombia, the peace process led to breakdowns in partnerships between drug cartels and guerrilla and paramilitary organizations, which resulted in a proliferation of dozens of autonomous groups. These are generally paramilitary in their origins and are even more violent and criminal than the groups that preceded them, who were rooted in remote regions and especially in indigenous territories that they subjugated and exploited. Recent years have also witnessed a geographical displacement, a shift to countries with very weak states, where local gangs are very strong and have transborder roots. This is especially the case in Honduras, the most violent country in Latin America in 2018. This is not to say, however, that violence has decreased in Mexico or Colombia. In 2017, there were more deaths in Mexico than during any other year of the country's history; the rate of deaths by homicide for every 100,000 residents was over 25.2, according to the Instituto Nacional de Estadísticas y Geografía. Massacres by cartels became bloody micro-conflicts, affecting neighborhood after neighborhood in all cities in which the criminal economy was still up for grabs.

In addition, two fundamental transformations in the drug economy took place. On the one hand, there was an expansion and diversification of global markets; having been global, these became at once global and local. Concretely, this meant that the importance of the US market for cocaine diminished significantly, while the market for amphetamines and synthetic drugs increased, especially the market for fentanyl, generally coming from China. (Fentanyl is 50 times more powerful and destructive than heroin.) Between the mid-1990s and the 2010s, demand for cocaine in the United States decreased from 70 percent to 31 percent of the global market. The main cause of the decline in cocaine consumption in the United States was not that the country's consumers were in recovery, but rather the emergence of

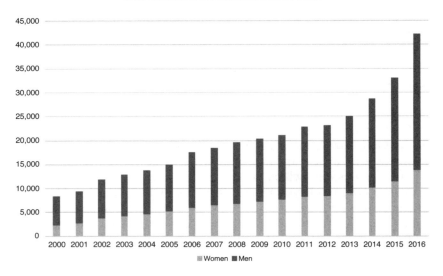

Figure 3.2: Number of Deaths Caused by Opioid Overdoses in the United States, 2000–2016

an opioid epidemic of enormous proportions, one that led to nearly half a million casualties from overdoses between 2012 and 2018 (see figure 3.2). This is more than the total number of US citizens who died in combat in both world wars. As the researcher Melina Sherman has shown in her doctoral dissertation (2018), these opioid drugs are obtained through legal prescriptions provided by doctors, then exchanged and paid for in networks of families and friends. And although a majority of opioid addicts are white, all social classes, genders, and ethnic groups make up the legions of those addicted to prescription drugs (especially painkillers) produced by "Big Pharma" and administered by the medical system under patient pressure. Paradoxically, the opioid epidemic has contributed to a new expansion in the minority market for heroin. This is because heroin, another opiate, turns out to be cheaper and more powerful in its effects, for the thousands of addicts who are unable to obtain drugs through the semi-legal market for medical prescriptions.

The decline in the US market for cocaine has been more than made up for by the growth of three new markets. We are referring to the markets in Europe and Southeast Asia, but also to the market for internal consumption in Latin America, which has grown exponentially in recent years, especially in Brazil and Argentina. This is a market for the consumption not just of cocaine but also of synthetic drugs, and its effects include trafficking and local violence resulting from fights over the control of markets. In 2017, the most violent city in Argentina was the marvelous Rosario, where death arrives by way of the city's majestic river, the Río Paraná. Soy travels over this river headed to China, and Chinese fentanyl travels over it as well, toward places beyond Rosario. During Castells' visit to the city in 2018, he was able to see a key site in its drug trade: the campus of the prestigious Universidad de Rosario. Here the market was largely made up of students and professionals, a far cry from the markets catering only to *gringos*. In Rosario, the struggle for control over the new market involved two family clans, the Funes and the Camino, who clashed in a series of violent vendettas.[3]

Drugs, Culture, and Society

It seems clear that the demand for ever more powerful drugs has no limit in today's world. At the root of this demand is the need felt by millions of human beings for chemically induced stimulation or, in other cases, for chemically enabled escape from the unbearable difficulty or absurdity of their everyday lives. This affects young people in particular, who were led to expect another world, different from the one into which they were brought without asking to be. These young people still do not have a solid spinal cord to make them resilient, because this comes only from withstanding blows. It would seem to be obvious, given the psychological need for drugs, that they should be legalized and that their use should be regulated and treated as a public health issue. Instead, the illicit traffic in multiple drugs creates a giant fog of death, imprisonment, and destruction. After all, the sale and consumption of marijuana led to the imprisonment of thousands of people until very recently, and this remains the case in many countries. By contrast, marijuana is now legal in several states in the US, since its therapeutic effects have been proven to relieve both illnesses and tension, and its harmfulness has been shown to be minimal, and in any case less than that of alcohol. But the social hypocrisy and the ideological interests that dominate our lives stand in the way of a rational solution to this enormous social problem. It is the repression of drugs that is the real problem, not drugs themselves. This problem continues to worsen in Latin America and to limit everyday life, politics, and governance. For most Latin Americans, violence is their primary concern. Almost a third of people in the region have experienced or know someone who has experienced violence at least once

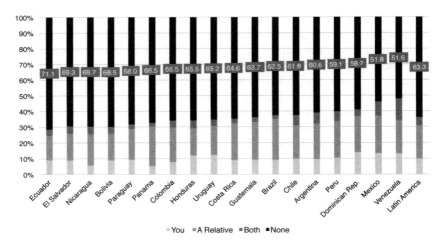

Figure 3.3: People who have been victims of a crime, Latin America, 2016 (%)

per year (see figure 3.3). Although this is partly an effect of informal mechanisms of redistribution in a context of enormous social inequality, much of the worst violence, which is caused by gangs, is related to drug trafficking.

Why Have Drugs Played Such a Prominent Role in Latin America?

Historically speaking, there are two reasons. On the one hand, the role of drugs in Latin America has to do with their traditional cultivation for local use, as in the case of coca, which is necessary for life and work in the Andes, or as in the case of marijuana, which was grown for medicinal uses. These were discovered by US youths traveling in Latin America in the 1960s, a period characterized by a search for new sensations, leading to a cultural revolution on university campuses. Networks of smugglers in Colombia and Mexico recognized the potential in this market and began organizing themselves to produce and export drugs. On the other hand, the second reason for the role played by drugs in Latin America follows from the existence of vast areas of South America that are outside state control, whether because they are in the hands of guerrilla or counter-guerrilla movements or simply because of the structural weakness of the state in some of its territories, as in the parts of Bolivia, Colombia, or Peru surrounding the Amazon. These are precisely the areas where one coca plant can be harvested four times yearly. Something similar led to the development of the traffic in heroin from Asia – for example from Afghanistan, Thailand, or Myanmar – which created new market possibilities. Once networks of production and export were formed, at first for the production and export of cocaine, drug traffickers expanded and updated their activities. The network became more important than the product itself; all kinds of drugs, including especially synthetic and derivative drugs, now circulated through this network. Laboratories for the production of cocaine began to produce amphetamines as well as the various kinds of new drugs that emerged in the market. The range of services that the network could offer, in terms of power, violence, and capital, made the criminal economy into a forceful economic sector, one ultimately connected to global financial markets.

Importantly, the drug cartels were marked for a long time by their cultures of origin, by their local roots, which provided resources, support when it was needed, and a sense of identity. The value of family, of tradition, and even of religion were central to the cartels, important to leaders as well as to hitmen. Added to this was a clientelist system in which many drug lords recruited local populations, who were offered shelter, schools, clinics, and of course employment and protection after the death or imprisonment of family members. There was one condition: absolute loyalty to the cartel, enforced by the threat of death. All of this explains both the regional and cultural identity of each cartel and the violence that marked confrontations between different cartels. To be sure, the structure of the trade developed continuously, that it was globalized, and that it led to the creation of a class of narco-financiers that operated almost independently of production. Many leaders in this class resembled – and became – corporate executives like any others in the business world. Still, in situations of crisis or state repression, they withdrew to their own territories and to the cultures from which they came. This happened, for instance, when, after it fell, the Guadalajara Cartel was replaced, with intense violence, by Jalisco Nueva Generación, which insisted both on its youthfulness and its shared cultural origins and identity.

Moreover, in local markets, both in the United States and in Latin America, youth gangs are in charge of the drug trade. They are in direct contact with wholesalers, without intermediaries, and they also arrange for the transfer of profits without relying on intermediaries. This is how the criminal economy takes root in the social fabric of large cities, becoming part of local cultures, consolidating itself in networks of collaboration that continue to function in prisons, which in many cases become centers for the coordination and control of the drug trade.

Gangs, like the *maras* that arose in the Central American communities of Los Angeles and other large cities, form transnational networks that operate on both sides of the border and in franchises run by Mexican wholesalers working in partnership with Colombian and Andean producers. Thus the old figure of the great cartels, vulnerable to repression because of their visibility, has given way to diversified, horizontal networks that are both socially and culturally integrated into their surroundings.

The traffic in heroin, which is much less important than cocaine in Latin America and the North American market, offers an alternative and innovative model of vertical integration, in which production, distribution, and marketing are brought together in networks originating in specific territories. A revealing case of this can be found in the state of Nayarit, in Mexico, which specialized in the production of black heroin. Immigrants from various cities in Nayarit, related through kinship or proximity, maintained, and still maintain, control over this heroin's distribution in the United States. The system is so thoroughly capillary that it even includes home delivery in the upper-middle class. In order to operate in local markets these groups rely on the protection of gangs in different territories whose diversified work includes both trafficking for themselves and serving as hitmen for others in their drug distribution networks.

These gangs, present in large cities throughout the Americas, are the direct causes of the everyday violence that has increased every year in the twenty-first century. Each gang's and each gang member's capacity for violence is a key factor in the competition for control over markets and suppliers. These decentralized, coercive apparatuses have destroyed the ability of institutions, beginning with the police in many countries, to ensure compliance with the law. Uncertainty among citizens has led to the proliferation of private security forces, frequently organized by the police themselves.

The culture of hitmen is a fundamental component of the criminal economy. So, too, is the direct or indirect experience of low-income youth. This is an example of what, some time ago in her book on *malandros*, or thugs, in Caracas, the Venezuelan sociologist Magaly Sánchez called "the culture of urgency" (Pedrazzini and Sánchez, 1992). This culture is a matter of speeding life up, living every minute as if it were one's last, because the orderly sequence of a life lived according to society's guidelines offers no perspectives on what

48

makes existence worthwhile or what gives life existential meaning. So the empowerment represented by wielding a weapon, or by enjoying the material and psychological support of other gang members, or by gaining immediate access to consumer goods that would otherwise be inaccessible (like expensive sneakers) is worth the sacrifice of years in prison or even death itself. Better to die after having been high on life than to languish through a long series of daily humiliations.

García Márquez, in his splendid work of non-fiction *News of a Kidnapping* (1997) described the psychology of the young hitmen whom he interviewed. For them, everything in society is rotten. There is no meaning beyond what can be felt in each moment. And for this reason, each moment must be lived with the greatest possible intensity, with free rein given to the instincts, to the will to power and violence. The only norms that matter are those of one's own criminal organization. Only family – especially the mother – has value in these hitmen's lives. That and a certain religious feeling, typically projected onto an individual saint or virgin, a feeling that offers them a vague promise of protection, a fragile hope that their lives might be prolonged. This culture, in which death is the only value for life, is present in all areas associated with the criminal economy.

In Tepito, the legendary and indomitable neighborhood in central Mexico City, where informal commerce, petty crime, and the sale of drugs mix with whatever else one can think of, there is a chapel in the entrance to an old house, presided over by a *santera* or priestess. The chapel is dedicated to the Virgen de la Santa Muerte, the Virgin of Holy Death, a local creation. The virgin here is a skeleton. And around her a colorful mural features an endless host of the dead, whose long procession extends all the way to the horizon. There are also the names of some in the neighborhood. New names are added to this list periodically. This is a representation of life as seen from the perspective of the "culture of urgency," enshrined in a fatalism about the world and an invocation of the moment lived here and now. This is the holy death that ends a life intensely felt.

Coca, Identity, and Social Movements

Cultural alienation involves the reinterpretation of a way of life in the prejudiced terms of another culture. This reinterpretation establishes a pattern of domination through the negation of the "other." Hence the history of colonial domination, which opposed the "barbarism" of indigenous "savages" to the colonizers' "civilization." In a way that is subtler but no less efficacious, coca has been identified with cocaine. And drug addiction in the dominant countries, which are also the main markets for drugs, has been rendered synonymous with the production, sale, and use of coca. Clearly the substantial increase in the production of coca leaves in the Andes beginning in the 1970s was related to the appropriation of most of the harvest by drug traffickers, especially Colombians, to be processed into cocaine and exported to profitable markets in "the north." Nevertheless, it is common knowledge that the coca plant has numerous uses, especially medicinal uses, and that it is inextricably bound up with the millennially old history of Andean cultures. Thus the United States Drug Enforcement Administration's violent and indiscriminate attempt to eradicate coca cultivation, with the participation of colluding governments and policies that served US interests, was regarded, and resented, as a pillaging presence by coca-farming communities in various areas where the plant was cultivated. The proposals for alternative crops (like bananas or rice) made no economic sense for those who had already dedicated themselves to the production of coca. In 1985, Castells visited the Chapare Valley, a key site for the production of coca leaves in Bolivia, as well as Las Yungas near La Paz. The communities that he interviewed were made up not only of traditional peasants, but also of miners displaced by the government in an effort to relieve unemployment in the mines and turn the country's tropical areas to profit. The plan was absurd given the absence of networks for transport and distribution from such a remote location. But the population of new peasants soon discovered the possibilities of coca leaves (including in the national market, which is considerable), and, for their part, drug wholesalers discovered the peasants and organized the transportation of their crops to Colombia. Something similar happened in Alto Huallaga, Peru, which was controlled by guerrilla fighters for a time, and in Colombia, where there were also areas that remained beyond the government's reach, though not that of its paramilitary forces.

Given their institutional instability, the coca-producing regions could not be development zones. Nearby cities like Cochabamba or Santa Cruz in Bolivia, were centers only for the modest accumulation of capital. In fact, in all of Latin America, coca farmers receive only 1 percent of the revenues generated by the drug trade. But without the agricultural raw materials provided by these farmers this trade could not function. There would be no value chain or value added. Hence the repressive actions taken especially by the United States. These included the massive deforestation of vast swaths of the woods without the relocation of their inhabitants, and they amounted to a veritable declaration of war for the coca farmers. This led to a wave of protests organized by unions representing territories, and this wave became a social movement. This was not just a response to grievances, but the articulation of a critique of a whole system of dependency on the United States, a system that ignored possible alternative markets for coca. The movement also included the denunciation of government corruption and the affirmation of indigenous culture. In this way, the Movimiento al Socialismo (MAS) was born, led by a charismatic coca farmer named Evo Morales, who was also from the highlands and would be elected president of Bolivia and begin a sweeping social revolution. In 2017, long after his first visit to Chapare, Castells returned to attend an event proclaiming the passage of the new Ley de la Coca, or coca law. Thousands of coca farmers representing their unions from throughout the country celebrated this victory. In cooperation with these unions, the government set limits for the production of coca in order to minimize its diversion into illegal markets as much as possible. But at the same time, the government created alternative production lines and export networks, making allowances for coca's medicinal and pharmaceutical uses. This was an act of national sovereignty in which Bolivia decided what to do with its own coca, affirming its ties with its indigenous cultures.

The struggles over coca expressed at once the producers' demands for control over their lands and processes of production, their affirmation of the identity symbolized by the mythic plant, and their defense against the geopolitical strategies subtending the international politics of control over the drug trade, which target supply rather than demand and are implicitly enabled by a vision of territorial domination.

The Criminal Economy and Latin American Societies

Despite the efforts of excellent Latin American economists, including Francisco Thoumi, Juan Mario Laserna, and Daniel Pontón, it remains difficult to measure the criminal economy and thus to analyze it. But in a study conducted by the Inter-American Development Bank, we find the estimate that in 2014 the cost of crime represented 3.5 percent of GDP in Latin America and the Caribbean (see Figure 3.4). Meanwhile, we can detect and even study the effects of these costs on Latin American societies, because all of them are marked by the criminal economy at various levels.

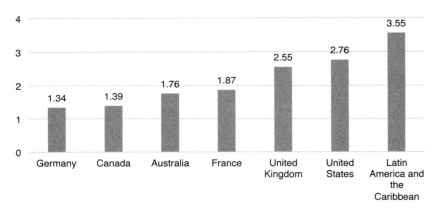

Figure 3.4: The Cost of Crime: Latin America and the Caribbean and Selected Other Countries, 2014 (% GDP)

The first effect to note is the appearance of narco-bourgeoisies in numerous local areas, classes that leave their mark on surrounding social norms and perceptions. The rapid accumulation of capital, with its consequences for consumption among *nouveaux riches*, combined with a sense of impunity and thus with ostentatious displays of wealth and power that were deliberately provocative to traditional local oligarchies.

In 1991, Castells observed in the supermarkets of Guadalajara a parade of *"narcas"* wearing jewels and leather (which must have made them sweat!), surrounded by maids who carried their purchases and by discreet bodyguards. This was not at all world-changing, but it did signal a shift in the social hierarchies that had long since been established and, in a sense, in the cultural models available for imitation and valorization. Throughout the region the appearance, in elite social circles, of characters whose legality and money were questionable led to the social acceptability of a certain kind of life and activity, even among political and business elites.

At a second level, popular and youth culture created a new imaginary based on fables of rapid self-promotion and unregulated entrepreneurship. These fables were nurtured by images from entertainment and by the visual normalization of violence.

The spread of feelings of insecurity throughout society is even more significant. And although it is the low-income sectors of the population that suffer most from the onset of violence, ruling elites and the upper-middle classes are those who see themselves as permanently under threat. This is, among other things, because of the numerous kidnappings that have made kidnapping into one of the most lucrative businesses in the underworld. The most direct consequence of public fear, apart from the creation of many jobs in private security, allowing clients to bypass the mediation of police suspected of corruption, was the self-segregation of affluent social sectors, whose members withdraw to wealthy ghettos removed from the city and guarded by their own militias. This can be seen in the north of Bogotá, for instance, or the south of Mexico City. Here the city is no longer a common space, and public space becomes a space of fear, except on the streets that serve as theme parks set aside for the protected use of tourists.

Moreover, the destabilization of local and global financial markets by the volatility of capital derived from money laundering generates insecurity for local investors and contributes to the permanent flight of capital toward parts of the world considered institutionally protected. This heightens the sense of dependence on the formal world, which contrasts starkly with the more local form of everyday life marked by informality and negotiations with the unexpected.

Of course, the volatility of capital results not only from the money laundering associated with the Latin American drug trade. In fact, here all kinds of capital converge in their ability to evade capture and control by states. This evasion can happen legally, through transfers to tax havens, or illegally, through global financial fraud arranged by specialized firms, many of them located in tax havens or lax states, often in Central America or the Caribbean. Here capital arrives by opaque routes from places throughout the world – most of it, in fact, from Asia or Russia. This might mean that, measured in monetary terms, the main illicit (not necessarily illegal, but a legal) economy in Latin America is not drug trafficking but the recycling of global finances.

Ultimately, the source of all of the forms of corruption involved in the criminal economy is the corruption of numerous Latin American states. But since this corruption involves various other processes, we need to expand our analysis in order to account for the range of factors that contribute to systemic state corruption in twenty-first-century Latin America.

— 4 —

HUMAN DEVELOPMENT, URBANIZATION, AND INHUMAN DEVELOPMENT

Human Development in Latin America

During the first two decades of the twenty-first century, the traditional indicators of human development improved considerably in Latin America, as we noted in chapter 1. This was especially true in those countries that saw the implementation of a neo-developmentalist model, one that sought to combine economic growth with the social redistribution of resources.[1] The percentage of the population living under the poverty line was significantly reduced, and reductions in rates of extreme poverty were even more significant, though with variations in different countries. Primary education became nearly universal, even if the quality of public schools remains for the most part deficient despite its teachers' best efforts. Rates of both secondary and higher education increased substantially, as schools and universities admitted more students, though this was often thanks to the expansion of private schools, which are more expensive than public schools and poor in quality (except for the private schools that cater to elites). Healthcare systems expanded coverage and improved their services, though millions of people were without stable insurance, and waiting lists in hospitals grew to such lengths that in some cases medical appointments came too late for patients. Social programs for the poorest populations, like the Bolsa Família program in Brazil, helped the least socially advantaged. Social polices relieved poverty in places that the market could not reach, and they even helped foster the emergence of new urban middle classes able to plan for the future, if only modestly.

There were also important improvements in levels of collective basic consumption (of potable water, sanitation, gas, electricity, and so on). Nevertheless, levels of inequality and marginalization have persisted or worsened. Moreover, there is no guarantee that the gains that we have mentioned will be sustained, especially given the periodic crises that currently afflict Latin American countries and their citizens. Using data from 2009–10, a UN Habitat study arrived at estimates of the Gini coefficient of social inequality for 32 cities in the region. The study found that in all of these cities the Gini coefficient rose above the "alert level" (a Gini coefficient above 0.40), and that in 13 cities the index was above 0.55. So, for example, Brasília had a Gini coefficient of 0.67; Santo Domingo a coefficient of 0.58; Bogotá a coefficient of 0.51; Montevideo a coefficient of 0.43; and Lima a coefficient of 0.40 (UN Habitat, 2016) (see figure 4.1). Moreover, levels of wealth concentration remained high. For example, in 2010 the richest 1 percent of the population in Colombia, Mexico, Brazil, and Chile garnered between 20 and 25 percent of national revenues. By contrast, in developed countries, except for the United States, this percentage was below 15 percent (ECLAC, 2016a).

Furthermore, increases in overall quality of life are associated with processes of environmental deterioration related to the conditions of urbanization in Latin America. In fact, as a direct consequence

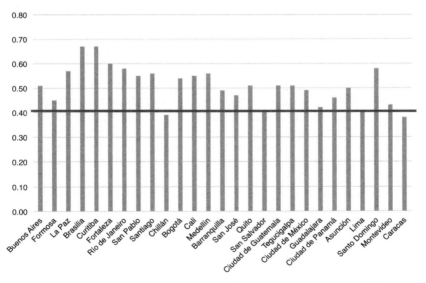

Figure 4.1: Gini Index of Inequality, Selected Latin American Cities, 2009–2010

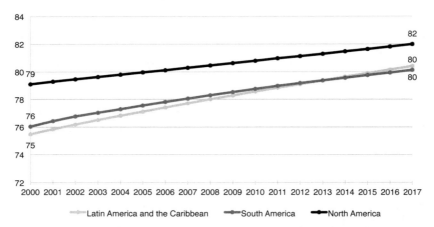

Figure 4.2: Urban Population as a Percentage of Total Population: Latin America and the Caribbean, South America, and North America, 2000–2017

of the acceleration of economic growth following the region's insertion into the global economy, there was an urban and metropolitan explosion in Latin America. In 2017, levels of urbanization both in Latin America and the Caribbean and in South America reached 80 percent, approaching North America's level (82 percent) (see figure 4.2). The highest percentages are found in Uruguay (95%), Argentina (92%), Venezuela (88%), and Chile (87%); the lowest in Paraguay (61%), Nicaragua (58%), Honduras (56%), and Guatemala (51%) (World Bank, 2018). But although urbanization concentrates much of the population in megacities like Mexico City, Buenos Aires, São Paulo, and Rio de Janeiro, it has also expanded consistently throughout many national territories. Indeed, only five cities in Latin America had over one million residents in 1950, while in 2010, 47 cities had populations this size. Similarly, the number of cities with between 20,000 and 49,000 residents went from 324 in 1950 to 1,739 in 2010 (Jordán et al., 2017: 83–92).

Urbanization is not in and of itself a negative factor in people's lives. In fact, there is a positive correlation between human development indices and levels of urbanization. In this sense, it is worth noting that the countries with the highest levels of human development in the region – Chile, Argentina, and Uruguay – are also among those with the highest levels of urbanization, with urban populations measured as a percentage of total populations.

A study by Ricardo Jordán, Luis Riffo, and Antonio Prado notes, for example, that Panama City occupies just 15 percent of Panama's surface area but generates 71 percent of its GDP and houses 51 percent of its population. Likewise, Buenos Aires and the metropolitan areas of Lima and Santiago represent less than 10 percent of their countries' surface areas but generate more than 50 percent of their GDPs. These tendencies are less pronounced in Bolivia and Ecuador, given that each of these countries has more than one main urban center (Jordán et al., 2017: 43). That is, overall, the region's large cities are motors of economic growth, innovation, social cohabitation in porous public and private spaces, and cultural creativity, as seen on the coast of San Juan in Puerto Rico, along the boulevards of Montevideo, or on the banks of the river in Rosario. At the same time, cities offer greater opportunities for improving quality of life than do rural areas or regions that have been marginalized by the dynamics of globalization. But precisely because these great metropolitan areas concentrate capital, employment, wealth, higher levels of education, and better healthcare, they attract migrants from areas that have been left behind, leading to extreme inequality in Latin America's metropolises (see figure 4.3).

Thus if the richest 0.1 percent of these cities' populations is separated out from the rest, multiple differences come into view. Guerrero et al. (2006) estimate that the potential income of billionaires in Mexico was 400 times greater than that of the richest 0.1 percent of the population according to income and expenditure surveys, and 14,000 times greater than the average income of all Mexicans. Consumerist, anti-fiscal, and rentier behaviors in the corporate sector have limited its own potentials for productive growth and those of the region as a whole. Likewise, construction, investments in urban infrastructure, and financial speculation on urban properties for rent all lead not just to new forms of wealth concentration, but also to forms of socio-territorial fragmentation and differentiation. Indeed, the concentration of wealth in families can lead to much more severe concentrations of corporate influence, through pyramidal structures of business ownership. These structures result in family control over assets and increases in effective ownership. This can also be seen in stock markets. For example, in Mexico, 15 publicly traded companies "represent more than 80% of the sample used in the Índice de Precios y Cotizaciones de la Bolsa Mexicana de Valores [Mexican Stock Exchange's Index of Prices and Quotations], and more than 40% of the stock market's total capitalization" (Guerrero et al., 2006: 8).

That said, the worst forms of income inequality and the most severe disparities in human development and social mobility occur

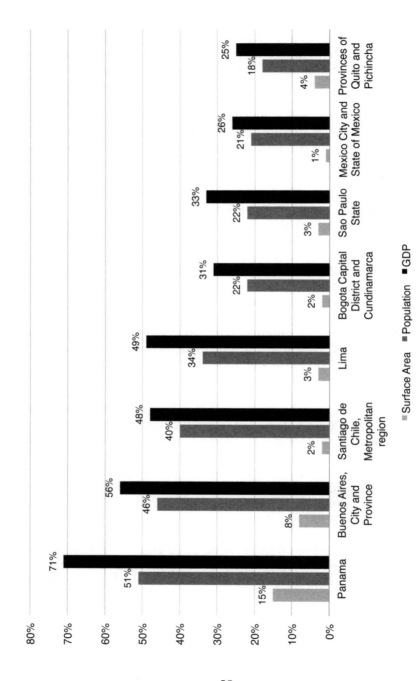

Figure 4.3: Metropolitan Areas, Surface Area, Population, and GDP: Latin American Countries, circa 2010 (%)

not within cities, but between cities and the rest of a country's territory, especially rural areas. For this reason, massive migrations to cities and to metropolitan areas have taken place. Once a critical mass is reached in urban and metropolitan areas, natural growth alone leads to increased population density and economic activity.

Here a sad paradox emerges: together with obvious economic and social benefits, urbanization under current conditions has created extremely serious problems, diminishing the quality of life and the experience of many people. In a certain sense, the development associated with the urbanization and "metropolitanization" of Latin America has produced an inhuman development. We will see why.

Metropolitanization and Inhuman Development

During the twentieth century, urbanization in Latin America was historically linked to migrations from rural areas as well as to international immigration. Limited industrialization led to an imbalance between accelerated urbanization and precarious industrial development, and to a concentration of employment in the informal, service, and tertiary sectors, where salaries are low and there are chronic deficits in levels of collective consumption. It also led to the growth of enormous masses of marginalized people, an "industrial reserve army" without industry, where state policies were incapable of satisfying urban social demands, despite significant efforts made.

Since the end of the twentieth century, and especially during the first decades of the twenty-first, globalization and the region's integration into the techno-economy of information and communication have caused significant changes in urbanization at the levels of culture, the economy, and space. The extreme inequality to which we have referred has consequences for urbanization. On the one hand, most migrations result not from the attractiveness of large cities, but rather from expulsions from rural zones or from regions in crisis, with migrants seeking better alternatives for themselves and their children. Globalization depends on connections among the world's major urban centers, and on networks of communication and transportation that create an integrated, highly dynamic global system, as both capital and labor abandon the territories disconnected from these centers. Because these networks simultaneously connect and disconnect, they connect what is economically, technologically, and politically valuable, and they disconnect what is uninteresting to investors and those who accumulate capital. Once people reach the big cities, most jobs accessible to people with limited qualifications and capital are in the informal sector, and they offer low salaries without social benefits or job security. Under these conditions, many cannot enter the formal housing market because prices and rents respond to speculative interests in contexts of extremely high demand, fueled by population growth. For this reason, the informal economy includes informal housing, which makes up a third of the housing stock in the region's large cities. Informal housing combines land invasions, accepted or legalized by local authorities after the fact, with makeshift construction, supervised by irregular real estate developers often associated with local organized crime and working in cooperation with city functionaries and politicians building clientelist networks of their own. Under these conditions, urban growth follows no planned pattern. Instead, it results from random speculative investments, often in lands not suitable for construction, subject to all manner of geological and climate-related upheavals.

Even in the formal market for the middle and lower-middle classes, speculation is the rule, and prices are imposed by semi-formal companies that benefit from the defenselessness of clients trying to establish new homes, clients who are often immigrants or young people. Public investments in transportation, infrastructure, and city services do not suffice to satisfy demand, intensified by low household incomes that do not cover the costs of these necessities. These difficulties are exacerbated both by the enormous investments needed and the high rates of growth in urban populations. So, on the one hand, city centers become saturated, their inhabitants crowded into neighborhoods nearing the point of collapse. And on the other, extensive sprawl in the peripheries of cities translates into hours-long daily commutes from home to work, with transportation systems in disrepair. Everyday life for the majority of the population reveals the dark side of development. The pattern of inequality linked to the exclusionary model of development directly influences urban space, leading to segregation by class and race. The wealthy segregate themselves in an effort to escape from the "dangerous classes," seeking refuge in peripheral settlements that are protected and exclusive. Such new spatial phenomena are the product of processes of severe socio-spatial and functional differentiation, in which the most privileged city dwellers build isolated and militarily protected homes, like islands of consumption in the midst of the "barbarism" that they fear and against which they defend themselves every day, even while they enjoy a way of life they share with global elites.[2] All of this tends to degrade public space. Caught between two socio-spatial poles, the unstable "middle class" experiences ups and downs, interacting daily with two different worlds, with fear and uncertainty about the future combined with the search for a better quality of life and projects that might lead to belonging. Or they combine with the demand for authoritarian solutions that might offer protection.

But there are very serious problems that cut across classes and that point to the need for a common response to threats to public health, which do not discriminate according to the size of their victims' bank accounts. Indeed, one problem common to the major metropolitan areas in Latin America is poor air quality. The World Health Organization (WHO) recommends that the concentration of particulate matter (PM10) not exceed 20 μg/m^3, but data from the WHO in 2014 indicated that no Latin American capital met this standard. On the contrary, in cities like Lima and Santiago, the average annual concentration of PM10 was 64 and 68 μg/m^3, respectively (see figure 4.4).

Major metropolitan areas in the region have grown dense and socio-spatially diverse, and this is true in cities of various kinds. According to the United Nations, Bogotá, Santiago de Chile, and

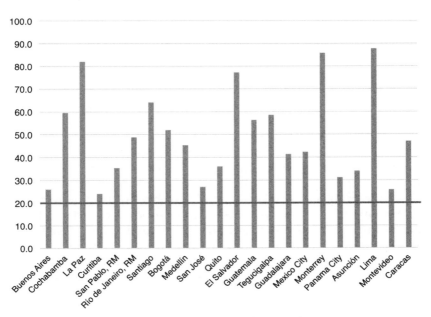

Figure 4.4: Average Annual Concentration of Particulate Matter (PM10) in Selected Cities, circa 2014 (μg/m^3)

São Paulo are highly congested cities (Jordán et al., 2017), where growth in the tertiary sector and particularly in specialized services predominates and is similar to that seen in comparably sized cities, where such services account for 80 percent of urban GDP. Industrial employment has lost its importance, and agricultural employment has also declined except in cases of agri-business linked to export. The result: new forms of marginalization with high degrees of social and functional differentiation associated with the diversification of professions and specializations in every area of the economy. If we add to this the high levels of pollution and serious problems affecting the resilience of cities faced with natural disasters and climate change, we recognize the generalized human fragility of these settlements (Jordán et al., 2017: 258–69). Cities have become dispersed, unequal, dangerous, segregated, functionally differentiated, and ecologically vulnerable. In this way, together with increases in levels of human development, we have witnessed an increase in inhuman development and its corollaries, violence and fear as forms of social relations.

The new frontier of inhumanity can be seen in another set of human products: climate change and its consequences. These include increases in inhumanity produced by earthquakes, tsunamis, hurricanes, tornados, wildfires, floods, and the effects of environmental pollution. Tragedies in several major Latin American cities and areas – including, for instance, San Juan, Valparaíso, Mexico City, the islands of Honduras, or La Plata, in Argentina, which has been flooded repeatedly – are examples of how the results of climate change severely affect the everyday lives of people and levels of human development.[3] These phenomena are worsened by the ineptness of states, corruption in networks of assistance, and the lack of solidarity at a global scale.

The recent modernization of cities produces inhuman development in Latin America's urban centers.[4] This is also a matter of the persistence of a dominant form of urbanization that is expanding in all countries in the region, a form of urbanization that reproduces the problems, tendencies, and challenges of twentieth-century urbanization, even while it introduces new problems related to the deterioration of social ties and formerly shared values. Changes in family structures, schools, and religion, especially Catholicism, have led to declines in the collective quality of urban life, especially in metropolitan areas and among the poorest, most excluded sectors of society. Territories and spaces thus arise that are not just monadic and isolated, but also distrusting of and opposed to one another. In these spaces, moreover, residents experience a brutal deterioration of the environment in a closed, "tribal" social context, where the decomposition of social ties and insecurity in everyday life are related to weak states, a lack of sustainable inclusion in markets, criminal economies, fear, and generalized human vulnerability at nearly every level of human development. All of these elements overwhelm subjects, who every day find themselves more isolated even while they are ever more integrated into a single informational market through cellular phones and communicate in a "tribalized" way, through participation in selective social networks.

An important cultural symptom can be found in works of young adult fiction like *The Hunger Games*, for example, or John Green's books. These contribute to both segregation and individualization. But the most inhuman symptoms are among groups of marginalized youth like those shown in television series and in films about "tribal" life in the *barrio*. Consider the Netflix series *El Marginal*, for instance, which, as its name suggests, is about marginal youth in Buenos Aires; or consider the various Brazilian television series and films on the same theme: *Elite Squad*, *City of God*, and *The Mechanism*, among others.

On the basis of such generalized disconnection, which ultimately leads to the dehumanization of the "other," violence arises. Violence as a defense and as a way of appropriating the resources that "should" belong to me and not to "them." When social relations are not human, they become more violent. In a document released by the Instituto Igarapé, in Brazil, we find that in more than 141 cities in Latin America (or 52 percent of all cities with more than 250,000 residents), homicide rates per 100,000 residents were above the regional average in 2016 (21.5 per 100,000 residents). In addition, the same year, 43 of the 50 most violent cities in the world were in Latin America. The list of the 50 cities in the world with the highest homicide rates is topped by San Salvador, followed by Acapulco and Ciudad Juárez (in Mexico), San Pedro Sula (in Honduras), Soyapango (in El Salvador), and Chilpancingo de los Bravo (also in Mexico). In all except the last of these cities were there more than 100 homicides per 100,000 residents (Muggah and Aguirre Togón, 2018: 5–6). According to the same institute, around half of all victims are young, between 15 and 29 years of age. Obviously these calculations are per city resident. In absolute numbers, the vast majority of violent deaths occur in metropolitan areas.

As a result of the criminal economy and especially the effects of drugs and increasing violence, which we analyzed in chapter 3,[5] a culture of conflict is expanding in an urban society that is ever more fragmented. A "clandestine" and complex urban society has arisen in the context of a "tribalization" of socio-spatial relations. The drug

63

economy is at the same time the result of, and a form of compensation for, social backwardness and inhuman development. Vast swaths of major cities are being organized in clandestine networks of criminal relations and "tribal solidarities" that lay bare the limits of states and of models of development. Thus the limits of social ties are redefined, and forms of life are altered in much of Latin America. Clandestine urban networks of power already affect everyday life in considerable parts of cities like Guadalajara, Culiacán, Ciudad Juárez, Rio de Janeiro, Bogotá, Medellín, and Rosario, among many others.

Nevertheless, urban society itself seeks ways to recover and reinvent shared forms of life, new social ties capable of restoring dignity to city dwellers, new kinds of work, consumption, and distribution that create templates for another life that remains possible. At the heart of these experiences, urban socio-cultural movements emerge, seeking transformations in everyday life.

Urban imaginaries are changing at surprising speeds, and very often they are associated with a new urban aesthetics that redefines, distinctively expresses, and at times even advances the changes that we have described. The graffiti artists of São Paulo are an interesting example. They not only forge a new, aesthetic critique of corruption and violence in the streets; they also display their street art on the internet, producing exchanges with other artists across the globe through various social networks. Their work stands out for, among other things, its engagement with the public in the streets and on the web, on the one hand, and, on the other, its participation in an expanding array of popular websites and virtual communities. Beatriz Fernández notes that graffiti connects to the masses, influencing publicity, fashion, art, and design (UNDP, 2009).

At the level of culture, not only has a culture of drug consumption arisen; an art linked to drug trafficking has emerged as well, as in Fernando Botero's paintings of the charismatic drug trafficker Pablo Escobar, shown in Medellín. A film industry has also emerged, one that displays, reproduces, and often valorizes this activity. All of this has become a key question for the population of Latin America: fear, insecurity, the continuing harassment of women, and brutal human rights violations affect millions of residents in many of the region's cities. In other words, a new culture and a new, pervasive social imaginary of delinquency has taken root.[6] Under these conditions, development is inhuman because it denies the humanity of "others," of all of those who are different from those directly bound together by family ties or selective social networks. Spatial concentration has generated social isolation.

— 5 —

A NETWORK SOCIETY

Individualization, Techno-Sociability, and the
Culture of Diaspora

Since the late twentieth century, the advent of the "information age" has not only produced socioeconomic and political changes under neoliberalism and neo-developmentalism, as we saw in the previous chapters; it has also brought about fundamental changes in the workings of multiculturalism. These changes are of such magnitude that culture has become not only foundational for power, development, and politics, but also integral to any possibility for meaningful ethical change that would be both intercultural and emancipatory. Today culture can give a distinctive meaning to power, economic development, and politics itself.

In the 1980s and 1990s, business and communications markets initiated a significant and complex process of expansion across several dimensions, including the proliferation of television networks; the increasing use of video, which was often informally acquired without royalties; the early incorporation of electronics networks; the use of fax machines; access to satellite communications networks through the use of parabolic antennas; and especially the massification of public consumption. According to a study conducted by the Economic Commission for Latin America and the Caribbean (ECLAC) and UNESCO (1992), for example, between 1980 and 1988 the number of telephones per thousand residents increased from 100 to 140, while rates of access to television rose above 130. Estimates suggest that Latin Americans, whose average life expectancy is 65, spend approximately five years of their lives watching television, especially commercials, *telenovelas*, and "canned" entertainment from the US (Calderón and dos Santos, 1995).

In this way, building on historical precedents for Latin American and Caribbean multiculturalism, new cultural transformations took

65

place, responding to the force of the techno-economy of communication and information and the functioning of social networks. In this chapter, we identify some of the most salient features of this new multicultural dynamic, which has for the most part arisen in the last 20 years.

The Emergence of Hegemonic Individualism and Consumption: The Centrality of New Media as Vectors of Cultural Construction

At the end of the twentieth century, the incorporation of digital technologies into everyday life had already begun, taking place at different speeds in different countries. But this process became especially intense and pervasive throughout Latin American societies during the first fifteen years of the twenty-first century. This suggests that both the workings of the global market for information and communications technology and state policies, mainly the policies of neo-developmentalist regimes, led to a truly spectacular form of integration. Indeed, this process of incorporation into the world of the internet was enabled by two sets of factors: on the one hand, the economic growth that took place in the first 15 years of this century, leading to a reduction in poverty, increasing social mobility, and changes in social stratification as well as to a reduction in the cost of access to digital services; and, on the other hand, policies and educational programs, like the Plan Ceibal in Uruguay, which explicitly sought to promote such access, especially among excluded social sectors (Rivoir, 2013).

In 2014, there were already more than 700 million mobile telephone connections and more than 320 million unique users, concentrated in cities, where new social and communication networks were used most heavily. In just over a decade, beginning in 2003, the number of internet users in the region doubled (ECLAC, 2016: 11 and 41). In 2016, it had already reached 56 percent of the population (ECLAC, 2018: 5). In 2014, among young people between the ages of 16 and 29, internet use reached 70 percent of the population (ECLAC, 2016: 182).

The questions are thus: what kind of incorporation has occurred, and above all what is the meaning of these changes in people's subjectivities and in Latin American societies? With respect to the type of incorporation, it is worth underscoring the intensity of increasing hourly internet use in the region. The average for internet consumption is 21.7 hours per month, one hour less than the global average. In Brazil, use is intense, and the average is 29.4 hours per month; in Uruguay, 32.6 hours per month. The averages in the United States and Europe are 35.9 and 25.1 hours per month, respectively (ECLAC, 2016: 61).

Another feature of this type of incorporation is related to the predominance of extra-regional consumption. Thus Latin American internet users prefer sites like Google, Facebook, and Wikipedia, among others, whereas, according to the study conducted by the Economic Commission for Latin America and the Caribbean that we have cited, users in China or Japan prefer local sites. It is likely that the structure of language is a relevant variable in this respect. Global platforms are hegemonic when it comes to internet use in the region, while groups like Televisa, the Grupo Clarín, and O Globo are still limited in their reach. The use of video is prevalent in Latin America, where there are even countries, like Mexico, that surpass the global average for video consumption. In Argentina, Chile, Colombia, and Brazil, these figures approach the global average.

While these platforms integrate more and more users, costs tend to be directly related to incomes. So, for example, it is possible to estimate the percentage of average monthly incomes represented by mobile broadband fees. In 2014, at one extreme, costs in Japan were ridiculously low, while costs in Nicaragua, Honduras, and Bolivia were considerably higher (ECLAC, 2016: 50).

Finally, this process of "extroverted" incorporation involves considerable levels of inequality among the region's different countries and, within these countries, between rural areas and cities, where the process takes place at different speeds. These phenomena are directly related to the levels of human and economic development in various countries. Figure 5.1 shows both inequalities in, and speeds of, incorporation.

When we consider the meaning of this process of integration, it is important to emphasize that the various processes of democratization that the region underwent, especially those related to the workings of the market and globalization, tend to redefine subjectivity and social relations through greater integration into the society of information by way of individual consumption. This changes standards of everyday life at different scales. It suggests that processes of social differentiation in the region are becoming more complex as societies are individualized. Individualization is associated with consumption and sustained alienation, a kind of reification in the market, and a form of individualist narcissism especially evident among elites at the

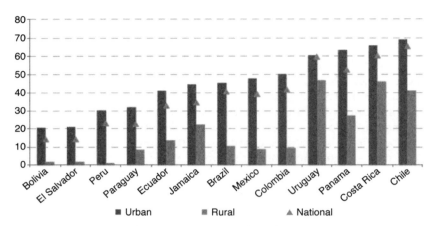

Figure 5.1: Homes with Internet Access: Selected Latin American Countries, circa 2015 (% homes)

highest levels of power. But we also see the emergence of a search for greater personal autonomy in projects of self-construction, a search for individual and collective alternatives for everyday life.

The key issue here is the population's active and increasing integration into the consumption of cultural goods like those discussed here. These shape the process of individualization at the level of whole societies, and individualization and consumption come to thoroughly alter the historical workings of Latin American multiculturalism. This is particularly true in urban centers and large cities.

And here a long-standing historical pattern begins to change, one relating to the nature of human relations. Differences become ever more apparent between people and their search for self-determination, on the one hand, and, on the other, institutions and systems of power, like the media, that act on an increasingly global scale. In this realm, individual people can have little or no effect. In this sense, the new multiculturalism seems to be increasingly organized around the individualization of persons, rather than by social or cultural collectives. This, at least, seems to be the tension characteristic of our new era. In this context, individualization becomes increasingly a matter of subjects in society, while collective actors lose their relative importance or are redefined. Paradoxically, this process of collective and differentiated access to the market and to the culture industry of new media is what produces individualization, which is sustained by processes of both social and functional differentiation.

The acceleration of demographic changes; new, more horizontal and flexible forms of family organization; workers' uncertain but persisting relations to unstable labor markets; new, more equal gender relations; changes in norms surrounding sexuality; constant digital communications; the valorization of instantaneousness in everyday life; the breakup of vertical monopoly power in education: all of these, among other factors, are vectors in a new process of multicultural construction.

The "Culture of Techno-Sociability": A Culture Centered on Individual Autonomy and as the Nucleus of an Emergent Youth Culture

We note that new information and communications technologies are making it possible to redefine or recreate the values, aspirations, identities, and beliefs that organize forms of self-understanding and coexistence in the new Latin American societies, and especially among young people. In this way, new forms of life and of "techno-communicational" sociability are generated, where information and communications technologies are not only tools, but also the ambient contexts or conditions that allow for the emergence of new identities, new values, and new visions of life. The time and the space between people from different societies and social strata are thus also redefined. But confrontations and new relations of power and domination also emerge, creating new fields of conflict proper to the information age and renewing the logic of conflicts that belonged to the colonial period or the period of industrialization and dependency in societies throughout Latin America. Today, both these abiding conflicts and new socio-cultural conflicts are displaced onto the web. According to one study of social conflicts in 17 countries in the region, 59 percent of conflicts recorded between 2010 and 2011 had a web presence (Calderón, 2012: 68, 298–305).

Techno-sociability modifies the cultural field and social relations on the web, allowing for daily personal interaction, which leads to the emergence of various fields of symbolic exchange, with consequences that were unthinkable merely 30 years ago. Sexual openness is constantly redefined. But we have also seen an exponential rise in anti-sociability on the web, the expansion of new forms of discrimination and rejection, and new ways to negate the other. Racism is thus renovated online, as is machismo, but so are new ways to question equality and diversity (Szmukler, 2015).

Latin America stands out at the global level, both for the intensity of its use of social networks and for the "foreignization of consumption" in the region. According to information provided by ECLAC (2016), 78 percent of internet users used social networks in 2013. Contrast this with 64 percent in North America or 54 percent in Europe. With 145 million visitors, Facebook was the social network with the largest audience, but considerable numbers of people in the region also visited other network sites like ShareThis or LinkedIn, which received 93 and 38 million visits, respectively. In addition, Latin Americans were found to spend more time on social networks than the inhabitants of any other region, with their visits lasting an average of 17 minutes in April 2014.

Another significant finding in the study suggested that the use of social networks was not directly related to incomes. Thus, for example, Mexico, Argentina, Peru, Chile, and Colombia are among the ten countries in the world with the highest percentages of social network users. In this context, the most salient finding has to do with youth participation in this new form of sociability. In fact, recent years have seen the emergence of what the Human Development Report for Mercosur, commissioned by the United Nations Development Programme, calls "the generation of technosociability."[1] Among this generation's most salient features, in addition to those mentioned above, are those related to processes of social exclusion and insecurity as persisting, daily experiences in the wake of failed neoliberal and neo-developmentalist policies.[2] Here the cultural experience of Latin American youth has been thoroughly diversified and multiplied by access to information and communications technologies. Figure 5.2 shows the impact of the internet on various aspects of young people's daily cultural lives.

Overall, new uses of technology in both communication and culture are redefining individual and collective lives for young people in the region. It is worth specifying some of the salient features of this new "generation of techno-sociability" in addition to those we have already mentioned.

New Life Experiences

What distinguishes the current generation of young people from previous generations is their life experiences, not only of the political and socioeconomic transformations of the last 25 years – transformations related to neo-developmentalism or neoliberalism – but also in their daily lives. These lives have been changed by the expansion of techno-sociability, an expansion that is both real and imagined. This is true

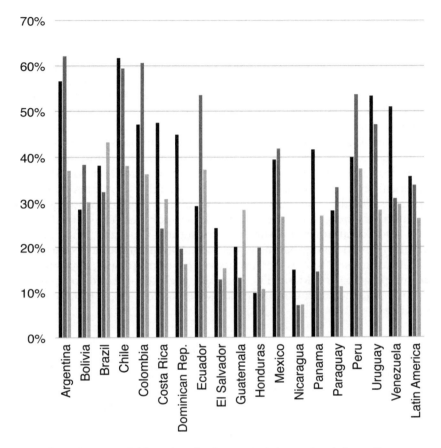

- ■ Searching or visiting sites for fun, entertainment or information
- ■ Participating in chats, social networks
- ▪ Searching or visiting sites for academic reasons

Figure 5.2: Youth between the ages of 16 and 25, surveyed on their three most frequent uses of the internet. Latin America, 2013 (%)

Note: Percentages do not add up to 100%, since categories are overlapping

above all of the functioning of people's minds. Today, there are uses of information and communications technologies that are socially inclusive and certainly motivating. Being on the web is part of a life lived with others. Techno-sociability, defined as an everyday, recurring experience of communication and intersubjectivity associated with the use of horizontal forms of mass communication (the internet, mobile phones and their multiple uses and constant updates, and so on), is changing patterns of knowledge and learning. This is expressed in various dimensions of the everyday: work, studies, home life, sex, amusement, politics, and so on. In other words, we are witnessing the use of technologies of communication not as tools or ends, but as environments that allow for new ways of being, spaces where values are put in play, identities are constructed, and cultural, social, ecological, aesthetic, and other sensibilities are expressed. New identities are created, and these make "the here and now" into everyday subjective referents, creating a glocal context for life in a practical, everyday sense and promoting a highly developed environmental sensibility. But this "techno-sociability" is not produced in a vacuum. It emerges, on the one hand, through networks of information and communication that are constantly changing, and, on the other, through young people's sociocultural and national experiences and traditions. But it is not exclusive to young people, though they are its principal builders. This last fact is closely related to their use of time and their location in space as well as to a range of new social practices.

Open Identities

The acceleration of time and the reorganization of space are important consequences of current changes. This might even suggest that a sort of gap in values, cognitive forms, and aspirations already separates generations from one another. Young people at all social levels connect with each other more rapidly than adults do, so that the more quickly social change takes place at the levels of knowledge and communication, the wider the gap between generations tends to be. An understanding of time as instantaneous organizes action among young people; the "now" occupies a central place in their imaginary. On the other hand, spatial scales change: the local and the global approach one another and come to overlap on the web. Young people's identities tend to be diverse in themselves; they are open, changing, and largely respectful of other identities. But they can also be discriminatory, alienated, and distant. Nevertheless, we should not forget that while for some young people global distances diminish, for others the distances between societies and nations are growing. How to articulate public values and identities in a shared public space, ensuring communication between the individual and the collective, the included and the excluded? Figure 5.3, which shows

72

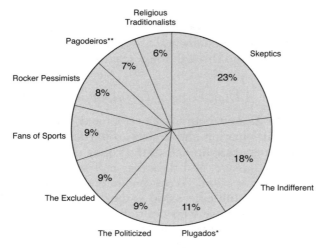

Figure 5.3: Youth Identities in Río de Janeiro, for people from ages 15 to 29, 2009 (%)

Plugados, or those plugged in, are people who were connected all the time.
**Those who dance or play *pagode*, a type of samba.

the kaleidoscopic dynamics of identification among youths from Rio de Janeiro, offers a good example.

Ethicopolitical Demands that Seek to Confront Insecurity and Strengthen Autonomy

Today, everyday insecurity shapes social relations in public. This insecurity is associated with fear of the "other," of those perceived to be different, but it is also a matter of fear of exclusion and violence, which both affect cultural responses to risk. For young people today, the most pressing question seems to be how to live together in the uncertainty of the irresistible night. In different ways, the social and digital gaps between young people affect the quality of their everyday lives. Everyone loses out if spaces for public coexistence shrink. In several cases, the state has acted positively by introducing public policies to promote distribution and the inclusion of youth, but there is also a negative side to these projects, as in cases of police repression. Young people are valorized in consumer markets, but they are also devalued in public life, especially when they are seen as threatening or "suspicious." In this context, in the study conducted for Mercosur that we have already cited, one finding notes that young people seek to develop strategies for reducing risk, but without at the same time restricting their own freedom and autonomy. Here information and communications technologies are fundamental. Even young people who break with norms do so in and through these spaces of communication.

A Dual Logic of Participation

According to the United Nations Development Programme's study for Mercosur, participation and desires to participate in consequential decision-making are split: half of the young people surveyed tend to be skeptical or passive, and the other half participate or express their desire for participation. To proceed in multiple directions is key for the promotion of full citizenship among young people. But how are we to ensure that those who desire to participate in fact do so? How are we to make it possible for poor people to transform their needs into actionable demands? How are we to work to convince those who do have opportunities to participate but do not want to do so find motivations to participate?

Here we present some key findings that would benefit from more in-depth study:

- There is a sort of coexistence among those who participate between a vanguardist logic and a spontaneous logic centered on questions of dignity, rights, and cultural subjectivity. Young people who are engaged combine a pragmatic culture, focused on provisional and local results, with a flexible approach to a broad range of demands for cultural and social recognition. In the study for Mercosur, among those who participate, three different orientations or sets of priorities are noted; these are not mutually exclusive, but involve: (1) the reaffirmation of cultural, religious, athletic, ethnic, and gender identities; (2) the protection of the environment; and (3) participation in more "classical" kinds of social organizations: national-popular or anti-globalization movements like social forums. In all of these cases, we see a demand for a new quality of life, a demand for both individual and collective dignity. Likewise, young people are conscious of the fact that fluency in the codes of digital communication is key to the attainment of their goals.
- Young people's ability to act varies. Women stand out for their ability to transform goals into results and dreams into realities, and for their ability to integrate demands for redistribution, recognition, and participation. Data suggest that women's ability to act tends to be greater than men's.

74

• The most active young people seek to integrate the future with the past and the collective with the individual. At least we can identify this tendency in the countries of Mercosur (Argentina, Brazil, Paraguay, and Uruguay), and hopefully in the rest of the region as well. Young people imagine a given future, but they do not set the past aside. In this sense, there is no generational break with their parents, but rather a sort of "intergenerational pact": their relationship to their parents is not one of breakage, but rather one of negotiation, associated with education and the logic of employment. On the other hand, young people value their autonomy and individuality, dialogue with others, and solidarity with those who are seen to be different. In this sense, we can formulate a normative hypothesis on emancipation: the collective is the result of a commitment made by autonomous people, and the individual results from a certain collective agreement or understanding.

A New Grammar for Social Conflicts

Both classical and new demands tend to be displaced into networks of communication and information. Young people are central to the management of this displacement. In this respect, the web has become a place where new forms of conflict and power are expressed and developed. The culture of techno-sociability not only changes the everyday lives of people and communities; it also alters politics. Mass-mediated politics plays an important role in social conflict, since organizing a demonstration or a march in which no vertical communications media (television, radio, and newspapers) are present, or especially one without the participation of horizontal media (the internet and mobile phones) decreases the chances that demands will be heard and makes it less likely that they will be positively responded to. Democracy is increasingly a democracy of the public. Protests take place both in public squares and on the internet.

New ways of communicating promote the intensive use of information and communications technologies in public space, where "public space" is understood as a place of encounter, a place where ideas and values are formed, transmitted, exchanged, endorsed, and contested. Information and communications technologies allow for more nimble, flexible, and spontaneous interaction among social actors, who can, thanks to these technologies, more actively participate in politics and social conflict. In this way, possibilities for collective action are amplified by the ease of access to, and the low cost of, both the internet and mobile phones. Taking part in a forum, keeping a blog, or participating in a group on a social network is easier and more accessible than other forms of political participation.

Increasingly, conflicts are native to the internet, since when people lodge a complaint or make a general demand, it is transmitted spontaneously to thousands of people in a relatively short time, now especially by way of social networks, but also through blogs, forums, email chains, or text messages. By way of these tools, citizens can organize themselves, respond to conflicts, and exchange information. A form of "cyber-activism" that promotes deliberation and acting in concert online and in the streets is now a given in Latin America and a global political reality. Globalization has not only produced concentrations of power and individualist consumerism; it has also consequently entailed the strengthening of individual and collective capacities in which spontaneity, voluntarism, and self-organization prevail. Thus it becomes necessary to individually redefine collective projects on the web, and conversely collective projects now presuppose the valorization of personal freedom and dignity. Later, we will offer an analysis of movements on the web and so return to these questions.

Migrations and the Culture of Diaspora

The phenomenon of migration is a fundamental structural feature of globalization and the crisis of multiculturalism that nearly all of the world is experiencing. Its dynamism and its effects cut across regions. This is now a matter of human and inhuman territorial dynamics within informational capitalism. Information and communications technologies are everywhere present in the complexity and variety of this phenomenon; they are present among migrants themselves, in countries that seek to expel migrant populations, and in countries that receive them.

Today, the phenomenon of migration operates online. The question is, then, how this phenomenon participates in and affects life in Latin America, and what role it plays in the workings of migration. How does it affect the labor market and informal economies? How are migrants integrated into the web and the culture of techno-sociability? A new culture of diaspora has emerged, and without understanding this culture it is impossible to understand the region as a multicultural and glocal territory. What, finally, is the cultural meaning of the new movements of populations, and how are these related to politics, democracy, and power?

General Tendencies

Figure 5.4 shows different flows of migration across the globe. According to a United Nations report on migrations, in 2017 more than 60 percent of international migrants lived in Asia and Europe, which had 80 and 78 million migrants, respectively. In third place, we find North America with 58 million migrants (UN, 2017: 5). According to the same report, 67 percent of all migrants resided in 20 countries. Here the United States was in first place, with 50 million migrants in 2017, followed by Saudi Arabia, Germany, and Russia, with around 12 million migrants each (UN, 2017: 5). On the other hand, of the total number of international migrants in the world (258 million), just under half (106 million) were born in Asia. In second place was Europe (61 million), followed by Latin America and the Caribbean (38 million) (UN, 2017: 9). In the case of Latin America, 10 million international migrants were registered in 2017, 3 million more than in the year 2000. The case of Chile is particularly striking: according to the United Nations, Chile had an average annual rate of growth above 6 percent, among the highest, together with Angola and Qatar, during the period between 2000 and 2017 (UN, 2017: 7).

It is worth noting that these data are limited, since not all migrants can be registered, given the repressive policies that they face when they are undocumented. In addition, the data do not register the new movements of migrants caused by the war in Syria, or by economic and social crises in Venezuela, Honduras, or Libya, for example. It is possible that the flows of migrants not registered and those too new to appear in the UN study would not change the overall tendencies that it identifies, but they do alter popular perceptions of migrants as well as the logics of policing and power. In this sense, the media play a central role by transmitting fear, contributing to a growing sense of insecurity, occupying the perspective of power, and generally stigmatizing migrants.

Migration takes place mainly between countries that are found within a single world region. In 2017, the majority of international migrants from Europe (67%), Asia (60%), Oceania (60%), and Africa (53%) resided in countries located in their regions of birth. By contrast, the majority of international migrants in Latin America and North America (84% and 72%, respectively) lived in a region other than the one in which they were born (UN, 2017: 11).

In the case of Europe, immigrants from Asia and Africa accounted for 31.5 million people, but Asia in turn received around 35 million

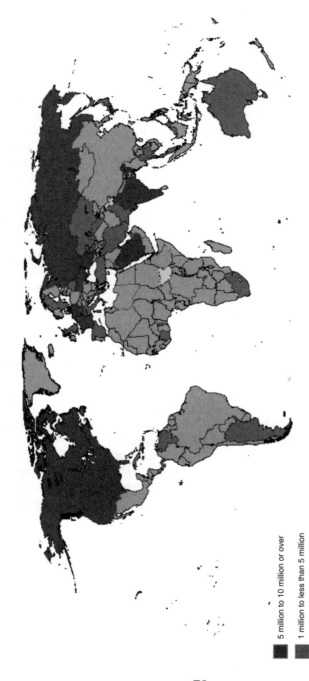

Figure 5.4: Number of International Migrants by Country, 2017

5 million to 10 million or over

1 million to less than 5 million

100,000 to less than 1 million

No data to less than 100,000

migrants. Still, many people left Asia for the United States and Europe. Overall, Europe and North America were the world regions that attracted most migrants, while Latin America, Africa, and Asia were the continents that exported most labor power. There are certainly regional differences. In Europe, for example, Portugal and Croatia also exported labor power, while the great migration of Mexicans and Central Americans has enormous repercussions in both national and global economies (UN, 2017).

In the case of South America, emigration to Europe represented 31 percent of the total. This meant especially emigration to Spain, where 70 percent of immigrants came from the Andes. In the United States, immigration from South America accounts for just 6 percent of the total, and here, too, most immigrants come from Andean countries: Colombia, Peru, and Ecuador. Still, in the US, the number of migrants coming from Latin America and the Caribbean overall represented 46 percent of total immigration. Mexico accounted for 26 percent; Central America and the Caribbean for 14 percent (UN, 2017).[3]

The Labor Market, Feminization, and Informality

Three features stand out when we consider recent migrations in Latin America: the feminization of migrant flows; migrants' exposure to the risks of being undocumented; and the presence of migrants in labor markets.

In terms of the feminization of the labor market, the situation is as follows: more than 50 percent of people who emigrate to North America are women. In addition, in the United States in particular, and in Europe, the rate reaches 54 percent. In these same regions, the participation of migrants in the workforce is greater than the participation of those who are native to these regions. More than 35 percent of female migrants work in the service sector. In North America, 75.5 percent of female workers in this sector are from Latin America. Domestic work and especially "care" work (especially work involving care for children and the elderly) are sectors that have grown, especially in Europe. These are also sectors that tend to be precarious in terms of working conditions. Therefore women are more exposed to such precarious working conditions (UN, 2017).

The number of migrants who are undocumented cannot be precisely determined. In the United States, in 2014 there were more than 11 million migrants who were undocumented, which means they were extremely vulnerable and exploitable. Such a situation also contributes to informality in employment and weakens migrants' ability to exercise their human rights (UN, 2017). So, for example, 29 percent of all migrants and 32 percent of migrant women are in jobs without contracts or social security. In Argentina, 67 percent of migrants from other South American countries work in this kind of informal situation; in the Dominican Republic, 84 percent do, and this number is made up especially of Haitian immigrants. In addition, these workers have almost no social organizations or unions to defend their rights. They are the most excluded of the excluded as well as being discriminated against and very often demonized. This is therefore not only a matter of economic and social marginalization or of perverse inclusion; it is above all a matter of cultural and ethical *negation* in global and multicultural societies in crisis. The dynamics of racism, degradation, social change, and resistance are distinctively expressed on social networks, through information and communications technologies.

Migration and Information and Communications Technologies

Techno-sociability and the integration of information and communications technologies into a range of migrant cultures influence both global society and the particular workings of migrant communities themselves. Some important effects of these processes include the following:

- New technologies of communication tend to redefine practices in, and understandings of, space and time among migrants as well as for particular individuals. The borders between here and there are no longer as clearly defined as they were in the past. Or at least cellular phones and the internet have weakened or redefined these borders. Instantaneous communication and the expansion and proliferation of means of communication allow for ongoing social and familial contact, redefining not only affective and cultural relations, but also systems of financial exchange and the movement of goods and persons. New strategies of resistance and new demands made by migrants appear online.
- On the other hand, information and communications technologies have allowed for increases in knowledge of other countries, where migrants can see living conditions, work opportunities, potential incomes, and ways of working in collective networks or as individuals for their own advancement. They can ask who will

respect their dignity more or at least denigrate them less. Migrants build their imaginaries around cities or places to which they will migrate, and they do so on the basis of exchanges of information and informal research. Information and communications technologies encourage rational deliberation on their expectations and their options.

- But these technologies also make ways of traveling through the world more rational and achievable. This follows from changes in the structures of travel companies as well as in the underworld of organized crime, in the criminal economy's dealings with migrants. Today the possibilities are more expansive, and the dangers are more complex than in the past.
- Likewise, the possibilities for migrating and exchanging cultural products are more varied today than in the past. Changes in patterns of global food consumption are an interesting example of the global impact of migrants in nearly all parts of the world. Not only is McDonald's consumed; an enormous variety – and sometimes a fusion – of Asian, Mexican, and Peruvian food can be found in all of the planet's major cities. The same thing could be said of the cultural exchanges in sports, festivals, and so on.
- However, it is also important to underscore the fact that information and communications technologies have enabled not only the rational mechanisms of police control and border patrol, but also the growth of networks of discrimination and xenophobia, particularly among the ultra-nationalist and conservative groups found in most host countries. This growing phenomenon is sustained by a culture of fear and a focus on terrorism, covered in distorted ways by many media companies and global communications corporations. The fear of the "other" is in the media and in global communications. Today the Crusades come alive again on the web. And at the same time a new culture of diaspora has emerged.

The Culture of Diaspora

By "diaspora," we mean a sense of belonging to a place of origin as well as the persistence and realization of this feeling through the maintenance of different kinds of ties with this place of origin: family, relational, and social ties as well as political, economic, and cultural connections. Moreover, these connections are asserted, questioned, or re-elaborated by groups of migrants coming from the same country, city, village, or region (Szmukler, 2015).

81

This culture is of course related to the daily practices of migrants. In host countries, migrants rethink and recreate relationships and actions; they reconsider their cultures of origin in ways that strengthen their sense of belonging as well as their psychological mechanisms for resisting the traumas of migration and discrimination. "*Se fue pa' volver*," says an aphorism from Ecuador: they went away in order to come back. Online, identities are recreated. Today, the real and the virtual are not separate; instead, they reinforce one another, forming part of a single reality.

When it comes to multiculturalism, cultures of diaspora suggest three important points. On the one hand, they strengthen relations among migrants in a reflexive way, especially in their relations to their communities of origin. On the other hand, however, these cultures question and critique societies and states and their mechanisms of discrimination, their tendency to negate migrants' cultures of origin and their human and cultural rights. Finally, cultures of diaspora also allow for the questioning of migrants' countries of origin and especially these states' inability to promote social inclusion and political participation.

From the perspective of migrants, their main demand has to do with human rights and with the construction of a dignified life. This is not just a demand for access to labor markets; it is a demand for acceptance, a demand that migrants be seen as equal in terms of rights and that they be allowed to live free from discrimination and xenophobia.

Families and social networks are the main sources of support for migrants. Informational networks have played a fundamental role in providing this sort of support. Thus, networks of information and communication increasingly connect migrants to one another and to other communities of migrants, as well as to their places of origin. The low cost of such communications encourages even more inter-communication among migrants. This has also allowed for the construction of "trans-territorial" spaces and centers of communication. Sites for diasporic communities on the web are at once the products of individual initiatives and the results of efforts to create and strengthen migrant organizations. The most dynamic factor in these organizations is the presence of young people belonging to the "culture of techno-sociability."

This informational process involving the reconstitution of identities is multicultural, and it gives a different meaning to globalization, highlighting its cosmopolitan tendencies and its intercultural workings. It draws our attention to the need for new forms of transculturation in the fields of law, ethics, and religion, among others.

In a context of conflicts and global changes, the role that migrants play is central, both to the emergence and development of new authoritarian and xenophobic cultures and to the creation of more human and cosmopolitan orientations.

— 6 —

PATRIARCHY IN QUESTION

Changes in the Family and the Crisis of Patriarchy

The family is one of the fundamental axes for the social reproduction of Latin America's multicultural network society, but it is also one of the main axes of the changes that this society has been experiencing across diverse social, national, regional, and political contexts. It forms a sort of knot that brings together, on the one hand, structural changes and, on the other, individual changes, with all that the latter imply for the everyday life of the family itself as well as for other key institutions of socialization like the school.

Changes in the family affect women above all, and they are leading to a questioning of the most arcane and universal form of power in these societies: the patriarchy. New types of protest have emerged to counter this patriarchy, and women have begun to demand opportunities to define themselves as new historical actors or actresses in the network society.

Generally speaking, "demographic transition" is a key theme. Presumably, all countries have seen a diminution in mortality rates and an increase in life expectancies. In fact, they have seen a growth in labor markets as a result of changing norms for women's reproductive labor. In this context, the male is no longer the sole breadwinner. As the data show, and as we will show in the empirical examples that we consider below, family members' participation in the generation of income is both growing and diversifying. At the same time, the typical age for marriage or civil union for couples has increased, and childbirths have also been delayed. Moreover, women have fewer children than in the past. These tendencies are all related to an increase in levels of education.

And with this increase, the extended and/or nuclear family in its patriarchal form is changing into another kind of family organization, one that is more open and complex. Today there are families with fewer children or with children from more than one parent (since the number of spousal separations has also increased), and statistically the number of female heads of household is also on the rise. There are now families that are interdependent, open, and shifting to include "ours, yours, and mine."

All of this entails changes to hierarchies in family structure. The father's monopoly on knowledge, or the presumption that his knowledge is greater than his children's, is being broken, but the father as head of household is also losing his authority in other ways, and other, more horizontal ties are emerging. Thus processes of individualization and techno-sociability have led to the formation of a new type of family. Overall, new family structures have implied greater diversity in patterns of family organization, and they have led to a deinstitutionalization of traditional family ties and the questioning of hierarchies and traditional divisions of labor within families. This process is certainly not homogeneous. There are variables including levels of education and unequal incomes. To these, we should add that national variations persist and remain significant.

We now turn briefly to an analytical account, based on studies of these new tendencies by Irma Arriagada; Eugenio Gutiérrez and Paulina Osorio; and Teresa Valdés and Ximena Valdés. This will allow us to show several things empirically, by considering several dimensions of the problem and presenting accompanying tables and figures.

a. Smaller Households

The most obvious consequence of the decline in fertility is a diminution in the size of households. Between 1987 and 1999 alone, this phenomenon can be observed in the 16 Latin American countries on which information is available (see figure 6.1). The wide range of national situations follows from different historical developments and, as we have mentioned, these developments are reflected in different stages of demographic transition. Uruguay is the country with the smallest average household size (3.2 people in 1999), and Honduras is at the opposite extreme (with 4.8 people per household on average

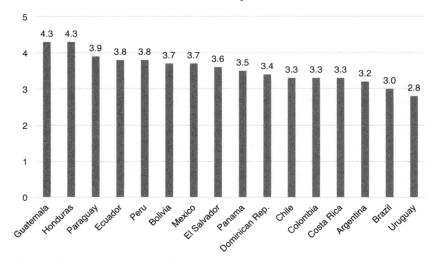

Figure 6.1: Average Size of Urban Households, by Income Quintiles. Latin America, circa 2014 (number of people per household)

the same year). Data from ECLAC (2018) indicate that in 2014 in both countries the average number of members of households was reduced in urban areas. These two countries, however, still occupied the same positions relative to one another.

b. Socio-spatial Differences

The decline in birthrates is greater in urban than in rural areas. In addition, fertility is higher in the lowest socioeconomic sectors than in the highest, and women with the highest levels of education tend on average to have fewer children than women with lower levels of education. In this way, geographic area, socioeconomic status, and education level all differently affect the size and composition of families. Generally speaking, the average size of families has been reduced by delays in first marriages or unions, declining numbers of children per family, and increasing space between them, so that there are currently fewer children per household, and differences in age between children are greater. At the level of the family, fewer children means less reproductive, domestic, and socializing labor for women, and this can mean, in turn, an increase in opportunities for work and autonomy.

c. Incomes

Household sizes also depend on socioeconomic status. A key indicator is family income, and especially the income quintile to which households can be assigned. If we compare urban households belonging to the bottom 20 percent of incomes (quintile 1) to those in the highest 20 percent (quintile 5), we can see a major difference in household size. In Honduras and Guatemala, households in the bottom income quintile are on average two members bigger than the richest households. The smallest such gap between income quintiles can be seen in the Dominican Republic, where it is 0.9 percent (ECLAC, 2018).

These differences follow from different cultural values relating to the ideal size of the family. Thus, countries that are at different stages of demographic transition have similar average family sizes, although the general tendency aligns family sizes with particular stages in this transition. That is, the more advanced the demographic transition (for example, in Argentina and Uruguay), the smaller the average family size.

The most traditional image of the Latin American family, associated with family principles from the last century, shows a household where grandparents, parents, and children live together with uncles, aunts, and cousins as well as other relatives at a further remove. This model of the extended family prevails less and less, given that extended families have shrunk in size in half of the region's countries. In 1999, they accounted for between 11 and 31 percent of families (in Argentina and Venezuela, respectively).

Similarly, mixed families in urban areas, which brought family groups together with other people who were not related to them by blood, have also diminished in size, accounting for between 0.2 and 5.2 percent of families in 1999 (in Mexico and Honduras, respectively). Members of the young rural population have migrated to cities in search of work opportunities since the 1950s, and this is especially true of the young people who make up the majority of paid domestic workers in cities. This has altered both extended and mixed families, while encouraging the formation of nuclear families as the predominant form. This, too, has now changed.

d. Increases in Single-Person Households

Processes of individualization can be seen in increases in single-person households, that is, households made up of people who, by choice, do not live in families. This choice is most often made by young people with economic resources.

Between 1987 and 1999, households made up of people who lived alone, including older adults, especially (given women's longer life expectancy) widowed women with economic resources, increased. These households are also formed by young people of both sexes, who decide to wait to be married or in a civil union, and who have access to their own economic resources that allow them to live alone. In fact, single-person households have increased markedly in urban areas: on average, just 7.9 percent of Latin Americans lived alone in 1999, while in 2014 the percentage rose to 11.8 percent. The greatest growth in single-person households during these years took place in Colombia, where they went from 6.9 percent of all households in 1999 to 14.5 percent in 2014. The country in the region with the highest number of single-person households during both years was Uruguay (ECLAC, 2018).

In some countries that make information from demographic and public health surveys available, we see that during the last decade there was an increase in the percentage of women between the ages of 30 and 34 who lived alone. These include Bolivia, Ecuador, El Salvador, and the Dominican Republic. During the same period, the percentage of women between the ages of 45 and 49 who were separated also increased in all seven countries for which information is available, as shown in table 6.1.

e. Female Heads of Household

One of the most important and visible phenomena related to recent changes in family structure is an increase in the number of single-parent households. These are almost exclusively households in which women are the heads of household. Traditionally, census measures and surveys of households define a "head of household" as the member of a married couple who is recognized as head of household by the other members of that household. This definition does not consider the real processes of domestic decision-making or the nature and size of economic input. Given these limitations of this definition of "head of household," some studies have sought to avoid the sexist biases implicit in this definition by simultaneously considering gender as a factor in both de jure and de facto head of household status (Gammage, 1998). Here "de jure" refers to the habitual understanding of the head of household reflected in census data and surveys, and "de facto" refers to the share of income generated in a family. This

Table 6.1: Changes in Women's Marital Status: Women from 30 to 34 and from 45 to 49 Years of Age. Selected Latin American Countries, between circa 1989 and 1998

Country	Year	30 to 34 Years of Age					45 to 49 Years of Age				
		Never Married	Married	Consensual Union	Widowed	Divorced/ Separated	Never Married	Married	Consensual Union	Widowed	Divorced/ Separated
Bolivia	1989	8.3%	75.8%	9.4%	1.4%	5.2%	4.1%	74.5%	5.9%	7.1%	8.5%
	1998	9.3%	65.6%	17.3%	1.0%	6.8%	3.7%	70.5%	9.1%	5.2%	11.5%
Brazil*	1986	10.5%	71.1%	11.2%	0.6%	6.6%	4.6%	74.0%	8.7%	4.1%	8.6%
	1996	10.2%	65.7%	14.9%	1.0%	8.2%	6.2%	67.7%	10.1%	4.3%	11.8%
Colombia	1986	15.5%	49.1%	25.0%	2.3%	8.2%	4.6%	57.6%	16.6%	8.6%	12.6%
	2000	14.5%	37.2%	33.3%	1.5%	13.6%	7.6%	42.5%	21.3%	7.0%	21.5%
Ecuador	1987	8.1%	58.9%	26.5%	0.8%	5.7%	2.7%	60.1%	19.6%	6.2%	11.3%
	1999	11.5%	55.2%	23.4%	0.8%	9.2%	5.1%	57.4%	17.2%	5.0%	15.3%
El Salvador	1985	4.3%	38.2%	41.5%	2.2%	13.9%	3.2%	35.1%	33.4%	7.5%	20.8%
	1998	8.1%	38.1%	37.2%	1.2%	15.4%	3.5%	43.7%	24.1%	6.6%	21.9%
Peru	1978	10.9%	65.1%	15.8%	1.4%	6.8%	5.2%	66.0%	13.2%	7.3%	8.3%
	1996	10.7%	49.5%	31.3%	1.1%	7.3%	4.3%	64.7%	15.5%	5.0%	10.4%
Dominican Rep.	1986	4.6%	32.3%	46.0%	1.4%	15.8%	1.6%	40.5%	33.2%	5.8%	18.9%
	1996	5.4%	35.7%	42.8%	0.7%	15.4%	1.1%	38.9%	33.9%	3.6%	22.5%

Notes: Figures in columns do not necessarily sum to 100% due to rounding

*Women from 40 to 44 years of age

Source: Arriagada (2004: 80)

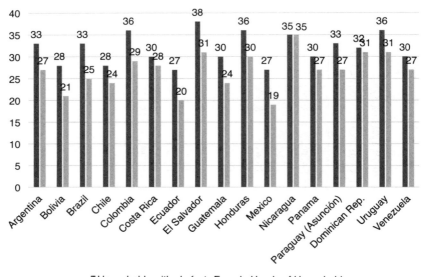

■ Households with *de facto* Female Heads of Household
▪ Households with *de jure* Female Heads of Household

Figure 6.2: Households with de facto and de jure Female Heads of
Household. Latin America, circa 1999 (%)

change in method led to the discovery of interesting relations between
the two types of female heads of household (see figure 6.2).

Setting aside for now the two types of female heads of household,
we note that the increase in these women's relative importance within
the home was notable. In 1999, 26 percent of all urban households
in Latin America had female heads of household; in 2014, this proportion rose by ten percentage points, to 36 percent. Single-parent
households with female heads of household rose, in urban areas,
from 9.6 percent to 11.5 percent (ECLAC, 2018). We can also detect,
if only in an inchoate form, an increase in single-parent households
with a male head of household, that is, an increase in the number
of fathers who live alone with their children, although the numbers
remain low. Clearly, both types of household respond to new models
of the family. In addition to having fewer adults, these single-parent
households highlight the existence of new family arrangements and
the need for support services to adjust to new realities.

Generally speaking, we can infer that although the work of socialization has lessened as the number of children per household has
declined, the number of adults in charge of this socialization has also

declined. This is especially noteworthy for women, who in a great many families have children in their care. Above all, the increasing frequency of separations and divorces has led to the appearance of complex families, a new and growing phenomenon in the region. These families can result from divorce, annulment, widowhood, or the breakdown of conventions resulting in the constitution of new ties. Nevertheless, statistical categories used in surveys of homes prevent us from measuring the size of these families, which are considered two-parent homes. For example, in Uruguay, where divorce was legalized at the beginning of the twentieth century (1907–1913), a continual increase in rates of divorce has been reported, but this has been especially pronounced in the last decades, specifically since the 1980s (Cabella, 1998).

f. Complex Families

Increases in the number of complex families in the region can help to account for decreases in the average size of families, since in complex families we can see the formation of new couples who want to have children with one another, as well as children brought together with the children of other parents, sometimes despite the fact that the latter are significantly older or younger. At the level of kinship, new, non-typical relations emerge, and these do not always have names or ways of being registered. Households headed by women exist at all social levels, reflecting diverse social processes. Increases in women's access to education, their increased participation in the labor force, and the growth in rates of divorce and separation during the second half of the twentieth century influenced changes in the ways in which households are organized. But in this sense conditions are different for different social strata. Among the highest-income sectors of society, households headed by women are the result of increases in rates of divorce as well as of aging (when older women live alone).

By contrast, low-income social sectors suffer the effects of macroeconomic policies and experience the crisis in the provision of social services most directly. Regressive redistributive policies begun during the dictatorships of the 1970s, and followed by policies of neoliberal adjustment during the 1980s, and especially the 1990s, implied increases in unemployment and underemployment for male workers. These policies also led to decreases in job security and a crisis in the provision of social services. The resulting pressure on households has been unmistakable and widespread, with the result that a greater number of women look for work in order to support their children.

In fact, as Geldstein shows (1999), the number of women living in poverty who have become the main providers for their households is greater than the number of female "heads" of household. There are a great many households that include unemployed men, in which women are the economic providers, although they are not recognized as "heads." Meanwhile, among the poorest sectors of the population, it appears that the increase in the number of female heads of household is an indication of the feminization of poverty. Gender discrimination in the labor force and the burden of responsibilities for women indicate that the expectation that women will play two or three roles at once persists. This expectation is socially unsustainable as well as unjust.

It is also clear that women who have become heads of household in urban areas are exposed to a great deal of domestic conflict. This is probably influenced to a considerable degree by the nature of their domestic partnerships. It is important to note that relations between female heads of household and their children are similar to such relations in other kinds of households. We can therefore conclude that the considerable amount of work that female heads of household perform, their greater decision-making power, and their frequent exposure to domestic violence do not lead to noticeable damage to their children or prevent them from handling intra-family conflicts.

g. Individualization and Differentiation

According to the analyses that we have cited, increases in inequality and exacerbations of difference result from the socioeconomic transformations that have been caused by the region's integration into the global economy. Without offering opportunities for stable employment in the context of a transformation in the nature of work, these changes have forced workers to be maximally flexible and have heightened competition, widening the gaps between poor and rich families.

Thus the expectations associated with consumption in fact generate indebtedness for families; economic expansion allows for expanded access to consumer goods that used to be unobtainable for broad sectors of the population (a home of one's own, color televisions, cellular phones, refrigerators). Nevertheless, this increased consumption implies excessive levels of debt. And this, in turn, implies a psychological cost that has consequences for intra-family relations. Frustrations increase, and the gap between desires for consumer goods and real possibilities for obtaining them widens. Paid work for women entails an excess of work for those who seek to reconcile family interests with their own. Although women's integration into the labor market has allowed them to contribute to the economic maintenance of households and thus led to improvements in families' standards of living, this has not led to a sharing of responsibilities or to an equitable distribution of unpaid domestic labor. Nor has it led to increased opportunities for women to develop autonomy. Their integration into the market and the dynamics of individualization have, on the one hand, led to serious pessimism, related to the insecurity that structurally unstable working conditions have caused, and that has given rise to growing inequalities in the distribution of resources. But, on the other hand, this integration has led to risks for families. The explosion of images and the aesthetic wastelands in centers of consumption fill the minds of young women with expectations that cannot be met. The weakening of the public sphere and a lack of the understanding that would make it possible to account for the speed of social change likewise affect women's integration into these spaces. On the other hand, we note more optimistically that individualization allows for technological inclusion and opens up spaces of action and communication, new knowledges, and new political possibilities.

h. Violence against Women

Violence against women is a structural and longstanding feature of Latin American and Caribbean society, for all its multiculturalisms and various social structures. For example, according to a study conducted by the Pan American Health Organization (Bott et al., 2014), this violence is widespread in the region. The study's authors indicate that the majority of surveys demonstrate that between one quarter and one half of all women have suffered from acts of violence in the home. Similarly, emotional abuse and controlling male behavior are common throughout the region.

The authors also note that violence is associated with the consumption of alcohol and drugs, and this of course affects women's physical and mental health. This phenomenon is even more urgently important and complicated given the early sexual initiations that are forced on many young women and their exposure to violence, which continues to have negative intergenerational effects. The data that we will consider below are eloquent in this respect. Against the backdrop of these structural features of the family and gender, changes in subjectivity, forms of collective action among women, and even sexuality itself can be observed in all Latin American societies. We will return to these questions in our chapter on new social movements.

— 7 —

THE CRISIS OF THE CATHOLIC CHURCH AND THE NEW RELIGIOSITY

In one of the most interesting paradoxes resulting from the techno-economy of information and communication and from global multicultural transformation, the changes associated with individualization have not further secularized societies. Instead, they have reactivated a number of religions, and they have done so in broad, diverse, and often enigmatic ways.

Thus religiosity had increased throughout the globe, according to data provided by Zeev Maoz and Errol A. Henderson (2013), who found that between 1990 and 2010, rates of religiosity increased from 83 percent to 89 percent (see figure 7.1). More recent data from the *World Values Survey* suggest that the number of people who consider themselves religious is considerable and grew during the years between 2004 and 2009, and again 2010 and 2014 in countries including Ukraine, Hong Kong, Taiwan, and Germany (Inglehart et al., 2014). By contrast, these numbers have fallen in Spain, Australia, Romania, Turkey, the United States, and Iraq, among other countries. For its part, Gallup International indicates that in 2017, 62 percent of people considered themselves religious, a percentage similar to the figure from 2015 (63 percent), but three percentage points higher than the figure from 2012 (59 percent) (WIN/Gallup International, 2017).

In this context, the religions that grew the most between 1990 and 2010 were Islam (which grew by five percentage points); Hinduism and Sikhism (which grew by three percentage points); and non-Catholic Christian churches (which grew by two percentage points, while the Catholic Church shrank by one percentage point). The non-religious also grew as a percentage of the population, by three percentage points (Maoz and Henderson, 2013).

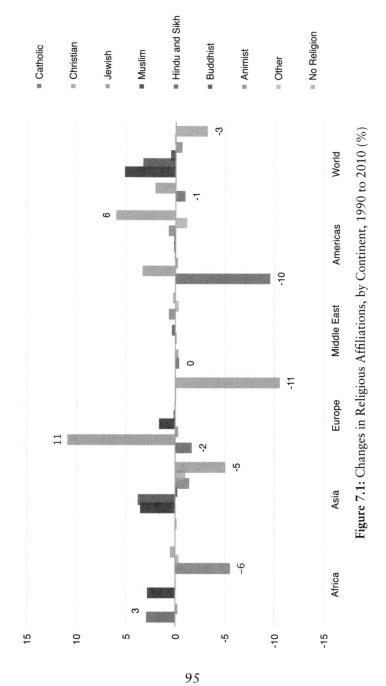

Figure 7.1: Changes in Religious Affiliations, by Continent, 1990 to 2010 (%)

Catholic
Christian
Jewish
Muslim
Hindu and Sikh
Buddhist
Animist
Other
No Religion

95

In Latin America, the situation is more complex and has evolved rapidly since 2010. Still, one basic fact has become clear, namely a decline in the importance of the Catholic Church, which still predominates both in terms of the number of adherents and in terms of the intensity of their religious practice. At the global scale, Catholicism went from accounting for 19 percent of the world's population in 1980 to 15 percent in 2010. In Latin America, between 1990 and 2010, the proportion of Catholics declined by 17 percent, while other Christian churches (mainly Pentecostalist, but including various other Protestant denominations as well) increased their influence by 12 percent (see table 7.1). This tendency has been heightened since 2010. Thus, according to the Latinobarómetro Database, the most reliable source among many contradictory presentations of data, the proportion of Catholics in the region's overall population fell from 67 percent to 60 percent between 2013 and 2017: an unusually rapid decline. Meanwhile the proportion of Protestants rose somewhat, from 15 percent to 19 percent, although variations by country invalidate this overall figure (Latinobarómetro, 2018). For example, Evangelical Christians account for nearly half of the population throughout Central America (except in Costa Rica and Panama). And in Brazil Evangelicals accounted for 27 percent of the population in 2017. But the most substantial increase in proportional terms was in the category "no affiliation," which went from 12 percent of the population in 2013 to 17 percent in 2017. Again, we need to make careful distinctions in order to understand what is happening, because this category includes agnostics and atheists, on the one hand, who in Chile and Uruguay now account for almost 40 percent of the population; and, on the other hand, it also includes the syncretic and Afro-Brazilian religions practiced in Brazil, where their adherents are part of the 10 percent of the population identified as having no particular religious affiliation.[1]

The causes of this crisis in the Catholic Church are numerous and interrelated. But studies undertaken by Catholic intellectuals have identified very concrete causes that are present to varying degrees in all countries (Strotmann, 2007). First of all, these studies point to the Church hierarchy's traditional complicity with dominant elites in all countries. As Nicolás Antonio Castellanos, the former Bishop of Palencia who became a missionary in Bolivia, complained in 1991, the bishops "live in their palaces." This critique was echoed by Pope Francis during his first visit to Brazil, when he addressed – and admonished – an assembly of bishops. This lack of Christian virtue stood in contrast to the missionary activities of various evangelical

96

churches in poor neighborhoods, and it was the first rift that began to call the credibility of the church into question. This was despite the pastoral dedication of many priests and other members of the clergy who received little support from the Church hierarchy. Another factor in this process was – and is – the Church's inability to situate itself in the culture of the third millennium. Changes in young people's sexuality, sexual diversity, and women's rights, including abortion in particular, have made the dogmatism and intolerance of the Catholic Church unsustainable. This Church dogma has remained anchored in the medieval world, as in the congenital patriarchal sexism of the Catholic hierarchy, which continues to marginalize and discriminate against women in the heart of the Church. Patriarchy is falling apart in all realms of society except in the Catholic Church. Thus, what is falling apart instead is the Church itself. Finally, the sexual abuse in which Catholic priests have engaged, and especially the cover-ups and the systematic protection granted to these priests by the hierarchy have gravely eroded the Church's credibility, and disgusted broad sectors of Catholics, including even the Pope. But his reaction has come late, undoubtedly. In Chile, the proportion of Catholics fell sharply, from 60 percent in 2011 to 38 percent in 2017. This was after the 2011 revelation of the sexual abuse that Fernando Karadima – a celebrated priest (sadly), pedophile, and friend of Pinochet – had engaged in for many years, targeting young men in particular. Reproached by the Pope during his visit to Chile in 2017, the Chilean bishops' only response was to resign all together. This might appear to be an acknowledgment of responsibility but was in fact a closing of the ranks against the Pope's authority, although the Pope did sanction various bishops responsible for cover-ups.

Norberto Strotmann, bishop of Chosica in Peru and a renowned philosopher, wrote an important text in 2007, addressing the ongoing crisis of Catholicism in Latin America, after the debates that took place at the Conference of Aparecida in Brazil, which gathered bishops from throughout Latin America. In one passage, Strotmann writes: "Five hundred years of Catholic religious monopoly have left us without arguments or creativity, confronting Latin American societies in which the Catholic Church is no longer the central institution of development. And here the Catholic Church is not the only church, nor necessarily the most attractive one on the Latin American religious spectrum" (Strotmann, 2007: 3).

Consequently, the key question is about the institutional weakness of the Church and the decline of Catholicism in Latin America, which has lost out to other, growing Christian churches, on the one

Table 7.1: Main Religions by Country: Latin America, 2013 and 2017 (%)

Country	2013					2017					Variation 2017–2013				
	Cath.	Evang.	None, Atheist, Agnost.	Other	No Response/ DNK	Cath.	Evang.	None, Atheist, Agnost.	Other	No Response/ DNK	Cath.	Evang.	None, Atheist, Agnost.	Other	No Response/ DNK
Argentina	77%	7%	13%	3%	0%	66%	10%	21%	3%	0%	-11	3	8	0	0
Bolivia	76%	17%	5%	1%	1%	73%	20%	4%	4%	1%	-3	3	-1	3	0
Brazil	63%	21%	11%	4%	1%	54%	27%	14%	5%	1%	-9	6	3	1	0
Chile	56%	13%	25%	5%	1%	45%	11%	38%	4%	2%	-11	-2	13	-1	1
Colombia	75%	3%	8%	14%	0%	73%	14%	11%	2%	1%	-2	11	4	-12	1
Costa Rica	62%	21%	9%	6%	3%	57%	25%	15%	2%	1%	-5	4	6	-4	-2
Ecuador	81%	12%	4%	2%	1%	77%	14%	7%	1%	1%	-4	2	3	-1	0
El Salvador	54%	31%	10%	4%	1%	39%	28%	30%	2%	1%	-15	-3	20	-2	0
Guatemala	47%	40%	9%	3%	1%	43%	41%	13%	2%	1%	-4	1	4	-1	0
Honduras	47%	41%	9%	2%	0%	37%	39%	21%	2%	1%	-10	-2	12	0	1
Mexico	79%	3%	7%	10%	1%	80%	5%	11%	3%	1%	1	2	4	-7	0
Nicaragua	47%	37%	12%	3%	0%	40%	32%	25%	3%	1%	-7	-5	13	0	1
Panama	72%	19%	4%	4%	1%	55%	24%	16%	1%	4%	-17	5	12	-3	3
Paraguay	88%	8%	2%	2%	0%	89%	5%	4%	2%	0%	1	-3	2	0	0
Peru	77%	10%	5%	7%	1%	74%	12%	8%	5%	1%	-3	2	3	-2	0
Dominican Rep.	65%	18%	12%	5%	1%	48%	21%	28%	2%	1%	-17	3	16	-3	1
Uruguay	41%	8%	38%	13%	1%	38%	7%	41%	14%	1%	-3	-1	4	1	0
Venezuela	79%	13%	6%	2%	1%	67%	18%	13%	2%	0%	-12	5	7	1	-1
Latin America	67%	15%	12%	5%	1%	60%	19%	17%	3%	1%	-7	4	5	-2	0

Cath. = Catholic; Evang. = Evangelical; Agnost. = Agnostic; DNK = Does Not Know hand, and, on the other, to forms of agnosticism. This dual erosion of the hegemony traditionally enjoyed by the Catholic Church is related to age and education. Older people tend to be more faithful to Catholicism. Likewise, social status, measured by level of education, is positively correlated with Catholicism. By contrast, evangelical churches attract the bulk of their followers from less educated and lower-income social sectors. Meanwhile young people have moved overwhelmingly away from Catholicism and are the most likely to consider themselves agnostic. This process of youth secularization is monumental, and it is new in Chile, and it has intensified in all of the countries where it already existed as a tendency, especially Argentina and Uruguay. The Catholic Church retains its influence in traditional, rural areas. By contrast, its presence diminishes in large Latin American cities, whose informal peripheries are the main sites for recruitment for evangelical churches. These peripheries' new middle classes, moreover, are the groups most likely to lose their religion, both in the sense of changing their religious affiliation and in the sense of becoming less devout in their religious practice. It is in large cities that we find the starkest contrast between the Catholic Church hierarchy's integration into the social elite, and the Church's ministry or social work – in other words, its defense of the rights and interests of the poor against established powers – work that the Church tends to devalue. In this context, a projection cited at the Episcopal Conference in Aparecida, which took place in 2007, predicted that in 2035 the proportions of Catholics and Protestants in the region would be equal at roughly 41 percent each, with those without any religious affiliation accounting for 16 percent of the population (Strotmann, 2007).

To be sure, however, the crisis of the Catholic Church in Latin America is inseparable from the crisis of the Catholic Church as a whole. This Church is enveloped in scandals and beset by the internal power struggles that have come to light in the last four decades. At the center of the self-destructive processes is the College of Cardinals, which seeks to control the Church apparatus from the Vatican and is reluctant to give up power. In several countries, investigations into the efforts to cover up systemic sexual abuses in churches, Catholic schools, monasteries, and orphanages have uncovered well-connected cardinals with ties to the College and the Curia. This is a testament to the popular adage according to which "all roads lead to Rome." And at the heart of these intrigues involving the Curia, we find the Vatican Bank, currently undergoing reforms and a facelift thanks to Pope Francis. Throughout the world, journalistic reports, books, and films about the Church have appeared, some accurate and some sensationalizing and best taken with a dose of skepticism or regarded from a distance. In any case, we will point to a few key facts here in order to show that the crisis of Latin American Catholicism should be situated in a broader context.

It suffices to recall the 1982 collapse of the Banco Ambrosiano, a screen for the Vatican Bank, its main shareholder. This led Roberto Calvi, director of the Masonic Lodge Propaganda Due (or P2) and president of the Banco Ambrosiano, to flee to London, where he was immediately assassinated lest he reveal the connections between the Lodge and the Sicilian mafia, which used the bank to launder money. In fact, the Vatican accepted "moral responsibility" for the bank's collapse and paid US$224 million to shareholders. In 1974, another bank's dealings had come to light at the moment of its collapse: the Franklin National Bank, which had ties to the Vatican Bank and was controlled by Michele Sindona, a mafia boss who was poisoned in prison before an investigation could run its course. Pope Benedict XVI sought to reform the management of the Vatican Bank, naming a financier friend, Ettore Gotti Tedeschi, as president. With Tedeschi, the Pope devised a law to prevent money laundering in 2010. This was only partly passed, and according to Tedeschi this was because of opposition from the Curia. In particular, it was owing to the hostility of the official then responsible for the Vatican's finances, the Australian cardinal George Pell, who ultimately had to return to his native country to face trial for sexually abusing minors.

Here we see an interesting convergence of two taboos in the Vatican. Tedeschi was replaced by Ernst Von Freyberg. Benedict XVI's last decision before retiring in 2013 was to dismiss Von Freyberg in an effort to exercise more direct control over the practices of money laundering that, according to trustworthy published reports, have made the Vatican into the eighth largest tax haven in the world (measured by volume of operations) and an efficient channel for this activity. As soon as Francis assumed the papacy, he picked up where Pope Benedict had left off, naming a new Bank President, the French financier Jean Baptiste de Franssu. He did this without consulting the Curia and ordered the closure of 5,000 suspicious accounts at the Vatican Bank. It would seem, however, that these steps were not sufficient. In November 2017, Giulio Mattietti, the Bank's subdirector, was dismissed, with the Pope's approval. Mattietti had been close to members of the Church hierarchy.

What is the meaning of this endless series of scandals and power struggles involving the Catholic Church's finances? This is not just a matter of bishops who "live in palaces"; it is a matter of the Church seeing its interests as aligned with those of finance capital. It has participated in the speculative practices and the kinds of money laundering that characterize some sectors in the financial system. And since the criminal economy and government corruption are essential components of large-scale money laundering operations, various groups have sought the Church's collaboration in their business ventures, with the likely, perhaps implicit cooperation of part of the Vatican bureaucracy. It is likely that these deals have involved the blackmail of clergy. For it is no mere coincidence that a sexual abuser like Pell was also apparently an obstacle to the reform of the Vatican Bank (officially the Institute for the Works of Religion) in his capacity as an official charged with overseeing Vatican finances. And if these conclusions were extended to the whole system, it would be logical to think that these sorts of problems have also affected the Latin American Church, which operates in a context of illegality and corruption. In such a context, the claim that the Archbishop of Guadalajara was assassinated by *narcos* because he was about to reveal that drug traffickers had infiltrated the Church becomes credible. How can a church shot through with global financial interests and exposed to a world of corruption and money laundering preserve not just its credibility, but its ethical culture?

The consequences of the profound crisis in the Catholic Church in Latin America go beyond the corporate interests of the institution itself or those of unconditional believers. A community of values is being dismantled, one that has been, and in some ways still is, an essential source of social cohesion, solace in times of suffering, refuge, and hope. In societies in which violence, extreme individualism, and nihilism envelop everyday life for the majority, the gradual loss of what the Catholic Church represented compounds the problems of social decomposition and personal desperation. To be sure, there are alternative forms of religion, and forms of agnostic spirituality, as we have shown in the foregoing analysis. But because of their relative historical novelty, these tend to involve the reconstruction of ethical and religious values in fragmentary and communitarian forms, in specific communities. They thus reinforce broader cultural tendencies involving the distancing of different worlds from one another and ultimately the fraying of any social fabric founded on coexistence, based on shared values. In this way, we are witnessing a decline in multicultural coexistence, in the ethics of respect for the other as a shared value, whoever this other might be and whatever her beliefs might be. The criminal economy is a paradigmatic example of this, one that has affected people's religious practices. Consider, for example, the case of the "Knights Templar" in Michoacán, Mexico, where drug trafficking is combined with the use of networks of information, and lethal territorial disputes coexist with a sort of familial religion practiced by gangs of drug traffickers.

Hence the importance of the possibility of profound reform in the Catholic Church in Latin America: a reform that would let the Church preserve its capacity for social integration. This is the kind of reform that, against the odds, Francis is working to implement. Compelled to confront a global crisis, the Catholic Church boldly chose to elect him and to confront the serious problems that we have mentioned with a charismatic leader. But it did so with a specific goal. If the former pope thought that the key was a reform within the Church, the current pope lays stress on problems and questions that are external to the Church, on its relation to society. This is not just a matter of stopping corruption in the institution of the Church itself; instead, it is a matter of revitalizing the Church's role as an instrument of social reform and a place of personal refuge.

Here we put forward the hypothesis that both the crisis of the Catholic Church's legitimacy and its consequences for subjectivity are expressions of a global ethical crisis. This implies the creation of conditions for the emergence of a new charismatic leader, one who can take risks and confront both dimensions of the crisis in complex and composite ways. In this sense the current pope's charisma is the result of a crisis that has occurred at both the socio-cultural and the institutional levels. When the institutional foundations of the church lose their legitimacy, when the global crisis of multicultural coexistence intensifies, or when intercultural coexistence becomes insufficient, demands for a charismatic leader like Francis become louder. When you do not change, you lose, but change always carries risks.

Pope Francis has a kind of gift that grants him unusual power. Appealing to an ideal of emotional community, he generates excitement, and he is in demand among the people, even while he is valued by those in power. A charismatic leader, he includes, protects, sacrifices himself, and demands sacrifices. He transforms passive subjects into active subjects.

Papal charisma, emanating from the modest convent of Santa Maria, has a Jesuit priest from Argentina as its agent. Francis is the son of poor migrants and was influenced by the populist culture of Peronism. He gives the impression that his political and cultural principles were built on these precedents. His approach, we think, is related to the *habitus* of the Jesuits in Latin America. In other words, his approach, like his subjective and personal world, is influenced by a cultural inheritance.

The idea that conflicts should be mediated by an ethics based on peace and the idea of a renewed Christian community are both key to the orientation that allows for a confrontation with the challenges of secularization, one that threatens to limit human coexistence. In fact, this orientation is an effort to renew the historical legacy and the experience of the Society of Jesus.

Consider the idea of a "communist community" first proposed and constructed in the baroque utopias of the Jesuit Missions of the Guaranís (Droz, 1972; Chinchilla, 2010), or the celebrated recognition of indigenous languages in the region, as in the translations from the Aymara and the creation of a bilingual, Aymara-Spanish dictionary by Ludovico Bertonio in 1612 (Bertonio, 1984). Or consider the various modern projects of "enlightened" education, guided by a pedagogy of personal meditation and undertaken throughout Latin America. Albó and Layme analyze the Jesuits' impact on Andean cultures, through to liberation theology and various other proposals for integrating modernity and community. Or consider, finally, the Jesuits' reflections on spirituality and secularization (Albó and Layme, 1984).

Here the community is defined as a process of building an everyday life in common, one that allows for the development of personal autonomy and self-reflexivity. This kind of community also allows for a secularization of time, where human time is not separated from religious time or from ecological time, and where there are no certainties. It is from within this time that a new kind of ethics and a new, more coherent and legitimate kind of institution can be imagined and proposed to the world and specifically to the world's poor.[2] Although it is too soon to reach any conclusions about the agency or the capacity of the new papal charisma, some tendencies in the public realm can already be identified.

In this connection, it is worth mentioning that the Church has regained some prestige as it has promoted inter-faith dialogues; worked to promote peace treaties, especially in Colombia; mediated politically between the US and Cuba; clearly supported poor migrants from the Third World in Europe and the US; and offered support and sympathy to ecological movements throughout the world. The recovery and promotion of an ethics based on peace and the valorization of human dignity, especially for the poorest, has been no less significant. These have offered the Church ways of countering a consumerist and hedonist form of secularization, which curtails human coexistence, destroys nature, and does not respect the rights of animals. Still, the scale of the institutional crisis and the persistence of benighted, ultra-conservative values that are deeply rooted in the Catholic Church, even while they are also tied in complex ways to various dark forms of power, rule out early conclusions on the tendencies that we have been considering in light of a profound global crisis in values. The most significant thing that we have seen, however, is that the Catholic Church could again become a global force that is proactive in decisive moments, one that acts on behalf of humanity and Latin America, while also coexisting with other majority religions and other Christian churches whose influence in the world continues to grow.

— 8 —

THE POWER OF IDENTITY
Multiculturalism and Social Movements

In a sense, multiculturalism is an intrinsic feature of Latin American history. Since its origins, the region has been home to diverse and densely interrelated cultures. At the beginning of the colonial period, the indigenous population was made up of approximately 100 million people. Today, indigenous people account for nearly 45 million in a total population of 538 million. Rates of self-identification have increased under conditions of democracy, and increases were especially marked during the period from 2000 to 2010. Estimates suggest that there are 826 different indigenous peoples in Latin America and the Caribbean (Denevan, 1976; Latin American and Caribbean Demographic Centre, 2010).

Aymara culture, for example, was heterogeneous and dynamic, as were the cultures of the Maya and the Amazonian peoples. Andean cultures were characterized by linguistic diversity and were constantly interacting with Amazonian cultures. The arrival of Europeans and the presence of Spanish and Portuguese cultures – which were themselves multicultural, as Carlos Fuentes showed so well in his book *The Buried Mirror* – further complicated the dynamics and the multicultural fabric of indigenous cultures. This multiculturalism was further enriched by diverse migrations of peoples from Africa, the Arab world, and Asia. A particular multicultural fabric, vibrant and complex, was a hallmark of Latin American identity. The origin of this multicultural Latin American world is reflected in the myth of the Ayar brothers, who in wandering founded an empire.[1]

With colonization, new forms of domination and power were introduced, centered on mineral extraction and agriculture. These annihilated populations appropriated vast natural resources, to such an extent that they go some way toward explaining the process of

105

primitive accumulation in Western capitalism. But these forms of domination also destroyed networks of roads, for instance, or cultural norms for working the land, relating to nature, responding to the movement of populations, and storing provisions to sustain complex reproductive systems (Murra, 2017 [1969]).

Colonization forcefully introduced a pattern of social stratification, typical of colonial societies and organized around *haciendas* and mines. This system was sustained by a culture that centered on the extraction of natural resources over long periods, a culture that shaped social relations throughout the region, and continues to shape them. Precisely by exploiting so many territories in this way, Latin American elites created the mark of their "distinction": a rentier ethic and a relation to luxury goods modeled on European patterns of consumption. This tendency was based on a sort of "dialectic of negation of the other," where the other (indigenous, Black, female, migrant, and so on) was, in being differentiated, also degraded and could thus be exploited and used to legitimize power in the system of social stratification that developed.

In response to this kind of stratification, and in response to this culture, which required the negation of the other, diverse forms of resistance, struggles, cultural movements, and multicultural systems for coexistence emerged throughout the region, with many local and national variations and hallmarks. These forms of interaction also responded to international changes, and they changed and overlapped during the course of various historical periods, forming multicultural, regional, and national networks or fabrics. This is a central feature of Latin American cultural politics (Calderón et al., 1996).

From this cultural morass or historical *chenko* (chaos, in Quechua), colonialism also generated new forms of cohabitation and coexistence, like those of baroque Latin America, which expressed new creative forms, tensions, and ways of interrogating dominant multiculturalism. In colonial Latin America, there were dynamics of assimilation, but there were also dynamics of resistance, creation, and transformation in the workings of colonial (and later neocolonial) power.

The baroque Guraraní, for example, introduced the idea of a social utopia to the Western world as well, as a volume recounting the history of the French socialist party acknowledges (Droz, 1972). Meanwhile, the baroque period in Potosí, Bolivia, or in Mexico indicated different paths for coexistence and mutual cultural enrichment (Castedo, 1966). Religion in its numerous regional, Afro-Portuguese manifestations also enriched and complicated the "universal culture" in Brazil. Later, the cultures of the colonial period developed new dynamics with the arrival of immigrants from Asia, the Arab world, and different parts of Europe. Today's regional and national cultures are only parts of or layers in this complex and rich dynamism.

In this context of multiple cultures, an important case of political "universalism" is the Haitian Revolution at the end of the eighteenth century. Argentina represents another interesting case of relatively successful multicultural coexistence, enabled by its public schools in the twentieth century. Maroon culture traversed the entire region, including its islands. It is perhaps not surprising, therefore, to find clear cultural similarities across distant regions. Such regions can be distant from one another and still have more in common with each other than they do with the nearest urban centers. For an extreme example, consider the Chinese migrations in both the remote past and recent history; these migrations created a multicultural dynamic throughout the region and particularly in countries like Peru, Mexico, Panama, and Cuba. Wilfredo Lam's paintings are at once Cuban, Chinese, African, and European, since they are inspired by the Cubism of Lam's friend Pablo Picasso and pay homage to the creative force of the Spanish Republic. These paintings then traveled to New York, where they inspired the Surrealist movement in that city. A similar dynamic can be observed in the careers of the painters Roberto Matta, from Chile, or David Alfaro Siqueiros, from Mexico.

In the twentieth century, the *hacienda* system was called into question, industrialization began, and national-popular movements began to appear. After the Mexican Revolution, Mexicans could reconsider their origins. Throughout the century, they sought to integrate the people into the nation through incorporation into the state. In many Latin American countries, people sought to make social integration and industrialization into mutually sustaining processes. The state became a central point of reference not only in political or economic conflicts, but also in the ethos or cultural life of these societies. Hence the contested, often polemical nature of characterizations and definitions of the state (Calderón and Jelin, 1987; Touraine, 1988).

The Force of Cultural Diversity: Indigenous and Afro-Brazilian Movements

For the past 36 years, the region has undergone processes of both democratization and integration into the network society. These processes were accompanied and enriched by the increased participation of indigenous peoples and people of African descent, by the "extraterritorial" dynamics of indigenous peoples' international emigration, and by new forms of cultural mixing or *mestizaje*. Particularly in the last decade, this has meant that a new, "culturally constructive" creativity has been exercised by those formerly excluded or repressed. This dynamism has been created by new socio-cultural movements like the Zapatistas among the Maya in Mexico, the intercultural peasants in Bolivia, the Mapuche in Chile, and people of African descent in Brazil.

Figure 8.1 illustrates this dynamism. According to estimates from the Economic Commission for Latin America and the Caribbean's Latin American and Caribbean Demographic Centre, there are 44,795,758 indigenous people in the region, and they can be grouped into approximately 896 distinct peoples. The data show the growth of a multicultural subjectivity that has been enriched and complicated by the emigration of indigenous and "mestizo" people to other countries in the region as well as to Canada and the United States. These emigrants generate a new form of multiculturalism that strengthens indigenous cultures in "foreign" lands, while also enriching and being enriched by new kinds of interaction, autonomy, and cultural production in destination countries. In this way, new dynamics and identities are generated that become cosmopolitan and global.

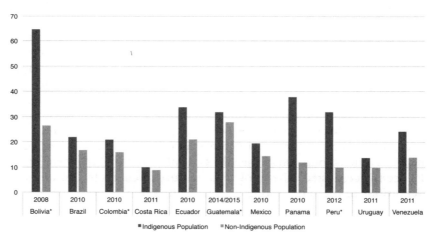

Figure 8.1: Proportion of the Population that Is Indigenous. Selected Latin American Countries, Census Data from 2000 and 2010

Notes:
*Data from 2000 refer to the *Encuesta complementaria de pueblosindígenas*, 2004–2005
**Data from 2010 refer to the *Resultados preliminares del III Censo nacional de población y viviendas para pueblos indígenas* (2012)

108

One peculiarity of these transformations derives from the fact that their strength is directly linked to an expansion in the use of online networks of communication. Between 2000 and 2017, according to a study conducted by the United Nations (UN, 2017), the number of Latin Americans who left their countries of origin increased from 24.8 million to 37.7 million people. In the countries where they settle, these emigrants create new spaces of communication and cultural creation, new networks of identity in a context of diaspora. Networks of communication facilitate everyday connections, beyond time and space. On the basis of these connections, people who identify as part of the same culture expand their creative and communicative capacities, and through this process of exchange they strengthen forms of recognition, citizenship, and belonging in the world. The force of these new social movements led by indigenous peoples and people of African descent would be unthinkable without communication networks, which are central to the culture of diaspora. And conversely, the influence of these movements on that culture is key. This is a question that requires further research.

In the dynamics of these movements of indigenous peoples and people of African descent, four particular movements stand out and can be seen to exemplify the movements' ability to structure identity in the region, as well as their ability to redefine multiculturalism in more pluralist and truly intercultural ways. These are: the *Zapatista* movement in Mexico; the movement of intercultural peasants in Bolivia; the Mapuche movement in Chile; and the protest movements led by people of African descent, which are present throughout the region and especially in Brazil.[2]

Zapatismo 2.0

The resistance and mobilization of mostly indigenous (Tzeltal, Chol, and Tzotzil) communities or commons in Chiapas and Oaxaca, in southern Mexico, since the early 1990s has been a point of reference for current mobilizations, not only in Mexico but throughout Latin America and even globally.[3] These mobilizations would be impossible to understand if we did not consider the force of the Zapatista movement at the beginning of the last century. This movement, too, had international importance. Here it suffices to recall how living in Mexico, and experiencing the Zapatista revolution, encouraged John Reed to travel to Russia at the time of the Bolshevik revolution.[4] Like Emiliano Zapata and Pancho Villa, who did not want to see political power remain in Mexico City, today's Zapatistas do not aim to seize political power through armed struggle, as did the liberation movements of the 1960s. Instead, they work to build on their indigenous and communitarian identities, to politicize democracy and development in a unique way.

The Zapatista movement has sought to combine renewed communitarian demands, tied to the land, for the improvement of their basic conditions of social reproduction and demands for cultural recognition and democratic participation at the national scale. Unlike other movements that arose later in the region, they have not worked to create a "Mayan nationality," but rather to achieve recognition as Maya citizens of the Mexican state. In addition, they have questioned neoliberalism and the North American Free Trade Agreement, which Mexico signed with the United States. The movement has brought together various "communitarian" values and aspirations in order to forge a political project in a context of conflict, making both regional and national demands. All of this was made possible by a strange charismatic leader: Subcomandante Marcos. "Marcos does not exist. He was born dead on January 1, 1994," according to a communiqué from the period (Le Bot, 1997: 13). His identity was a mask, and so "any Mexican can put on one of those balaclavas and be Marcos, becoming me" (Le Bot, 1997: 16).

The organization, made up of communitarian peasants, was at first supported by the Catholic Church and strengthened by appeals to liberation theology. This was especially true at the time of the organization's beginnings. Thus "cadres" of peasants were formed on the basis of progressive doctrines, which strengthened their "communitarian unions." Communitarianism was further strengthened by the willingness of religious organizations to confront local powers, including ranchers and the PRI (Partido Revolucionario Institucional, or Institutional Revolutionary Party). Later, Marxist ideologies became influential, but these were ideologies typical of the region and were increasingly subordinated to the cultural imaginaries of the indigenous people of Chiapas and the Lacan Dona Jungle. Later negotiations with the Mexican state involved the direct participation of local communities.

It is impossible to imagine the character of this rebellion unless we take the historical *longue durée* into account: the period extending from colonization to the present of the movement. The protest in San Cristóbal de las Casas, in Chiapas, on October 12, 1992, against the 500th anniversary of the "discovery of America," included the destruction of a statue of the conquistador Diego de Mazariegos. This was a decisive movement in the formation of subjectivity in the movement.

The movement's participants connected this historical questioning to what they saw as a sort of reincarnation of colonial logic in the Free Trade Agreement, and in the place of Mexico in the new world order. The Zapatistas see themselves as legitimate rebels, as patriots, and as communitarians committed to democracy, questioning the political order created by just one party in power.

A phenomenon related to its growing local, national, and global prominence was the internet and other media (Castells, 2010: 101). This was the so-called "first informational guerrilla war." Through the media, the Zapatistas could disseminate their ideas even in the midst of very violent conflicts. But the use of force was a resource for bringing their demands to the local and global public sphere, in order to the claim legitimacy for their ideals and force the state to negotiate on various viable demands. Mexican public opinion spoke eloquently in favor of the Zapatistas: in December 1994, 59 percent of Mexico City residents had a positive opinion of them, and 78 percent thought that their demands were justified (*La Reforma*, December 11, 1994, quoted by Castells, 2010: 102).

It is important to underscore that the use of the internet and other media is tied to the creation of "la Neta" in Mexico as well as other Mexican NGOs and the Institute for Global Communications in San Francisco, founded by young computer scientists who supported the movement (Castells, 2010: 103). Women's use of these systems of communication is also noteworthy; this led to the creation of connections between the uprising in Chiapas and women elsewhere in Mexico and the rest of the world.

Even beyond the complex political processes that it has undergone, the movement in the Lacan Dona Jungle and in Chiapas launched a new form of politics in the region. It not only challenged the dominant logic of globalization; it sought to build a new meaning for politics by innovating democracy and the very idea of indigenous community. The Zapatistas sought to bring new horizons of possibility into being, together with a more participatory and deliberative democracy, based on substantive values centered on the intercultural recognition of indigenous peoples.

The Intercultural Peasants of Chapare

In order to understand this recent experience, it is important to situate it in a longer history. It is related to colonial domination in Charcas, Boliva, and to the indigenous uprising that took place there in the

111

colonial period. But it is also related to the long, various, compli-cated, and conflictual process of constructing social institutions in the Bolivian nation, with its multiple peoples indigenous to Charcas. Today's Plurinational State of Bolivia is built on a land with an intense and strange history. In Bolivia, society makes institutions, and this probably accounts for the country's strength as well as its weakness: its strength, because it shows a capacity for acting and for collective crea-tion; its weakness, because institutions have not become efficacious or legitimate for the society that created them. The absence of "constitu-tive minorities," to use a term elaborated by Norbert Lechner, goes a long way toward explaining the limits of the country's institutions as well as the exploitation and dependency from which it has suffered, despite the Revolution of 1952 and the return to democracy 30 years ago, to mention only two moments in the twentieth century.

In this context, there are constant problems, including the strati-fication of classes traceable to colonialism and the persistence of a culture that negates "the other." These problems have changed, however, in their manifestations, and today it is crucial to carefully consider Bolivia's real chances of intercultural democracy.

But what set of social actors currently drive the change? What options for development are compatible with this quest for democ-racy, and how sustainable are they in a global risk society? Social movements in Bolivia are diverse and intense, both in the Andes, as in the case of the *katarista* movement (which is inspired by Tupác Katari, who led an insurrection in the late eighteenth century), and in the Amazon, with the indigenous movements formed by Amazonian peoples and especially the recent mobilization in the Territorio Indígena y Parque Nacional Isiboro Sécure (TIPNIS, or Isiboro Secure National Park and Indigenous Territory) in 2012. All of these experi-ences highlight the intercultural tensions and conflicts involved in the process of change.

Here we will try to characterize one set of actors strategically involved in this process: those formerly called "peasant settlers," especially in Chapare in the Bolivian Amazon. Today they call them-selves "intercultural peasants." Without them neither the temporality of the process of change in Bolivia nor the leadership of Evo Morales, who remains the most powerful labor leader in the movement, would be explicable.

The "settlers" or "intercultural peasants" are the result of the exhaustion of mining in the western part of the country as well as the policies driven by the state after the Revolution of 1952. They are migrants, mostly peasants, from different cultural and social contexts

112

in the Andes, regions with important cultural features and communities, like the north of Potosí, or regions where the ownership of small farms already had a long history, as in the valleys around Cochabamba. But they are also the result of crises and economic failures in different historical moments, like the tin mining crisis and the structural reforms of the 1980s, and from the force of inertia exercised by the coca economy and the price of coca. In any case, they are the founders of a new multicultural and social configuration. Their capacities for survival and development begin with the very act of their integration into the tropics. Here they have to confront a nature that is harsh and aggressive, living in precarious conditions and growing rice, plantains, coca, and so on with difficulty. In the beginning, they thought productive diversity would allow for economic victory in a confrontation with aggressive markets and intermediaries. Gradually, however, it became clear that only coca was profitable and could allow them to survive, at times accumulating resources and some capital, though at the cost of operating semi-legally and having to confront the US Drug Enforcement Administration (DEA). Various alternative policies promoted by the Bolivian state and the United States were relative failures. As we know, all of this was related to the power of the international market for cocaine and to developed, consumer societies that were somehow in decline. The "American way of life" has serious problems with both local and international recreation.

Still, what we want to highlight is that as a result of all of these experiences, a stoic and shrewd spirit was formed, a rugged class forged through all kinds of resistance. This was not a "liquid" but rather a solid social class, which organized itself into unions as a way of life, both local and every day. United on the land and creative in their confrontations with enemies, this class could survive.

Unlike miners' unions, which took the form of "isolated masses," today's unions of "peasant settlers," or those who call themselves intercultural, are more open and plural. Their relations with others are peasant relations of reciprocity with indigenous communities. In some cases, as in the valleys around Cochabamba, these are relations with family economies that are diversified and interrelated. Their relations with Amazonian indigenous communities have often been ambivalent and marked by mutual suspicion.

Their political presence on the streets of Cochabamba and La Paz has been crucial during the last two decades and especially important to recent events in Bolivia. They form a rugged class and union, with pro-peasant, intercultural, and radicalized, revolutionary ideologies, but above all with concrete and flexible practices, with the capacity and skill to articulate maximalist demands and still achieve specific results. We can conjecture that the political force of the Movimiento al Socialismo (MAS, or the Movement for Socialism), the diverse and changing social alliances in Bolivia, and the political force of President Morales himself depend largely, though not entirely, on them. Who would have thought that poor, migrant peasants could form such complex alliances with, among others, intellectuals, the middle class, neighborhood organizations in the city of El Alto, and even the Bolivian state, businessmen from Santa Cruz, and transnational gas and oil companies?

But perhaps even more significantly, this movement, working together with other popular and protest movements, after complex confrontations with the state and various regional elites, created a new constitution and a new, pluralist institutional order called "intercultural democracy." Institutionally, the Plurinational State of Bolivia was created, and so a new and complex process of change began, one that we have elsewhere called "indigenist neo-developmentalism" (Calderón, 2007).

This neo-developmentalism has, on the one hand, entailed the return of a state that plays a structuring role in the economy and politics, and it has led to a concentration of power in the hands of the charismatic President Morales. On the other hand, it has entailed the strengthening of an indigenist and at times a communitarian logic, one that has redefined the institutional political order, producing substantive changes in liberal and republican democracy and introducing communitarian forms of participation at the regional and national levels. A dynamic and ambivalent tension was thus generated, between the state and a communitarian or semi-communitarian logic that is profoundly indigenist. On this basis, social and political relations with the rest of Bolivian society and its various forms of organization and power were restructured. The question is whether these strategic actors, the intercultural peasants and their allies and the new political elites in positions of state power – with their identity, their conflicts, and their various orientations – will be able to build a new pluralist, intercultural democracy (Mayorga, 2018).

The use of information and communications technologies has been and still is very important in this movement as well. These technologies have been resources in the peasants' struggle, and today it suffices to look at their web page to understand the key role that these technologies play in the movement's politics and social relations. The peasants' conflicts and deliberations are now "alive and kicking" online.

114

In terms of the "neo-developmentalist-communitarian-indigenist model of development" that, together with other priorities, has driven the movement, it is worth underscoring the hypothesis according to which this model was made possible by the conjunction of a developmentalist state, on the one hand, and, on the other, a communitarian and indigenist orientation that prevailed in the early days of the movement. This led to a new constitution, and we now see the former prevail over the latter. The "model" in question is ever more centered on the state, the executive, and the charismatic leadership of President Morales. This center is the place where the movement's politics are now articulated. This means, on the one hand, a macro- and microeconomic form of management consistent with international practices, with extraordinary levels of savings and investment plans never before seen in the country's economic history. On the other hand, however, this means a political economy that is increasingly neo-developmentalist and that depends on an export economy, especially on the export of raw materials, and on massive investments in national integration, whether in the form of infrastructural investments (in roads, equipment, and so on) or in satellite communications. Finally, both economic management and developmentalist policies are complemented by populist policies that seek to integrate and give national and popular legitimacy to social investments and political mobilizations. Not only have levels of poverty decreased and indices of equality improved; many, though not all, indigenous and communitarian majorities that were traditionally discriminated against and denied social and cultural power during long periods of domination have now been empowered and gained self-esteem. It seems that a process of national development begun 50 years ago and long left unfinished is now culminating: an effort to complete the unfinished work of the Revolution of 1952, as well as opening new horizons in a global society.

It is in this context that new and innovative possibilities for intercultural democracy are suggested, in a community of citizens. Without denying important advances, and while appreciating the diverse and complex reality of Bolivia, it is still necessary to acknowledge the tensions, weaknesses, and ambiguities that have accompanied this political and intercultural process. These were evident during the conflict over the TIPNIS and during the actual process of debate during the drafting of the new constitution, as well as during other key moments in Bolivia's recent political history.

It is perhaps worth clarifying that a simplistic and instrumental vision of the intercultural, defined as a limited "tolerance" for cultural heterogeneity, as a sort of "plural monoculturalism" in the Andes, predominates. This may be related to the weakness of exchanges between the country's diverse cultures, or to the quest by one of these cultures to achieve hegemony over the others at the level of ideology.

Still, politics continues forcefully on the streets. Bolivia is one of the countries with the highest level of social conflict in the region (Calderón, 2012). Today it would seem to be undergoing a struggle over distribution linked to a revolution in expectations that the process of social change has itself generated. Government parties and the opposition have not fully processed this struggle, especially at the institutional level.

Overall, the situation creates the impression that the intercultural democracy that is largely, though not entirely, driven by the movement formed by intercultural peasants in the tropics near Cochabamba, arrives at a sort of contradiction between political pluralism and state hegemony. The old practices and political orientations of what was called "*democracia pactada*," or the form of democracy that privileged pacts and prevailed in the neoliberal period but is now fragmented in its electoral force, now rest on the basis of this contradiction.

Intercultural, political pluralism is necessarily conflictual and inclusive, but it is also incomplete, because every democracy needs to reinvent itself constantly. It is not only the responsibility of the government and the opposition, but rather the whole society's responsibility, to undertake this reinvention, for the sake of its capacity for action and autonomy. This is the only guarantee of a sustainable intercultural democracy. In this sense, the only democratic hegemony possible in a country like Bolivia would be one involving political pluralism. This is also the best, though not the easiest, way to progress democratically. In this context, ideals of "living and getting along" or of "citizens' autonomy" or of a "community of citizens" acquire a different meaning. It is clear, however, that just as Bolivian society shows remarkable creativity and deliberative power, including as it does different peoples seeking equality, it also has features that are factionalist, clientelist, and paternalist. These limit the very processes of change that have been set in motion.

Here we can identify two sets of issues that might prompt further reflection at a theoretical level on the indigenist movements that we have considered here. First of all, although social and political processes in Mexico and Bolivia are different, in both cases these take place in plural and complex societies that are increasingly integrated into the network society and the global economy, societies with interdependent and increasingly diverse and heterogeneous international relations. Their common field of action is centered on the search for equality: in the case of Mexico, this search emphasizes state recognition; in the case of Bolivia, it has sought to create a new form of democratic institution. In both cases, communitarian or neo-communitarian logics and demands are present.

Second, both of these movements, in different ways, interrupt the practice of politics in their respective countries. Equality, recognition, and inclusion, together with innovation, appear to be the key demands of these movements, which in this way perhaps propose a new type of politics. We are dealing, then, with two sets of social processes that have reorganized not only the political process in their respective countries, but also the field of political analysis.

The Mapuche Movement

The Mapuche movement in Chile, and also in Argentina, forms part of a new cultural dynamic involving both indigenous peoples and people of African descent, who have put the issue of the recognition of their identities and cultures at the center of debates about democracy, development, state forms, and politics itself in the context of new global changes.

In the case of the Mapuche, this new dynamic is part of a continuous, long-term historical process traceable to resistance against the Inca empire, Spanish colonial domination, and especially the consolidation of the Chilean state with the Chilean settlement or "Chilenization" of Mapuche territories. This process allowed for the expansion of haciendas and agricultural projects throughout the twentieth century. Perhaps only in the progressive movements under the Partido Demócrata Cristiano (Christian Democratic Party) governments and especially the Unidad Popular (Popular Unity) government did Chile implement policies and undertake experiments that valued the Mapuche people. A party that broke away from the Christian Democrats, "El Mapu," was even part of the Popular Unity government of President Salvador Allende, suggesting that the Mapuche are key actors in the process of change in Chile (Cantoni, 1978).

Recent Mapuche mobilizations arose as concrete responses to a series of changes introduced by the model of development to which Chile has been subjected during the last 20 years. The mobilizations,

117

in other words, respond to transformations in the environment, to the ecological and socioeconomic consequences of "informational extractivism," to the politics of national imaginaries as communicated by major media outlets.

An important point of reference for the current mobilizations began in the region of Lomako, where a group of Mapuche advocate, in addition to the burning of logging trucks, an autonomist path for the Mapuche people. Here memory, territoriality, and identity emerge as values and as the foundations of an emancipatory possibility (Tricot, 2009: 18).

It is worth clarifying that the Mapuche people are marked by heterogeneity, especially in regions VII, XIX, X, and XIV.[5] There are also various interpretations of the movement and diverse organizations within these regions. The Mapuche do not constitute a homogeneous subject, but rather a range of actors, perhaps in the process of constructing a shared project. Similarly, the movement is supported by NGOs, human rights organizations, and a network of indigenist movements throughout Latin America.

The Mapuche movement, based in one of the poorest regions in Chile (UNDP, 2006), responds to several, sometimes violent forms of action on the part of the businesses that have been established on their lands (not all of them legally established there). They also respond to discriminatory practices and those that negate their identity and deny their rights, as well as to radically repressive police measures undertaken in the name of "anti-terrorist" state policies, which legitimate repression without considering the historical causes of Mapuche demands. The vision of Chile's historical elites, who built their force by subordinating and limiting the culture of the Mapuche, among others, seems to predominate.

But these oppositions and conflicts take place in an international context that is "friendly" to the demands of indigenous peoples, a context characterized by a global revalorization of indigenous cultures with very positive consequences at the national, regional, and international levels. This has entailed new and increasing communication among indigenous peoples, and especially an increasing international legitimacy, as indicated by new United Nations accords protecting indigenous peoples' rights.

However, the new dynamics among the Mapuche are also associated with the dynamics of democracy and with modernization and the expansion of education in Chile. Today an "enlightened and educated Mapuche elite" exists in Chile, with the capacity for questioning and critically reflecting at the highest levels on Mapuche history and contemporary reality. As in the other cases that we have considered, the monopoly of knowledge held by Chile's historical elites has been broken, and as a result a new context of debate has emerged, one that is unique in Chile's intellectual history and that has implications as well for social dynamics among the Mapuche living in Argentina.

In this way, in the past years and especially since the events that took place in Lumako in 1997, we can see a movement centered on the values of, and practices involving, greater cultural autonomy, which has become an axis for institutional political organizing among the Mapuche. This organizing is centered on the ideal of communal lands and on the effort to exercise territorial sovereignty.

The movement has also been characterized by various forms of struggle that express its visions and internal tensions. These range from violent practices or acts to the most advanced forms of political deliberation. As we have mentioned, Mapuche demands for the recovery of lands are linked to the construction of a sort of "territorial communitarianism," where the land is thought of as a place for the reconstruction of cultural identity and historical memory. This presupposes a constant search for greater participation and an effort to achieve consensus in the community, both in Mapuche lands and in urban spaces and other realms of the Chilean state and Chilean society, where the Mapuche have established a new presence, as in the poor neighborhoods of Santiago and Valparaíso, in universities and teacher training centers, and in the headquarters of new student and environmental movements that have emerged in Chilean society since 2011.

Thus, as José Bengoa (2009) argues, we have witnessed an "indigenous reemergence," the appearance of a movement whose demands have begun to be perceived as legitimate in Chilean society and abroad. The question is what logics will prevail in this movement: the absolute logics of identity, logics that negate and destroy the other, or a set of deliberative logics capable of forging consensus and based on the substantive values of pluralism, human dignity, and rights. To be sure, this is directly related with the politics and orientations of all of the actors, interests, and political cultures in Chilean society. If the authoritarian and conservative logic of the past prevails, together with the instrumental use of law in repressive and punishing conditions, then this may sustain and reinforce a conflictual, violent logic in response, one that is destructive of the democracy that Chile has worked so hard to recover. Today more than ever, this democracy must be reinvented.

119

The Afro-Brazilian Movement

Afro-Brazilian demands for equality, participation, and inclusion have been present throughout Brazilian history. Afro-Brazilians' struggles and mobilizations for the recognition of their human rights and cultural identities can be traced back to the abolition of slavery at the end of the nineteenth century, and they would seem to converge today in an effort to achieve the recognition of a national, multicultural – and thus also an African – identity for Brazilian society. But the recognition of this culture comes up against very specific limits under the conditions of a dominant, monocultural matrix characterized by the conservatism of elites. The movement also confronts the complexity of a society that is regionally differentiated, in which semi-modern features persist, together, as do para- or quasi-institutional behaviors.

People of African Descent

Overall, mixed-race, black, and indigenous people constitute the majority of the Brazilian population. According to the national survey of households conducted in 2012, 53 percent of Brazilians identified themselves as of African descent. Nevertheless, ethnic differences historically tied to strong forms of social stratification, in which social and ethnic differences overlapped, have not substantively changed. The processes of modernization, industrialization, and democratization in Brazil did not substantively transform a pattern of social stratification that had its origins in colonialism and that was, in fact, reproduced and further complicated under new conditions. This can be seen, for example, in the labor market, where improvements in levels of incorporation into the formal labor force have been made, but differences between the white population and people of African descent persist, as figure 8.2 shows.

Despite these improvements, men of African descent earn salaries that are 30 percent lower than those earned by white men with the same level of education. Women of African descent earn 60 percent less than white men with the same level of education (Olbemo 2012). In figure 8.3, we can see the inequality that persists in the distribution of incomes by ethnicity, as well as changes in this distribution under the PT government, when there was an effort to change the patterns of socioeconomic differentiation that we are analyzing.

Such inequalities can be seen not only at the socioeconomic level, but also in forms of ethnic and cultural violence and discrimination.

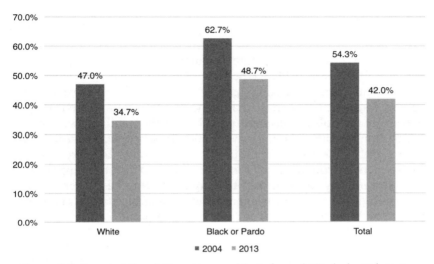

Figure 8.2: People 16 and Over Engaged in Informal Work, by Ethnicity. Brazil, 2004 and 2013 (%)

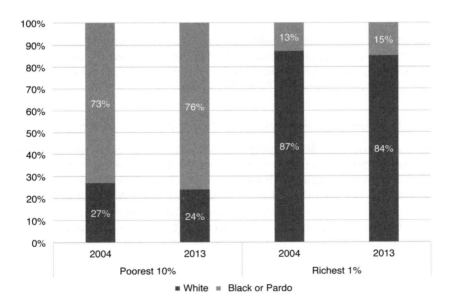

Figure 8.3: Distribution of Per Capita Family Incomes among People 10 and Over in the Poorest 10% and Richest 1% of the Population, by Ethnicity. Brazil, 2004 and 2013 (%)

121

So, for example, racism against people of African descent is one of the causes of the lynchings that took place in 2014, and the homicide rates among people of African descent from 2002 to 2012 is much higher than rates in the white population.[6] In this same context, between 2009 and 2011, 61 percent of those killed by police in the State of São Paulo were young people of African descent, between the ages of 15 and 29. The most striking fact in this connection is that 79 percent of the police officers responsible for these killings were white. In 2012, in the same state, for every 100 black people, 35 were caught in the act, while for every 100,000 whites, only 14 were caught.[7] These facts surrounding the violence practiced by state apparatuses and paramilitary forces linked to drug trafficking have been key factors motivating social movements and especially movements among people of African descent from 2005 to the present.

Among other policies that have sought to ensure cultural recognition for people of African descent, in 2007 a law was passed that banned religious intolerance. It is worth remembering that African-American religions have historically been persecuted, criminalized, and controlled by the Brazilian state. Although this law represents a step forward, it comes up against clear limits in its enforcement, given the enduring, racist rejection of Afro-Brazilian religions. In 2013, however, the First National Plan for the Sustainable Development of Traditional Peoples and Communities, which centered on populations of African descent, was introduced. The plan focused on the following areas: guaranteeing rights, land and culture, social inclusion, and sustainable development (IPEA, 2015: 446).

The Emergence and Dynamics of Afro-Brazilian Movements[8]

With the process of democratization begun in 1978, the Afro-Brazilian movement begins to form, various organizations coming from different parts of the country all seeking to reclaim their identity. These included the Centro de Cultura e Arte Negra (CECAN, or Center for Black Art and Culture), the Grupo Afro-Latino Americano (American Afro-Latino Group), the Câmara de Comércio Afro-Brasileira (Afro-Brazilian Chamber of Commerce), the journals *Apertura* and *Capoeira*, the Grupo de Atletas (Group of Athletes), and the Grupo Artistas Negro (Group of Black Artists). This led to the creation of the Movimento Unificado Contra a Discriminação Racial (MUCDR, or Unified Movement against Racial Discrimination), with the aim of countering discrimination and advocating "a real racial democracy" (Ríos, 2012: 44). The movement's first activity was a public repudiation of the racial discrimination that four young men had faced in the Club de Regatas Tietê in São Paulo. This was also a protest against the killing of Robson Silveira da Luz, a worker and father who had been tortured to death in the Guaianases district of São Paulo. Within a few days, they incorporated the word "black" into their name as an organization, becoming the Movimento Negro Unificado Contra a Discriminação Racial (Unified Black Movement against Racial Discrimination), later shortened to the Movimento Unificado Negro, which today has a presence in various Brazilian states. Among the demonstrations that the movement has organized, several stand out: the march on the centenary of the abolition of slavery (1988), the 300th anniversary march for the resistance hero Zumbi dos Palmares (1995), and the night marches for racial democracy (1998–2010).

In its origins, the group was influenced by left political movements, the new trade unionism of the period, and student movements. A significant number of black intellectuals brought the Marxist understanding of class and the social critique of racism together to create the ideological foundations of the movement (Ríos, 2012: 46). The centenary of the abolition of slavery in 1988 was a key moment for the national black struggle against racism. The wave of protests that this occasion produced was a great achievement and a political opportunity that made it possible to consolidate the movement on the national political scene. The União de Negros pela Igualdade (UNEGRO, or Union of Blacks for Equality), a national organization, was founded at this time in the city of Salvador de Bahía.

The marches honoring the memory of Zumbi were another significant moment in the formation of the Afro-Brazilian movement. During the 1980s, there was an increase in yearly pilgrimages to Serra da Barriga and in public celebrations on November 20 on the streets of several Brazilian capitals. The ritual marches culminated in the creation of the Memorial Zumbi in the state of Alagoas, offering evidence of a renewal of action on the part of black activists and a strengthening of collective identity, anchored in the memory of slavery. This movement's followers began to spread the figure of the warrior Zumbi throughout Brazil, as a symbol of political and cultural resistance. The demonstrations reached their apex during the 1990s, with an important set of protests organized by the movement to commemorate the 300th anniversary of Zumbi's death. Activists from different states collaborated to organize a national demonstration that united a social movement made up of various organizations. The march through the Explanada de los Ministerios in Brasilia took place on Monday, November 20, 1995, under the rubric "Against Racism: Citizenship and Life." Economic, educational, and political demands were key, as were denunciations of inequality and discrimination. This movement opposed a mestizo vision of the country and called for the strengthening of black pride, especially for black women, whose autonomous identity had been gaining ground in the previous years and whose claims were connected to those of the feminist movement (Ríos, 2012: 57). The demonstration in November 1995 gave evidence of greater and more explicit support for the movement on the part of community organizations, unions, and rural popular movements.

At the state level, one achievement of the tricentennial protests was the construction of the Fundação Cultural Palmares, an organization linked to Brazil's Ministry of Culture. The Foundation is centered on the movement's cultural demands, but does not have the institutional capacity to intervene in efforts to reduce inequality. Thus an institutionalization of the movement began, through the work of activists who worked with the state bureaucracy, promoting responses to the movement's demands (Ríos, 2012: 62–4).

In 2006, a new movement was formed, one made up of mothers demanding justice and truth after the deaths of their sons in what are popularly known as the "crimes of May," an episode that led to the deaths of nearly 500 young people, the majority of them black and poor. "The group still believes that many of its demands have not been addressed, and that the deaths were covered up by the political structures of the state. But they have updated their demands with the passage of time. They now ask for improvements to the prison system, and they demonstrate energetically every time they believe there has been an excessive use of police force."[9] One novel feature of this movement is that it expresses discomfort with and protests against insecurity, organized crime, and the abuse of power by parapolice forces in Brazil. In addition, the movement has supported other demands: its participants have demonstrated against the World Cup, lent support to unions, and connected social protests to marginalized communities and left parties.

Despite the movement's force in demanding the creation of a new public institution centered on the issue of racial discrimination, like the Secretaria de Políticas de Promoção da Igualdade Racial (SEPPIR, or Special Secretariat for Policies to Promote Racial Equality), as well as the formation of specific, sectoral initiatives, increases in the population's coverage by social policies in the last 25 years have not significantly reduced racial inequalities (Jaccoud, 2008: 59). Still, we should recognize that the movement's achievements in terms of universal social policies have expanded opportunities for the Afro-Brazilian population.

In any case, the various protests and struggles led by the Afro-Brazilian movement, like those led by indigenous people, are linked to their situations of poverty and inequality as well as their demands to be recognized in their difference as both citizens and agents of their own development.

Conclusions

In this chapter, we have analyzed several of the cultural transformations that have taken place in the era of information. The following are among the most significant.

First, culture is increasingly systemic in the ways it shapes the order and dynamics of conflict and change in the new Latin America. The multicultural changes that we have analyzed exceed the state's administrative capacities and attest to the limits of democratic institutions and political systems for decision-making. Although conflicts over social reproduction and inequality as well as properly institutional conflicts are expressed at the cultural level, multicultural changes that are the products of the information society, like those we have studied here, shape power and political possibilities for development in the region.

Second, demands for a dignified life – in the context of the great multiplicity of changes that we have analyzed, apart from their structural or thematic specificity – are one of the organizing axes of a new sociocultural conflict. Here eco-territorial issues stand out, as do questions of patriarchy and the ethics of human rights.

Third, multicultural dynamics are asynchronous and have many meanings, trajectories, and orientations. Their component parts are functionally differentiated, leading to different logics of power and change in societies that are increasingly polycentric.

Fourth, the new Latin America is the product of changes both in neoliberalism and in neo-developmentalism, and it includes and integrates into its current dynamics a cross-section of pre-modern, late industrial, and information-age social worlds.

Fifth, the processes that we have analyzed have produced, or are part of, a dark side of development: inhuman development in Latin America. It is impossible to understand the institutional and political dynamics of the region if we do not understand the pervasive character of violence and the criminal economy. Here those most affected are absolutely those cultures that give a primeval identity to Latin America's diverse societies.

Sixth and finally, the emergence of a new form of politics associated with new sociocultural movements like those analyzed in the chapter is fundamental to the new dynamics of innovation in politics and development. The most important thing for actors and states to learn is how to "sail against the wind," combining productivity with equality, and pluralism with institutionality, in order to enhance the capacities and the agency of a *human* form of informational development.

— 9 —

DIGITAL COMMUNICATION AND THE NEW PUBLIC SPACE

Introduction

Public space in the information age is different from public space in the industrial era. In the latter, national borders went a long way toward constraining public space, while in the network society, the techno-economy of information and communication and its global functioning exceed strictly national spaces, privileging instead a relation between the global and the local. Or, as we have recently seen, new public spaces are marked by strong tensions between the local, the national, and the global.

With the multicultural changes produced by new technologies of information and communication, the public sphere that is typical of republican democracy has also changed, and questions about its capacity for expansion and representation and for citizens' participation have even emerged.

In relation to the impact of these changes, political communication tends to renew itself through four new practices produced by the web: (1) the online action of sociocultural movements that make claims on subjectivity and seek new forms of life; (2) local and horizontal experiences of political decision-making; (3) horizontal communication among masses of people enabled by social networks; and (4) direct communicative action produced especially by charismatic leaders and society in an informational public sphere.

If in addition to this we consider the importance of the industries of online techno-communication, the market, the culture industry, technological sociability, and the various other phenomena (including advertising, scandals, the growth of audiences, the visibility of acts of various kinds, with unpredictable effects) that affect politics because they take place in mass-mediated ways and especially go viral online, we can easily see that a new public sphere has emerged. It is crucial to reflect on this new space in order to understand the new cultural and political reality of the region. The public sphere is increasingly a space of internet interaction, although more unidirectional mass media still do predominate among older populations.

Having identified these issues as points of departure, we can ask ourselves: What role does politics play in public space in the information age? How do new forms and technologies of communication and information enhance possibilities for a more democratic public sphere, one shaped by the demands for greater dignity made by diverse social actors? Or, on the contrary, how has the public sphere increasingly limited democracy? What changes have taken place in public space in Latin America, given the expansion of new communication platforms and the dynamics these platforms make visible and generate? But also, what are the limits of their democratizing possibilities or their implications for an expansion of citizenship? What factors come into play in the construction of public space today?

What Is a Public Sphere?: Transformations in the Information Age

From a constructivist perspective, a public sphere is a space of social interaction, communication, and intersubjectivity that cuts across the state's boundaries and encompasses the public system as a whole. In a public sphere, conflicts and diverging interests are expressed; it is a space for debate and confrontation, for argument, but also for the kinds of demonstrations that often do not generate rational discussions, but still allow for the expression of ideas and disagreements. To the degree that citizens and social and political actors are autonomous, public space can be above all a space for the formation, transmission, and exchange of ideas and values, a space for disputes and encounters that lead to the collective discussion of priorities and aspirations for a community of citizens.

Public space has now been redefined. It is national and "glocal," and today it is shot through with uses of information and communication technologies that promote new practices of communication, allowing, among other things, for exchanges between different actors that are much more rapid and spontaneous, and for more horizontality in these communications. This allows for the possibility of more

128

direct participation in the public sphere, but it also enables new forms of control and power, exercised through the same web.

Although in the industrial period, democracy was central for the growth of public space, such growth is not a direct consequence of democracy. Nor is it guaranteed, because public space is shot through with conflicts, relations of power, and diverse interests, and shaped by a history and a political culture that "condition" and give meaning to the interactions that take place there.

As an example of how history and political culture come into play in public space, we can consider the importance of populisms or of national popular regimes of the "first generation" in Latin America, which reached their peak in various Latin American countries in the middle of the last century. These regimes had their own communicative practices that, on the one hand, were used to affirm national culture in scientific and technological production, education, and popular culture. But, on the other hand, these practices politically constrained the debates that could unfold in public space, distorting these debates through an ideological hegemony that powerfully curtailed pluralism at the level of ideas and political positions.

There were nevertheless several events that led to the reaffirmation of a democratic and pluralist orientation in public space in the region, especially in moments when this space was restricted by dictatorships. This was the case, for example, in the movements for human rights throughout the region, or in the mine radio stations in Bolivia, which became means of resisting the dictatorship. It was also the case in the rock festivals and "open theaters" in Argentina, after the return of democracy in the mid-1980s, or in the national plebiscite of 1988 in Chile, which led to the victory of the "No" campaign. And this is just to mention a few of the moments when communication through various media played a key role in the democratic construction of public spaces.

In public space, the market and the state manifest themselves, but so do politics, society, the community, and culture. To the degree that it generates greater plurality, public space also becomes more democratic, but not for all that less conflictual.

Several factors contribute to the democratization of public space. These include: pluralism in the production of information; the strengthening of a culture of freedom of the press and of expression; the expansion of access to information and, consequently, of participation in the analysis of this information and of social, cultural, and political diversity; and deliberation and public debate. But, especially in the context of a mass culture industry, public space is also appropriated by the market economy, by consumerist individualism, by the political marketing of "lying truths" (a phrase inspired by William Isaac Thomas's theorem),[1] and most of all by a culture of violence that promotes fear and the negation of the other.

Now, what significant changes have taken place in public space? Current processes of globalization and the impact of new technologies of information and communication have redefined the central role of media. Today the media, as means of mass communication, and above all the internet, play a central role in politics, in advertising and marketing, in the circulation of public opinion polls, and in the visibility of social movements, which rely on traditional media and on the web. And above all the media are central to the demonstration of conflicts both on the web and on the streets. This prompts us to consider the emergence of a new and complex form of communicative politics, both in terms of its ethical implications and in terms of its expansion of the field of the possible. All of these processes occur at the same time, and they disclose the limits both of representative democracy and of the state's autonomy. All of this has led to a redefinition of public space in the information age.

We are witnessing the vertical integration of multimedia conglomerates at the global, national, and local levels. These conglomerates significantly restrict the contents of communications in all spheres, in keeping with the proprietary business interests of the media, despite the daily, heroic efforts of journalists who seek to defend their profession and their independence.

In Latin America, we have witnessed an oligarchic concentration in the media, exemplified by multimedia corporate conglomerates like Televisa in Mexico, Clarín in Argentina, and Globo in Brazil. These conglomerates are also connected in strategic alliances that follow the logic of the multimedia networks that control the world of communication (Castells, 2013). Transnational media conglomerates in the region coexist with other large and medium-sized business groups whose reach is only national, as well as with others that are smaller. Here the tendency is toward the concentration of media that are also aimed at different publics and that allow for the diversification of platforms. In other words, the same conglomerate includes newspapers, television stations, and radio stations, all of them differentiated according to the sectors of the public and the places (cities, countries, and so on) toward which they are addressed. In addition, these conglomerates tend to produce their own content in order to gain traction locally.[2]

130

How, in this new media context that pervades public space, can we safeguard pluralism and diversity? How, in other words, can we secure the expansion of democracy and citizenship? This is a key question for the future of democracy, and analytical responses to it remain weak. On this point, for example, Thompson proposes a principle of "regulated pluralism" as a means for guaranteeing an institutional space that can ensure the expression of difference, which can tend to disappear under the conditions of the free market. This would be a matter of institutionally safeguarding the ability of different voices to express themselves in the media, through their organizations and through independent media, where "independent" implies independence from the state, but also from the major media monopolies.

But this proposal does not imply the construction of an institutional realm linked only to nation-states, because today national boundaries have been overcome by transnational communications conglomerates and especially by the expansion of the internet, which enables the circulation not only of material goods, but also and above all of symbolic goods. This substantially changes the public sphere, which, as we noted earlier, can no longer be understood as a set of spaces that are nationally delimited. Not only the economy, but also politics, is now a power game that is global, national, and local.

Today the possibilities for greater pluralism in national public spaces are not only tied to events occurring at the local level, as was the case in the industrial era. Transnational flows of information and communication cut across these national public spaces, and as a result the diversity and pluralism that are features of the international realm (or, conversely, the restrictions on diversity and pluralism in this realm) have effects on national public spaces. In this sense, nation states come up against a limit, one that indicates that they wield only a certain degree of power, and not "total" power, over transnational flows of information and communication, which cut across various, politically unpredictable publics. Today this is especially visible and conflictual in the United States (Castells et al., 2017).

Given that the media are the main sources of information for most people, there are more possibilities for the development and strengthening of deliberative democracy to the degree that the diverse and pluralist character of the media is assured. This is why Thompson's proposal for a principle of regulated pluralism is so important; it allows us to envision an institutional space for media that guarantees diversity and pluralism. The key question that follows has to do with the international viability of such a space.

New Forms of Communication: The Dynamics of Consumption, the Frustration of Expectations, the Generation of Techno-Sociability, and the Power of Media

The globalization of media and of the culture industry has, together with the revolution that has transformed technologies of information and communication, produced at least two tendencies in cultural consumption. On the one hand, these changes have led to a massification of cultural, technological, and communicative consumption. On the other hand, they have led to a fragmentation and "elitization" of technological and cultural markets, whose products and services are now geared toward the wallets, and not only the tastes, of consumers, and thus made to mark differences. These tendencies also affect interactions in public space, given the ever-greater importance of information and communication technologies in these spaces and the impact of mass media in the formation of public opinion.

But in addition to this, levels of consumption of media and of information and communication technologies have been increasing, especially as a result of the politics of social integration and consumption forged by neo-developmentalist or progressive governments. These increases have continued despite the recent stagnation or even decrease in wages, and despite the fact that the gap between expectations for consumption and the reality of what can be consumed has continued to grow. Technological and cultural markets are thus open to ever more consumers of technology, advertising, information, networks, and so on. This opening generates new desires and aspirations for consumption that cannot be satisfied in users' real lives, and this leads in many cases to the frustration of expectations for much of the population. This process was already evident in the 1990s; it was noted, for example, by the United Nations Economic Commission for Latin America and the Caribbean in 1990 and confirmed in greater detail in the later analyses made by Calderón (2018).

Another tendency also affects the public and leads to the expansion of public spaces. The expansion of the internet and increases in the use of cellular phones lead to a range of practices of communication, which expand the available alternatives for participation, diffusion, opinion, and expression for many groups, identities, and individuals. Here social networks play a key role. These technologies allow for the construction of a new public space, one that today cannot be contained by the formal channels of communication characteristic of traditional public space. Instead, social networks allow for the appearance of alternative voices, different cultures and identities, and a multiplicity of opinions. Today a so-called "generation of techno-sociability" has thus been created in Latin America.

With regard to the size of communications conglomerates, trans-national corporations reach across the region, and they work across all "platforms" (written and graphic media, audiovisual media, web platforms, mobile applications, radio stations). One example is the Grupo *Globo* in Brazil, which owns more than 25 print publications, ten radio stations, four television stations, and five web platforms. Some conglomerates do not work in all of these formats but can still be considered major players given the quantity of media that they own in one format. An example of this latter type of conglomerate is the Grupo de Diarios América, which includes 11 of the most widely circulated newspapers in the region, among them *El Comercio* in Peru, *La Nación* in Argentina, and *El Nacional* in Venezuela. This corporation's newspapers have a total daily circulation of more than ten million copies.

There are large corporations with only national reach that never-theless work across various formats at large scales, even if they remain within a single country's borders. Consider, for example, the Grupo Clarín in Argentina, which owns daily and weekly newspapers, free and cable television stations, AM and FM radio stations, and national and local internet platforms and services. Small corporations, by con-trast, are defined as those that own only one or two press outlets and that do not participate in global networks of communication or diffusion. Examples would include *Página/12* in Argentina, *Expreso* in Ecuador, and the *Jornal do Brasil* (IFJ, 2017).

Thus, using various platforms and following different trajecto-ries, mass media cut across public spaces, and this has profound implications for the formation of public opinion, the identification of priorities for public discussion, the diffusion of information, the "spectacularization" of everyday life, and the growth of expectations.

The Politics of Media

In our societies, politics is fundamentally mass-mediated because it is conducted in and through different types of media. Currently, the mass media constitute a privileged place for conflict and power. These media create a mass-mediated "political game," played in keeping with the set of rules that the media generate. Various social and political actors accept this game in order to be able to participate in conflicts over, and projects requiring, power in society. The existence of various media enables the expression of a range of interests and representations, but each of these seeks to expand and consolidate its space and to ensure its access to different publics. Meanwhile, traditional media generally enjoy the advantage of a certain credibility, and in today's societies they remain the main sources of information, of news, and of politics for most people.

Politics occupies a central place in the media, and various actors compete in order to appear in the media, because they know that it is here that the construction of political power is at stake. At the same time, and conversely, the relationship between the media and politics depends on the use of the information that the media make available, information that provides inputs for various strategies aimed at the construction of political power.

The characteristic features of mass-mediated politics include: the importance of personification (in which political proposals or orientations become associated with the images of particular political characters, images that are constructed in and through the media); the use of the media for electoral campaigns, in which media outlets become the most important spaces where candidates can make themselves known (as people even more than for their proposals); and the daily processing of political information. Here the question of charisma in the media is central.

The media are so important that, in keeping with their own orientations, interests, and relations with others (including government agencies, business corporations, and the other communications companies with which they compete or collaborate), they set agendas, identify priorities, and contextualize or decontextualize information. Ultimately, we do not know whom they are working for. And it is not entirely clear who is using whom. Economically speaking, mass-mediated politics is very costly for political actors, and technologies of information are, like mass-mediated public space itself, very expensive. This is one reason that political parties seek financing from businesses and interest groups; these organizations do not have sufficient financing on their own. This in turn constrains politicians and thus politics in general, because in addition state regulations in this realm are often disregarded or insufficient, and there is often a lack of transparency around the funding of political campaigns and mass-mediated politics more generally. Here is one of the principal sources of the corruption of political decision making, as we will discuss in chapter 11. Here we are also at the root of one of the main issues in democracy's crisis of legitimacy, and at the root of the major political scandals that are sweeping across much of the region. The main problem in Latin America is that these kinds of scandals take place through traditional forms of corporate, para-institutional, familial, and clientelist mediation. They are a constitutive and historically ingrained part of the relation between the state and society in the region. The arguments offered by members of Brazil's parliament in favor of the impeachment of Dilma Rousseff are one extraordinary example.

On the other hand, politics itself is undergoing a process of functional differentiation sustained by new and useful forms of specialization. Politics is increasingly informational. That is, it increasingly develops through professionalized practices that require the participation of experts and consultants (professional technicians), who analyze political conjunctures, future scenarios, the composition of political proposals, the construction of candidates' images, and the general running of campaigns. Here advertising, in all its complexity, plays a key role.

But politics is also increasingly informational because its practitioners use new digital technologies to conduct opinion polls, publicize proposals, run advertisements, follow events and track political developments in real time, and so on. The use of technology in this realm allows experts and consultants to make rapid adjustments to messages, for example, and to adapt their communications strategies so that they suit rapidly changing contexts. The use of "scandals" to vilify political rivals is a common political practice in today's information society, although the effects of this practice are not always predictable, and it does not always end up benefitting the candidate it is intended to. Still, the spreading of a "scandal" generally does benefit the interests of media corporations, as it creates a kind of "entertainment" that can appeal to broad sectors of several publics.[3] The case of Donald Trump has proven paradigmatic: with the majority of media outlets against him, he has created a reality show 2.0 and relied on scandal as strategy, thus managing to become part of the media that he seems to oppose, in a relationship that, though conflictual, has become mutually beneficial.

The crisis of political legitimacy in Brazil – a crisis affecting the political system as a whole – is more complicated, given that it affects not only political parties and republican institutions, but also the business world and the very self-esteem of Brazilian society.[4] Politics is a key factor in the regulation of forces and actors in markets as well as in communications. In Latin America, mass-mediated public space is very important, because it is in the media that political agendas and alternatives are constructed, in a game of interests that is often limited but that is highly influential. Here public space takes shape in a new way, with interests and relations of power vying with one another. How can we ensure that this mass-mediated public space is not wholly absorbed by the logic of business? How can we ensure that it is democratized and pluralized, becoming again a realm of expanded participation for various actors? How can we make it more diverse and egalitarian? We think, in fact, that various uses of new communication technologies can contribute to the creation of a more horizontal and democratic dynamic. In this sense, they can become a counterweight opposing the power of the major media corporations, because spectators have stopped being passive, and they now interact with the media. They watch television or listen to the radio, but at the same time they rely on social networks to fact-check what they hear said, or they seek out alternative sources of information on the web. And this is to offer just one set of examples.

Social Networks and the Construction of Political Power

Today multimedia social networks are absolutely relevant public spaces. In social networks and in multimedia communications in general relations of power are contested and constructed, but there is room for the representation of more diverse interests in a context of communication that includes the possibility of communication in real time. Processes of social change require the reprogramming of networks of communication, and networks allow for more horizontal forms of communication between people and groups. They give space to a certain spontaneity in participation; they make direct participation (without institutional intermediaries) possible; and they allow for the construction of greater autonomy for social actors. The defense of these aspects of online communication will depend on people and groups, since, as we have said, the logic of power also operates through social networks.

Sociocultural movements use these networks and other internet spaces and resources as well as the mass media to spread their ideas and proposals. There is a diversified dynamic that depends on more and less privatized spaces (as well as on mass media and social networks) for outreach and collective debate.

The expansion of wireless communications technologies in the last few years has, moreover, made communication more rapid and messages exchanged between users more trustworthy. Messages transmitted on cellular phones, coming from people and groups of friends and acquaintances, generate more trust. The individual is thus more important in the construction of collective actions, like social protests, for example. As we will see below in our analysis of three youth movements in the region, in the network society revolts acquire a new significance, with increased potential for influence and political resistance.

Thanks to information and communications technologies, communication can be instantaneous, interactive, and multimodal. Its repercussions are amplified by the apparent trustworthiness of the messages that we individually receive on cellular phones. And in this way all subjectivity is redefined. Free and horizontal communications technologies give rise to key social tendencies that are characteristic of the network society.

These are tendencies toward *networked individualism* and *communalism*. The former refers to a culture in which individual values and projects interact, and individuals interface with one another in order to achieve their goals. "Communalism" refers to a set of vulnerable identities with changing values. Where these two tendencies intersect, we find social movements "that respond to perceived oppression and then transform their shared protest into a community of practice, where that practice is resistance. That is, networks of individuals become communities of insurgency." We can therefore conclude that, "[j]ust as wireless communication is sustained by networks of shared practices, this communications technology allows for the spontaneous formation of communities of practice implicated in resistance to domination – in other words, the formation of instantaneous insurgent communities" (Castells, 2012: 472).

So these kinds of mobilizations, which emerge on and from social networks, often challenge traditional political practices and make democratic participation more dynamic. They even place limits on the power of institutions and thus create a new type of political practice through the web.

That said, social networks are not in and of themselves instruments of social change. Nor do they necessarily deliver authentic experiences of communication. The experience of the first 15 years of internet-based social networks (the first such social network, Friendster, was created in 2002) shows that, while representing sources of democratic potential, they constitute sources of manipulation and disinformation, as well as increasingly allowing for the usurpation of communication by robots programmed by wielders of power like Russian or US intelligence agencies. The novelty of communication through social networks derives from its multidirectional and interactive nature, and the proprietors of these networks have an interest in increasing horizontal communication to sustain the traffic on their sites. The monopolies of information once held by large corporate or state conglomerates have been broken. But it would be naive to think that social networks escape the logic of power. They level the playing field of communication by enabling masses of people to communicate with one another. But all kinds of interests and powers also act on this same playing field, often seeking to reestablish forms of control over citizens' self-determination.

Even so, the expansion of free, horizontal communication has had important consequences for the control exercised by apparatuses of power and for the democratization of information. The Anonymous collective is an especially suggestive case: an anarchist online movement that does not seek but rather questions power, with political and cultural effects that are sometimes notable. Anonymous opposes all forms of online censorship, seeking freedom of expression and criticizing and contesting the privatization of information by powerful political systems and corporations. The collective also supports human rights, gender, and ecological movements, and they are consistently critical of censorship. This, as Morales et al. (2017) emphasize, is by turns a cyber-activist and a hacker movement. Its collective use of networks is horizontal and leaderless, and it operates without directives from politically powerful sources. It insinuates itself into the information systems of powerful institutions, using complex techniques of analysis and engineering abilities to declassify information. Its slogan is, "We are anonymous. We are legion," and together with other movements, it has created a new, nodal type of political culture.[5]

Charisma, Communication, and the Web

When the institutional foundations of society are relatively weak, and national and social integration are insufficient, the demand for charismatic leaders increases. In Latin America, these actors have been key throughout the region's political history.

The negative results of the structural reforms that privileged the central mechanisms of the market and reified a merely institutionalist form of politics were the main causes of the return of "neo-developmentalist, national popular regimes" and the rise of new leaders with strong charismatic features. Here the state and the neo-developmentalist model played a key role in the context of changes in global geopolitics (Araníbar and Rodríguez, 2013).

This type of leader has a sort of gift that lends him extraordinary power. He creates an ideal of emotional community, produces illusions, and is claimed by the people. This leader includes, protects, sacrifices himself, and demands sacrifices. He transforms passive subjects into active subjects, into participants in movements.

Here references to the past are fundamental. Moscovici (1993: 373) argues that "impressions of the past are also retained in the mental life of masses as mnemonic prints. In certain favourable conditions, they can be retrieved and revived. As a matter of fact, the older they are, the better they are preserved."

"Neo-developmentalist, populist" leaders use the idea of a return to the past, one generally associated with the most beloved populist histories and leaders in the region: Emiliano Zapata and Pancho Villa or Lázaro Cárdenas in Mexico, Juan and Evita Perón in Argentina, Simón Bolívar in Venezuela, or Túpac Katari in Bolivia. Here we find a combination of past and modern traits, including leaders and societies that are "semi-industrialized" and "quasi-modern," on the one hand, and, on the other, leaders in a society of information and communication and virtual networks. The demand for community is associated with inclusion in a society of communication and cultural consumption.

The demand for an active state with a forceful presence in the economy is one fundamental explanation for the emergence of leaders with populist and charismatic features, who promote neo-developmentalist policies based on state intervention in the economy. According to the Latin American Public Opinion Project's report for 2014, over 70 percent of Latin Americans favored an active role for the state. In individual countries, figures ranged from 62 percent in Venezuela to 82 percent and 80 percent, in Paraguay and Chile, respectively. This sense of powerlessness is stronger in the poorest social sectors, which are precisely those that tend to call for leaders with populist characteristics.

The implementation of communications technologies has two important effects on citizens' attitudes and potentially on their leadership preferences. On the one hand, the mediatization of politics sets a complex process in which leaders and populations relate to one another, with the possibility that actors in the population can exercise certain critical faculties. On the other hand, the citizens' participation in the spaces of techno-sociability produces new patterns for social relations and political participation, which privilege the social over the state and suggest an autonomous citizenry.

But we should emphasize that the mass-mediated politics associated with the crisis of legitimacy of public institutions, especially of parties, favor the formation of cults of personality, in which exchanges between the leader and society deteriorate even more than institutions do. Today leaders practice a global politics and communicate with people through multiple systems and networks of communication. Tweeting is favored by today's leaders because of the "theoretical density" of the messages that circulate on Twitter. Trump's case is an especially notable one. Charisma does not have an ideological character, but it is sustained by the crises of institutions in the public space of the web.

Some Tendencies in the Reconfiguration of Public Space

Latin America has been integrated into the processes of globalization in an uneven way; levels of integration differ from one subregion to another and one sector of the population to another. This means, among other things, that there are masses of people more or less excluded from the information society (see figure 9.1). Nevertheless, we can affirm that the region, despite this unevenness and exclusion,

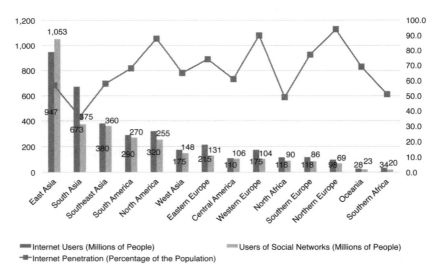

Figure 9.1: Internet Users, Social Network Users, and Internet Penetration. Selected World Regions, January 2018 (in millions of people and percentages)

140

is shot through with a global culture that affects young people with particular force. Today the world has "gotten smaller," and the distant has drawn close thanks to information and communications technologies.

The media have a forceful impact on the construction of public space because they not only generate and disseminate information; they also elaborate and represent collective imaginaries. In this sense, current possibilities for individual and group participation in the generation of information and content more or less successfully disrupt the discourse of the major media outlets. Such participation allows a good part of the population (especially young people, who have grown up and been socialized in this interactive technological context) to debate, express, respond to, reject, or accept what the media say (see figure 9.2). The media no longer confront a public incapable of responding or arguing, because there are now technologies that allow for the interrogation of the imaginaries represented by the major media outlets. These technologies also allow for the exploration of alternative representations. This is not to deny the power that mass media continue to wield or their ability to reach large segments of the population with a discourse that mainly depends on the market and its private interests. We mean simply that today it is possible to participate differently in communicative processes involving masses of people, because technology has made this possible, and because users want this kind of participation, which

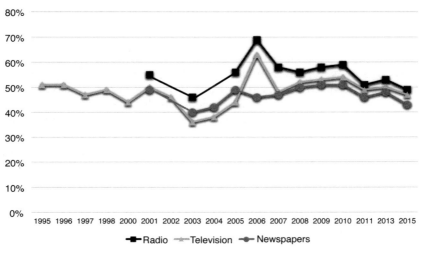

Figure 9.2: Trust in Mass Media, Latin America, 1995–2015 (%)

141

is consistent with a more open orientation in new systems of communication. In any case, interaction through media has a dynamism now caused by constant change, and its perceived legitimacy among people is relatively high, and much higher than that of political parties or parliaments.

This, then, changes the idea of intervention in public space, precisely because there are new mechanisms for both individual and collective action. In the present, we are seeing new forms of practicing politics, of participating and acting in conflicts and exercising political choices in various and complex ways. To the politics that takes place in institutions, as well as to the broader politics that happens in street demonstrations, we should now add a mass-mediated politics and another, more democratic politics on social networks. None of these forms of politics excludes the others, because the space of the web is complemented by action on the streets. This means that the different forms of participation, whether in new territories like the virtual or in older, mass-mediated spaces, are related.

New forms of communication and participation also change what we mean by public space. For example, conflicts that do not have a media presence would seem nonexistent. The social actors who lead movements know this, and they also know that the impact that they achieve depends largely on media coverage, which means not only television coverage, but also increasingly coverage on the web, of which television is now a part.

The relation between media presence and conflict is key. The presence of conflicts and of various actors and movements in the media relates to the topics that are "debated" or "addressed" in the public sphere, and to decisions about which issues and problems to prioritize. Still, the possibility of "disrupting" this dynamic through social networks or web platforms that reach large audiences also influences what can be discussed by the media. Today it is not so easy to say "anything." And in this sense, citizens can be more active in public space without having any organizational affiliation, and without hitting the streets, although hitting the streets does reinforce, on the ground, the kinds of protests staged and demands made on the web. Thus today people, independently of their political and ideological orientation, together with other social actors and movements, have more possibilities for carrying out direct action in public space, as in the case of recent youth protests in Chile, Mexico, and Brazil, protests that began on the web.

The State and the Shaping of a New Public Space

It seems crucial to investigate the problematic relations between the state, social actors, and the political system, as Calderón suggested in his book *Tiempos de cambio: Nuevas consideraciones sociológicas sobre la democracia y el desarrollo* [Times of Change: New Sociological Considerations on Democracy and Development] (2012a). In these relations, we can recognize an ineffectual state that does not respond to social actors' demands through political and public mechanisms of decision, administration, and implementation. In a democracy, such responsiveness requires a state that communicates in different ways with social actors and with society as a whole, above all through the political system itself. In *Tiempos de cambio*, Calderón refers to the need to forge a "state that serves the public," that is, a state that would support the formation of spaces for deliberation through the creation of political mechanisms and the establishment of the procedures necessary for citizens, whatever their social, economic, and cultural particularities, to come together to debate policies, by appealing to social priorities and values. Such a state, in addition, could ensure that specific demands made by social actors would not lose sight of the coexistence that should be guaranteed in a multicultural community, a coexistence that implies, especially in our region, fighting at once for greater social justice, against inequality, and for the recognition of the right to differences, whether national, territorial, or cultural.

In this sense, public space could be seen as the expression of conflicts, where the state and the private intersect, where it is possible to debate and deliberate on demands, alternatives, and proposals, but also where questions are resolved on the basis of what is shared. Hence the claim that there must be a public sphere where differences are in play, but where there is also a sort of social "unity." Here public space is seen as a common good, as a space for debate and the construction of public opinion by citizens and social actors who participate politically and socially. This would be the construction of a public sphere where open debate is really fostered, one that accepts conflict but allows for its resolution in ways that respect diversity, treating freedom, deliberation, and democracy as inseparable from one another.

It is not easy to achieve this. It will require ideas and values that can serve as goals and that can enable communication among the different actors involved as well as the institution of the state, so

143

that everyone understands that this kind of public space is built collectively, by various people with different responsibilities. Such a space is a good in and of itself, for everyone. This means beyond the practical achievements, the concrete policies that are implemented, and the conflicts that are resolved in it, this space can be seen not just from a pragmatic point of view, but from an ethical one, centered on dignity. This would be a unified and dynamic perspective on human rights. The idea would be that it is necessary to preserve the public sphere because such a space allows for a better democracy and makes it possible to create better conditions for different social actors. This implies again accepting rules and procedures in order to create a space that would ultimately benefit all social actors (even if it would not completely fulfill the expectations of each of them), whatever their particularities. In this way, a "modern form of political community" could be achieved, one "underpinned by the link forged by public interest. [Such a community] does not have a predefined form, because it is constantly under construction" (Calderón, 2012b: 152). And above all it depends on the conflicts and capacities of new political actors.

A Novel Challenge: Public Space and Democracy

By way of conclusion, and considering the conflicts in the region, we can inquire about the features of and possibilities for a renewed public sphere.

In different ways, the various actions and sociocultural protests that we have considered seek a public sphere that would contribute to a sort of libertarian, democratic development. If this is the case, then such a public sphere would have to contain values that could determine shared procedures. The functioning of such a public space would ideally allow for a redefinition of politics and of the institutional goals and the development in every society according to its interests, values, purposes, and priorities. But this would also be a plural and substantive democratic public sphere to the degree that it provided and protected adequate institutions, freedom of expression, and the diversity of the various actors who make up the region's societies. In this sense, Thompson's understanding of "regulated autonomy" is an important step.

By becoming a space of deliberation among actors who consider themselves equal participants even when they are different, the public sphere could make the achievement of consensus possible. It could allow for agreements on priorities for policies (in keeping with values) for a renewed political system. At least some important goals shared among different actors who participate in deliberations in public space could emerge, goals also capable of guiding the search for more freedom and for development, centered on people and collectivities defined as autonomous subjects. The more comprehensive this public space is in terms of its inclusion of diverse voices, the more universal the agreements reached there will be.

In a democracy the idea of agency is related to that of citizenship, because the citizen is understood as part of a network of social relations within which he or she acts and in which he or she shares responsibilities, rights, obligations, and commitments. The citizen is at the same time part of a community of citizens. One cannot be a citizen in isolation. And this kind of community leaves a trace in culture. But to be a citizen implies, as well, the ability to exercise rights and fulfill obligations through appropriate institutional channels. In this sense a democratic state plays a key role, because it seeks to ensure citizens' participation and expand it as well as defending the rights of citizens and overseeing the fulfillment of the duties defined as such. The public sphere in this sense is a key space for the expression and exercise of citizenship.

This perspective on development suggests that it centers on the agency of social actors. The state and market play key roles, but it is people, acting in their capacity as agents, both individual and collective, who are really the keys to the renewal of democracy and development. People have a will, goals, interests, and various capacities for acting to achieve their goals. They relate to other actors in order to modify their surroundings, and, in the process, they also modify themselves. The collective and the individual are not two categories that can be thought apart from one another, because the individual is born in a context that is historical and collective. And conversely the collective is sustained by individual capacities. In this dialectic, ideally mediated by processes of deliberation in a democratic framework, societies are constructed, and proposals for development are created in response to the aspirations, cultures, and histories of people who relate to broader contexts.

From this perspective, it becomes clear that the issue of inclusion is central, where "inclusion" is defined not only in a socioeconomic sense, but in terms of the exercise of political citizenship.

Inclusion requires decent living conditions for everyone, and it also requires the recognition of differences at many levels, but for the

145

sake of constructing a field of political and juridical equality in which various liberties can be developed. It requires nothing more and nothing less than the political, social, and civil exercise of citizenship. For this reason, under democratic regimes, the citizen is the subject and object of development and democracy itself" (Calderón, 2012b: 155).

Thus the link between citizenship, deliberation, and development is key, and it strengthens and expresses the capacities and the agency of different (political, social, and cultural) actors and people in public space.

A more democratic public sphere is therefore one that is more representative of the diversity that makes up society as a whole, one that gives different actors the ability to make proposals and decide on priorities and policies. In such a public sphere, it is possible to think of a more inclusive political system, in the context of a global scene that changes rapidly and generates new codes.

But what capacities do current sociocultural actors and democratic institutions have? How can they confront the challenges of a deliberative politics that is reshaping public space? How can citizenship be expanded, and how can the various actors who are devalued in public space be encouraged to participate, so that they are able to implement social, economic, and cultural policies that are more representative of the diversity of our societies? As a regime, democracy guarantees a framework. But it is people, with their deliberative practices, their representation, their actions, and their capacities, who give content to a democratic public space, obviously not without conflicts, but one in which debate can take place and policies can be devised for democratic development.

It is clear that the perverse logic of many online actors, including the ultra-nationalist right that is present in much of the region and closely connected to the authoritarian culture of past dictatorships, also redraws public space in ways that are relatively restricted and instrumental, as in the case of the political conjuncture in Guatemala or of the candidacy of Jair Bolsonaro in Brazil, or even the case of the counter protesters in Nicaragua. Thus authoritarian alternatives are also present – and strongly so – on the web. These also seek to become alternative responses to the decomposition and chaos that is not only national or regional, but global as well. This is the other side of the coin.

— 10 —

CONFLICTS AND SOCIAL MOVEMENTS

In Latin America and the Caribbean, there is a hallmark of historical continuity: social conflict. We cannot understand culture, development, or politics in the region without considering this abiding and dramatic human history. Latin Americans, for all the diversity of their experiences, have been formed by protests and movements against various and complex forms of domination.

A particular feature of this has been the persistent presence of the state in all spheres of social life, whatever the state's political and economic orientation. The State has often, though not always, been a producer of society. Thus social conflicts in general have more often been expressed within state frameworks than directly between social actors. Political projects of development almost always have the state as their point of references.

Since the 1980s, a range of forms of collective action have been central to the collapse and failure of authoritarianisms, to opposition to neoliberalism, to the emergence of neo-developmentalist and progressive governments, and most recently to the new sociocultural movements – including indigenous and Black movements as well as movements of women and young people, seeking various kinds of sociocultural and global transformation and, at the same time, new ways of practicing politics (Calderón, 1985; UNDP, 2009).

The Dynamics of Social Conflicts

Recent social conflicts, at the center of dynamics of and possibilities for politics and development in the region, show that the vast majority of countries in Latin America share these features: chronic mechanisms of exclusion and inequality largely questioned by the citizenry; complex conflicts that link such inequalities with the number of conflicts and their intensity; a combination of social protests expressed both on the social-national plane and at the cultural-global level; practical rationalities engaged in conflicts over social reproduction, conflicts that coexist with demands for more institutional efficacy and legitimacy as well as with cultural conflicts that are systematic. Likewise, omnipresent states appear in all spheres of the conflicts, seriously limiting the ability to process them. At the same time, societies confront conflicts that are ever more fragmented, in new public spaces forged by systems of communication in which these conflicts are represented in contradictory ways. The conflicts themselves tend increasingly to be displaced onto the web, with ripple effects in new scenes of power.

The analysis that follows below exemplifies this dynamic. It is based on some conclusions from a study of social protests in Latin America, which analyzed the conflicts recorded in 54 newspapers from 17 countries between October 2009 and September 2010. In all, 2,318 conflicts were detected and analyzed (Calderón, 2012: 121) (see figure 10.1).

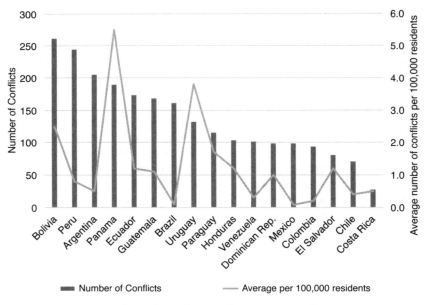

Figure 10.1: Number of Conflicts and Average Number per 100,000 Residents. Latin America, October 2009-September 2010 (in Numbers and Percentages)

The logic of these contexts of conflict is differentiated. Conflicts over social reproduction involve mainly demands for the fulfillment of basic needs, for the sake of wellbeing or the maintenance of a minimally dignified life. Work, health, education, housing: all of these allow for the reproduction of individuals and human collectivities, and conflicts over these essentials are essentially pragmatic. Conflicts at the institutional level seek more efficacy in the functioning of the state. Their logic is tied above all to the legitimacy, efficiency, and efficacy of institutional administration. Cultural conflicts seek to achieve a change in ways of life. They are ideological and deploy a more strategic logic.

Conflicts over Social Reproduction

We use the phrase "social reproduction" to refer both to the basic areas of human development (work, income, health, education, and housing, among others) and to issues related to the general wellbeing of society and quality of life. Conflicts in this realm, according to the study to which we have referred, follow a practical logic, since they are linked to concrete demands, related to the conditions of people's daily lives. (Such demands might include demands for higher salaries, for jobs more generally, for healthcare, for higher-quality education, for dignified housing, and so on.) These issues are the most important sites for conflicts, in numerical terms, in the region.

It is worth emphasizing that conflicts over social reproduction arise mainly around issues that are socioeconomic in nature, and they are especially closely associated with employment and collective consumption. Other issues that lead people to mobilize include the discussion and/or application of measures perceived to be destabilizing or prejudicial to workers, or economic issues more generally, or questions related to property, productivity, and the land. Fifty-nine percent of the conflicts over social reproduction were tied to work- or income-related demands. This gives an idea of the key role that work plays in Latin American societies. In nine of the 17 countries addressed in the study we have cited, conflicts over work and the economy accounted for more than 50 percent of the total number of conflicts.

Information on conflicts over social reproduction shows that socioeconomic problems occupy a central place in people's anxieties. At the regional level, these conflicts represent 47 percent of the total number, and they were the most numerous kinds of conflict in 12

149

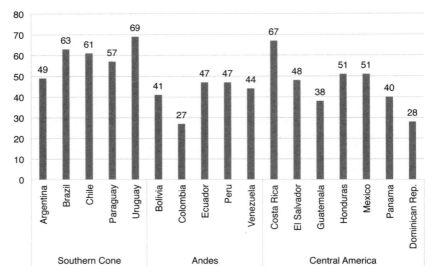

Figure 10.2: Conflicts over Social Reproduction, Latin America, October 2009–September 2010 (% of the total number of conflicts in each country)

of the 17 countries considered. When the findings are divided into subregions, we see that in the Andes and Central America conflicts over social reproduction represent approximately 42 percent of the total number. It is striking that in the Southern Cone this figure rises to 58.7 percent (see figure 10.2).

This situation places the problem of development on the table. Decreases in inequality and poverty will be substantial and sustainable only if they are rooted in quality work for people and in optimal levels of social wellbeing.

Although conflicts over land represent just 5.3 percent of all conflicts in Latin America, it is these conflicts that have the greatest tendency to be radicalized, something that occurred in 53 percent of the cases analyzed in the study. However, conflicts over work and/or salaries, and conflicts resulting from measures whose economic consequences are considered negative by the population, were also likely to be radicalized: in 49 percent of cases when it came to conflicts over work, and in 42 percent when it came to conflicts resulting from measures taken. Conflicts associated with problems relating to land would seem to be related both to a lack of institutional spaces and/or mechanisms for processing these problems and to the complexity

150

that they often entail, in that they market a place of intersection for demands from particular ethnic groups and other demands from political interests, and local economies. On the other hand, many of the countries analyzed are characterized by historical delays in terms of their implementation of the kind of land reforms that would allow for a break with traditional social relations tied to the *hacienda* system.

Institutional Conflicts

These conflicts follow from people's demands for more efficacy and efficiency in institutions, and they indicate the distance between these demands and the limited capacity of state institutions to respond in satisfactory ways. More than a formal critique of the institutional system, these conflicts question the functioning of these institutions, although in many cases a critique of the system is part of the discourse in the context of these conflicts.

Demands expressed in this context are connected to a call to improve public administration and management, to increase provisions and the quality of public services, to update and give transparency to the justice system, and to improve the legitimacy of the authorities. In this context, conflicts negatively affect the quality of social reproduction. In general, these are demands that have more to do with fragile institutions and shortcomings in the application of norms in many countries in the region than with the absence of institutions. It could be argued that in this context the state is a "producer" of conflicts, and that this problem has been exacerbated overwhelmingly during the last years.

Institutional conflicts are in second place in numerical terms in Latin America, where they make up 38 percent of the total number of conflicts. The issues noted most frequently include complaints about inefficiency in administrative management and protests against the unsatisfactory provision of public services (generally on account of shortfalls or deficits in funds for public works in particular places, or limits in the provision of basic services that should be guaranteed by the state).

At the subregional level, both in the Andes and in Central America, Mexico, and the Dominican Republic, these conflicts represent on average 41 percent of the total number. By contrast, in the Southern Cone they represent 29 percent of all conflicts, and in Uruguay only 20 percent.

151

In terms of the tendency of these types of conflicts to be radicalized, those that are most likely to be radicalized are those related to problems caused by political and administrative limitations (56 percent), the nonfulfillment of agreements (53 percent), and the questioning of or lack of confidence in public authorities (49 percent). Around 40 percent of conflicts related to administrative inefficiency and the provision of public services are significantly radicalized. The fact that such a high percentage of institutional conflicts lead to radicalization shows the structural weakness of government institutions in the region.

There is a "para-institutional" side to this kind of conflict that marks the relation between the state and social actors. This "para-institutional" side follows from an important feature of the region: a flow of interests that compete in the spaces and through the formal and informal mechanisms for processing and resolving conflicts. One hypothesis for explaining this phenomenon has to do with the coexistence of social relations based on networks and hierarchies, "legacies" of the colonial past, with modern institutions. An example of this would be clientelism. This type of informal relation can be seen in all spaces of social interaction, even formal contexts. It therefore provides a basis for corruption in the political system and for the impact of criminal economies.

Cultural Conflicts

Cultural conflicts call into question forms of life and social organization, and they seek to achieve new forms of coexistence and social interaction among cultures, people, groups, and institutions. They emphasize the quality of everyday life, posing not only objective and practical questions, but also subjective questions and others related to values. For this reason, these struggles can be considered strategic, because they point to a search for profound changes in ways of living together in our societies. The high levels of inequality – especially socioeconomic, but also cultural inequality – and the weakness of institutions in Latin America are important factors that we find at the basis of these kinds of conflicts. In this context, conflicts over security, political and ideological conflicts, and increasingly environmental conflicts stand out in the region. In this last type of conflict, we find a prevailing opposition to a model of development linked to exploitation and the exhaustion and contamination of natural resources. Another type of conflict that has become increasingly widespread in recent years involves gender relations and follows from the questioning of patriarchy. Thus many cultural conflicts in Latin America seek to redefine social relations in order to achieve better forms of coexistence among citizens and greater security.

Although cultural conflicts are relatively less important, given that they make up only 15 percent of the total number of conflicts in the region, their impact is considerable because of the social networks made possible by new technologies of information. These networks also make it possible for movements to question not only practices with economic implications, but also values, including especially those that are foundational for societies. In other words, these conflicts often pose questions about the type of society we want and what kind of development is possible. Because of their cultural impact, it is possible to consider these struggles strategic as well; they can affect the relationships between our societies and the state, as well as the relationships between these societies and globalization. They can even reach the point of questioning democracy itself.

Twenty-eight percent of cultural conflicts center on the effort to achieve more security for citizens confronted with crime, and 26 percent occur on the ideological and political level. In general, the latter are led by political parties' opposing visions, which can lead to confrontations between friends and enemies. These are also the kinds of cultural conflicts that are most often radicalized, followed by those that demand more security.[1] Meanwhile, 24 percent of cultural conflicts are environmental conflicts that question the management of natural resources by public and private bodies, or that demand control over these resources. Given their universal nature – that is, the fact that environmental issues have global implications – and the fact that they question a form of development based on the exploitation of natural resources, environmental conflicts have major repercussions, and it is very difficult to dispute their logic. Consider, for example, the conflicts related to informational extractivism, which has increased throughout the region, or those related to the building of infrastructure, especially in the Amazon.

Two actors stand out for the key role they play in the context of these conflicts. We are referring, on the one hand, to young people, who stand out for both their participation in spaces of mobilization and their issuing of new demands. Techno-sociability, conflicts on the web, and new forms of politics are the features that characterize youth movements in this context. On the other hand, we are referring to women, who stand out for their proactive nature and the potential for cultural, political, and social change that their movement represents (UNDP, 2009).

153

Overall, then, there is more complexity in social conflicts related to political systems and states with increasingly limited capacities to manage them.

Youth Protest[2]

As we noted in chapter 5, new forms of communication involve the intensive use of information and communications technologies in the public sphere. The latter is understood as a place of encounter, where ideas and values are formed, transmitted, exchanged, endorsed, and contested. Information and communications technologies allow for more nimble, flexible, and spontaneous interaction among social actors, who can, thanks to these technologies, more actively participate in politics and social conflict. In this way, possibilities for collective action are amplified by easy access to and the low cost of both the internet and mobile phones.[3] Taking part in a forum, a blog, or a group on a social network is easier and more accessible than other forms of political participation. Increasingly, conflicts are native to the internet, since when people lodge a complaint or make a general demand, it is transmitted spontaneously to thousands of people in a relatively short time, now especially by way of social networks, but also through blogs, forums, email chains, or text messages. By way of these tools, citizens can organize themselves in response to conflicts and exchange information. A form of "cyber-activism" that promotes deliberation and acting in concert online and in the streets is now a given in Latin American and global political reality.

Globalization has not only produced concentrations of power and consumption; it has also consequently entailed the strengthening of individual and collective capacities in which spontaneity, voluntarism, and self-organization prevail. Thus it becomes necessary to individually redefine collective projects on the web, and conversely collective projects presuppose the valorization of personal freedom and dignity. Castells has called these new, multicultural forms of collective action at the global level "networks of outrage and hope."

These are protest movements like those we have analyzed in the cases of the movements made up of indigenous people, people of African descent, women, and environmentalists. Their strong demands are ethical and subjective, and these are made in nearly all societies and cultures. They place questions of ethics, human rights, the environment, and personal dignity at the center of political debates. They tend to be spontaneous, horizontal, deliberative, practical, viral

154

(alternating between different spaces), multicultural, polycentric. Overall, they demand channels for the expansion of democracy, and they produce a critique of power that is ethical but also practical.

Some features of online protests led by young people in Chile, Mexico, and Brazil are part of a new dynamic that is also operative at a global scale, for example, in Tunisia, in Egypt, in Iceland, in Spain, in the United States, in Greece, and in Portugal, and so on (Castells, 2012).

Chilean youth, recovering the memory of Salvador Allende at the Alameda in Santiago (not least with the slogan, "Se siente, se siente / Allende está presente"), seek to project a new form of life, education, and politics. Their numerous demands are centered on nothing more and nothing less than the strategic role that inclusive, high-quality education has in building a new, democratic society. In May 2011, young Chilean university students began protests to call for free, high-quality public education. Their concrete demands were for increases in, and payment of, grants for students, the lowering of interest on student loans, student participation in the design and administration of university policies, and greater state control over private universities.

Although the movement was centered on the educational realm, it generated reflection and debate throughout society and gained legitimacy (according to Adimark's findings, in August of 2011, 76 percent of Chileans were in agreement with "the demands that university students and secondary school students have put forward recently"). This led to a questioning of other kinds of power in the public sphere (the healthcare system, housing, pensions), and these were articulated around the demand for a new, more "Latin American" way of life, one that would reject the neoliberal perspective on public policies and seek inclusion and social justice, the extension of citizens' participation in politics and the strengthening of democracy as well as the extension and recognition of rights. (This meant a questioning, for example, of the state's actions in relation to ethnic minorities, especially the Mapuche, but also a critique of the environmental degradation, racism, and sexism present in Chilean society.) Likewise, participation in the movement went beyond the limits of political parties and also questioned them.

The movement began on social networks, but it gradually gained strength on the streets, and started a process of negotiation with the government. Ideologically diverse, it included leftist strands (communist and anarchists) as well as independent students who wanted to participate in the construction of another kind of university and

155

a society different from the one made in the image of markets. The democratic character of the movement can be seen in the public debates it stages and in the decisions taken by majorities during assemblies.

Although the movement has not yet reached its goals, the difference it has made to the political and cultural agenda in Chile are evident. Will the system of political parties be able to integrate these demands? Or will the protests begin again, creating a new dynamic of conflict and change?

A recent event that is of particular importance is the national election of 2017. Here the movement chose to transform itself into a new, autonomous political force and managed to obtain over 20 percent of votes. None of the leaders was over 35 years old, an institutional precondition for running for the presidency; they had to rely on the feminist journalist Beatriz Sánchez, an independent candidate, to participate in that election. Whatever Sánchez's merits, this situation points to the gap between the old political dynamic in Chile and the reality of new forms of leadership.

In the context of the **Mexican** national elections in 2012, the **Movimiento YoSoy132** emerged as a response by a group of students at the Universidad Iberoamericana in Mexico City to events that had taken place in May of that year. After a presentation given by Enrique Peña Nieto, then candidate for president for the PRI, at the university, he justified his decision to repress a youth demonstration in 2006, when he was governor of the State of Mexico. This incident was recorded on cell phones and circulated on the internet.

After these events, which forced Peña Nieto to leave the university under the protection of a security detail after seeking refuge in a bathroom, the media and university authorities downplayed what had happened, claiming that it was not an authentic expression of students' views and did not represent their opinions. By this account, the incident had been set up by people not affiliated with the university.

After these statements, students from this same university posted a video in which they asserted their participation in the incident and reaffirmed their position. They signed as "131 students," and they included their first names, surnames, and matriculation numbers as well as the departments in which they were enrolled. The video was immediately reproduced by thousands of people on YouTube, and it went viral on social networks, where the slogan "YoSoy132" (or "Iam132") emerged to signal support for the group of young students.[4]

156

Days later, the movement that had originated on virtual networks appeared in street demonstrations and numerous assemblies. Its main demands were for the strengthening of democracy, transparency, and the defense of freedom of expression. In addition, the movement expressed grave dissatisfaction with the political class and corruption, and it questioned the manipulation of information in and by the mass media. The movement defined itself as a student movement that was non-partisan, plural, non-religious, and anti-neoliberal. It opposed Peña Nieto and was pacifist and humanist in its social and political orientation. It emerged in a private university and then formed bridges to students in public universities, something that reflected an increasing sense of discontent among youth, a dissatisfaction with the Mexican political system. This was a movement created by a new generation of young people who questioned both the political culture led by the traditional parties in Mexico and the country's two television monopolies, Televisa and Televisión Azteca. It sought new ways to participate and defend human rights and citizens. The future of this movement is uncertain, but what is certain is that it has had an important influence on youth and on poor and middle-class educational institutions. Its acceptance made it into a key point of reference in Mexican politics.

In **Brazil**, in early June of 2013, a series of protests began in response to public transportation fare increases. These protests continued to intensify until June 14, when police violently repressed them. In São Paulo, the demonstrations, initially organized through social networks, blocked main roads. These demonstrations were led by the **Movimento Passe Livre** (or Free Fare Movement), among other organizations. The Movimento Passe Livre had fought since 2005 for reductions in the costs of public transportation and had organized itself through social networks (Rolnik, 2013; Castells, 2015). The movement was formed by independent youth, left and anarchist political parties made up mostly of university students, and professionals. Poor people from the city's peripheries also participated. The movement was organized in a decentralized and online way and was horizontal in character.

Although the seed of these demonstrations was an increase in public transportation fares, which significantly affected the middle and lower classes, their demands later multiplied on the streets, especially those demands that opposed the costs involved in Brazil's role as host country for major sporting events (the FIFA Confederations Cup in 2013, the World Cup in 2014, the Olympics in 2016), while public services were insufficient and expensive. But the protesters also called for greater access to healthcare and education, transparency in public institutions, a struggle against corruption, the end of police militarization. They demanded rights for indigenous people. They put forward demands for an expanded role for the state in the public sphere and for increased citizen participation and, especially, for attention to be paid to society beyond the traditional political system, which they also called into question.

The initial protests, which began on social networks and in which debate unfolded, reached their goal of putting an end to the fare increases. New demands and claims made by citizens were generated in the following months, though in more fragmentary and sectoral ways.

Nevertheless, the events recorded during some demonstrations – police repression, on the one hand, and looting and property destruction by a racialized minority, on the other – divided public opinion and affected the movement's legitimacy. The vast majority of Brazil's population opposed this violence.

Some analysts maintain that these protests constituted a revalorization of public life and of the street as the site of political expression, as a public space where concrete results could be achieved. At the same time, it would appear that what the movement questioned was an economic and social model that, despite gains made in the reduction of poverty in the past ten years, has not managed to respond to the multiple demands that intensified with the improvements made. In other words, we see here a generalized dissatisfaction, especially in the middle classes, which had to make strenuous efforts to remain in the middle class. Others saw a questioning of the exercise of political power: behind the concrete demands, there was an ethical demand for substantive changes in participation in political decision-making, an expansion of the political system, a greater form of citizenship. This was even recognized in the discourse of President Dilma Rousseff (Nogueira, 2013).

These movements in the streets, which combine concrete demands and demands for the expansion of citizenship, show that there are many people who do not believe either in the "privatization" of cities or in their segregation. They make us think of new models for urban development and coexistence, and they point to the exclusion or the partial inclusion of broad sectors of society who live in cities and their surroundings and who want to be part of them, to give a meaning different from the one promoted by the market economy. There were signs at the protests that said: "Sorry for the inconvenience, we are changing the country." This would seem to signal a search for change, an effort to depart from the discontent generated by the conditions of urban life and its unfair costs, and a critique of politicians' ethics as well.

However, other social movements have also emerged in Brazil and in other places in the region, conservative and far-right movements that have given support to politicians like Jair Bolsonaro. Authoritarian and even fascist interventions on social networks are reviving older authoritarian cultures, which are being reinforced by references to neo-fascism in Europe and the leadership of Donald Trump. The politics of the far right are also mobilized on the street and on social networks, with new forces vying for power and the return of a stratified culture traceable to colonialism. In this way, social networks and the street are likewise part of a new, ideologically diverse public space.

Women's Demands and Agency

The most significant antecedents for the changes in the subjective agency of women are related to the human rights movement that has taken place throughout the past decades. From the demonstrations and hunger strikes staged by the mothers of Bolivian miners in the 1970s – which culminated in the installation of democracy in Bolivia – to the cultural and political importance of the Madres y Abuelas de la Plaza de Mayo in Argentina, the Mães de Maio in Brazil, or women in Colombia and Guatemala, to the more recent movements of mothers and women for human rights, women's roles in society have been changing throughout all of Latin America.

The symbolic force of feminist movements made up of enlightened middle-class women with forceful critiques of androcentrism and demands for changes to everyday life have also been very important. The claims that they made on the state and on international bodies, especially the United Nations, were very important in encouraging women's participation in various spheres of public life, and in strengthening women's human rights.

With these antecedents, a new logic began to emerge, a series of demands made and struggles fought by women in the most diverse contexts of the public and private spheres. These demands and struggles increasingly question the patriarchal regime of power and domination. Thus women's movements and other gender movements have politicized the private realms of domination, placing them in public view and altering relations of power, both public and private, in the process.

159

One fundamental movement is the struggle for the right to abortion. In 69.5 percent of countries in the world, abortion is not a legal practice, and according to reports by Amnesty International, Latin America is the most unequal region in the world when it comes to access to sexual and reproductive health services. Restrictive abortion policies – together with social understandings of the issue – compel millions of women to seek clandestine abortions. According to estimates from the World Health Organization, more than 25 million women and girls seek recourse to risky abortions (World Health Organization, 2017).

In this context, the site Women on Web is a digital community of women who seek to facilitate access to information on how to provide abortions to women who need them, using medications included in the World Health Organization's list of essential medications, Mifepristone and Misoprostol.[5] In Latin America, Mifepristone can only be obtained legally in Uruguay, where the legalization of abortion up to 12 weeks was approved in 2012, by Law No. 18.987.[6] In Argentina, Peru, and Colombia, Misoprostol can be acquired in pharmacies, although its cost varies significantly between countries.[7] In addition to being a place of encounter and support for women who voluntarily terminate their pregnancies, fully enjoying their rights, Women on Web works against the de facto inequality, discrimination, and violence that women suffer.

Another creative and increasingly widespread movement on the international scene is **Ni Una Menos**. "Ni una menos, ni una muerta más" (or "Not one less, not one more dead woman") was their original slogan, taken from a poem denouncing the killing of women in Ciudad Juárez, in Mexico. This is a movement formed by urban women, begun in Argentina but with a growing presence in Chile, Bolivia, Uruguay, Mexico, Guatemala, Spain, and France. Its main objective is to eliminate gendered violence and to increase the participation and recognition of women as subjects, with the right to question the macho imaginary of gendered violence in the media and to promote laws against all kinds of violence. Between 2015 and 2017, three major demonstrations were organized through the widespread use of social networks, which had considerable social impact. In this way, Ni Una Menos questioned patriarchal power and the political class, and they demanded laws to prevent violence and the domination of women.

The movement enjoys broad recognition in public opinion as well as the explicit support of artists, intellectuals, journalists, NGOs, and cultural agencies, among others. The text and websites cited here show various moments in the life of this movement.[8]

160

One fundamental consequence of the enormous change in gender relations is a tendency not just to develop new and diverse forms of protest, and new social actors and movements, in all Latin American countries, but also the capacity of these movements to change their goals and projects. Their actions follow from both a search for concrete results and from a pedagogy of intercultural and democratic communication among their various leaders. In this sense, perhaps one of the most extraordinary changes in Latin American society, or rather in its societies, is an increase in women's agency, in their capacity for action.

One important empirical example can be found in the findings on youth, especially youth in large cities, in the *Informe de desarrollo humanopara Mercosur* (Report on Human Development for Mercosur) (UNDP, 2009). Here we find a series of quantitative indices of objective, subjective, and democratic agency. And in almost all national cases, as well as in all social and generational contexts, among young people of different ages, women were found to have significant capacity for action. So, on one hand, women had a greater ability to articulate their demands as citizens, and this was related to more efficacy in their demands for distribution, participation, and recognition. Among the poorest women, demands centered on distribution; among the most educated and those with highest incomes, they centered on participation; and among the youngest women, they centered on their recognition as persons.

With respect to subjective and objective indices of agency, the report found that seven out of every ten women had higher capacity. In the case of men, only five out of every ten had a high capacity (UNDP, 2009: 33). Thus, on the one hand, the new women's movements struggle for women's rights and call for policies that question the very foundations of cultural power. On the other, they show a tendency to increase women's capacities for action, their ability to manage concrete problems in everyday life. We can therefore affirm that a new historical subject is emerging in the region. At issue here is a subject who seeks to achieve cultural change and give new meaning to life and politics. This subject finds a key point of reference for everyday human life in the search for dignity. These movements seek to change the patriarchal order and end sexist violence in Latin American societies, and in this way they work to redefine the kind of change that is possible in politics and in the historical field.

Finally, it is worth mentioning another key issue: the gay, transgender, and lesbian movements, directly linked to changes in the family and to the dissolution of the patriarchy. These are new subjectivities and new protests that revolve around expanding forms of self-definition, both in terms of sexual orientation and in terms of sexual identity. These are cultural forms of life centered on the formation of couples and relationships that increasingly exceed the norms and customs founded on the family and traditional, religious values. A new culture of sexual and affective relations is emerging from a rejection of heterosexual patriarchy, a millennial culture of domination that seeks to prescribe whom we can love and whom we cannot.

Environmental Protests

Global public opinion and many countries have come to acknowledge the existence of global climate change, which entails effects that are destructive for nature and, without exception, for diverse human realities. This recognition has been accompanied by a recognition of the impact of the industrial, capitalist model of development in nearly all spheres of production, as well as the impact of a form of individualist consumerism that legitimates and incentivizes the growing environmental crisis in much of the world. According to the Latinobarómetro report for 2017, 83 percent of Latin Americans are in agreement with the idea that humans are those most responsible for climate change, and 71 percent believe that the fight against climate change should be made a priority, even if this has negative implications for economic growth.

Processes of environmental degradation and destruction have been driven by the most industrially developed countries and businesses, while the countries that suffer the main consequences of this development have been those most polluted and those with the least ability to confront climate change and environmental depletion. Data from the Human Development Index and other global reports are conclusive in finding that the countries with the highest levels of human development are also the countries that cause more pollution, while those with low or very low levels of human development suffer more from the consequences. This shows that inhuman development is also global. In fact, according to the Human Development Report for 2007–2008, carbon dioxide emissions per capita in 2004 in countries that are members of the Organization for Economic Co-operation and Development (OECD) came to more than 11.5 tons, while per capita emissions in the countries of Sub-Saharan Africa and Latin America and the Caribbean were 1.0 and 2.6 tons, respectively (UNDP, 2008: 69). Data from the World Bank for 2014 show a decreasing tendency in carbon dioxide emissions in countries that are members of the OECD, but the disparities between regions remained (World Bank, 2018).

This phenomenon and others – including especially the new forms of "informational extractivism" (see chapter 2) – have led to important transformations in Latin American public opinion, a notable expansion in networks of NGOs, especially those of a sectoral nature, and a significant proliferation of protests by environmental resistance movements, especially in areas where new, extractivist enterprises have been expanding. All of this generates significant political problems for states and for businesses. In this context, we see the emergence of environmental cultures among indigenous people and the revalorization of forms of life in harmony with the healthy reproduction of nature. This is a matter of a right to life for nature itself. And so here we also see a new field of historical conflict taking shape.[9]

Some Examples in the Andes

An emblematic case is the mobilization around the Isiboro Secure National Park and Indigenous Territory (Territorio Indígena y Parque Nacional Isiboro Sécure, or TIPNIS), an Andean-Amazonian region of 1,200,000 hectares. This was a mobilization promoted by the Tsimané, Yucaré, and Mojeño communities. In the TIPNIS, there are three bioregions, all ecologically diverse, that need to reproduce themselves under natural conditions in order not to lose their ecological equilibrium. The government, neo-development, Andean, and indigenist in its orientation, promoted the construction of a highway through the middle of the TIPNIS, in an effort to bring about more territorial integration and create conditions for greater economic growth.

In response, a major community march was organized, one that went from the north of Bolivia, in the Department of Pando, to La Paz, more than 1,000 kilometers away. The protest began with around 600 people, who arrived in La Paz to be joined by more than half a million supporters. The relation between the march, public opinion, and the support of global environmental networks was formed through networks of information and communication. And so a space of conflict was created, where the conflict was over territory and pitted a neo-developmentalist government against the indigenous communities of the TIPNIS, who defended their right to a cultural reproduction based on sustainable eco-territorial practices. At stake in this conflict was the defense of the TIPNIS, on the one hand, and, on the other, a complex system of business interests, in oil in the cases of the Total and Petrobras corporations, in the expansion of the soy economy, in logging, and in the strengthening of the strategic integration with Brazil, Asia, and the Pacific. Ultimately, the communitarian approach prevailed, and changes in favor of TIPNIS were introduced into the constitution, although in real terms the resolution of the conflict remains pending and may favor state power (Aramayo, 2018; Fundación Tierra, 2018).

In a study of social conflicts and extractive industries conducted by Anthony Bebbington, some of the profiles of these various industries and accounts of political conflicts in Bolivia, Ecuador, and Peru stand out. The study centers on the role of governance. Bebbington writes that "institution building is a political process in which socio-environmental conflict can play a potentially constructive role" (Bebbington, 2011: 71). One of his conclusions underscores the fact that

[a]cross the case studies, it is manifestly clear that the final determination of conflicts and outcomes is due to the interaction between these relational and structural factors, on the one hand, and local factors, on the other. Local social and political economic histories have much bearing on how extractive industries are interpreted, on the probability and nature of conflict, and on the ways in which conflict – if it emerges – is handled (Bebbington, 2011: 72).

In the majority of cases, this is a matter of populations defending their territories against extractive megaprojects that generate social uncertainty related to means of subsistence (water, land) and control over territories. In all of these cases, this is in the context of "Latin America, a region relatively poor in financial capital but rich in biological and cultural diversity, where entrenched social and economic inequalities and weak state institutions pose very specific challenges for policy design and implementation" (Rival, 2011, 2).

"For despite the varying political inclinations of the presidents of Bolivia, Ecuador, and Peru, they each pursue economic development models based upon the extraction and exportation of mineral and hydrocarbon resources" (Humphreys Bebbington, 2011: 135). Polarized debates on the "resource curse" converge on an understanding of "the importance of institutional quality and context in determining the effects of extractive industries on development" (Bebbington, 2011: 67).

In many cases, local, national, and international dynamics come together in conflicts that also connect governments, markets, and civil society. The environmental conflicts studied by Bebbington involved Bagua and Camisea in Peru, Chaco and Pilcomayo in Bolivia, and the mining mandate and the Amazon in Ecuador.

Another particularly complex case was the environmental conflict among those living near Gualeguaychú, the plants owned by the Finnish company Botnia, the states of Uruguay and Argentina, and a complex system of private interests and local politicians. This was a lasting conflict over the effects of river pollution caused by the plants' processing of cellulose. The construction of a cellulose processing plant led to environmental changes that affected political life and the relationship between Argentina and Uruguay and made evident the difficulties of national politics in efforts to resolve the environmental demands of a local society. The study by Vicente Palermo entitled "El Gobernador pasó en helicóptero" [The Governor Passed by in a Helicopter], shows in detail the complexity of this kind of environmental conflict, the limits of politics and even states themselves (Palermo et al., 2009).

To sum up, if we view this new type of conflict and movement holistically, we can conclude that a new historical field has emerged, and that it has perhaps reorganized the new Latin America in the information age. We would thus be responding in an anachronistic way to a new kind of politics that has redefined the very fields of politics and power. The region is undergoing cultural changes related to chronic problems of inequality, insecurity, pollution, sexism, poverty, and inhuman development. These changes are porous and inherently related to chronic realities. But at present, although new types of conflict have multiplied, they remain fragmented and their dynamics remain largely associated not just with new forms of social differentiation, but especially with new, complex mechanisms of functional differentiation in various techno-informational and communicational processes and in networks of information that are almost infinite but not always interconnected.

— 11 —

STATE CORRUPTION

During the first decades of the twenty-first century, Latin America went through a series of profound socio-political crises in nearly every country. These called the stability of the state into question, affecting the process of development as a whole. At the root of nearly all of these crises was a triggering factor: corruption. What military coups were to the state and society in the twentieth century, systemic corruption is to the twenty-first. This corruption disrupts the state characteristic of all political regimes and destroys the bonds of trust between citizens and the state, the bond that is the psychological and cultural basis for the legitimacy of democracy. This is why corruption is serious: because at a moment Latin America seemed finally to have achieved the ideal of liberal democracy for which so much blood, sweat, and tears had been shed, a specter – the specter of state corruption – is corroding the institutions on which people's everyday lives depend. In fact, the political centrality of corruption is something of an enigma. Because there has always been political, corporate, and social corruption in Latin America, and not necessarily more so than in the rest of the world – Europe, Asia, the United States or Africa – where corruption takes more or less disguised or sophisticated forms, depending on historical differences, cultures, and legal contexts. Consequently, the real question is not why there is corruption, but why it is so much more decisive in political terms than it was in the past. And why citizens are so sensitized to corruption that they hit the streets and help to overthrow presidents. There are several possible hypotheses. It could be that there is much more corruption in quantitative terms, so that it has reached a critical mass that makes the system dysfunctional and unbearable for people. Or it could be a matter of a systemic form of corruption that erodes trust in institutions because these simply function according to rules to which the majority do not have access. Or it could be that more information is available, circulating through media who have understood that corruption sells, or through ubiquitous, uncontrolled social networks. This last fact makes it impossible for the media to hide information.

Or it could be that state corruption is part of a new way of practicing politics, part of the mass-mediated politics that we analyzed above: a politics based on the personalization of leaders, who become the embodiments of the trust placed in them. The corollary of this would be a politics of scandal, in which political adversaries leak relievable, partially false, or outright falsified information in an effort to destroy the image of their rivals. And since everyone (or almost everyone) does this, politics becomes an effort to determine who is most corrupt.

Perhaps it is all of this at once. The result is that corruption, its image, shapes politics and corrodes the state. But why is the state so decisive and so vulnerable? In fact, the state has always been the structuring nucleus of Latin American societies, whatever their autonomy or their dependency on national or foreign economic bodies or on social actors mobilized in efforts to control public resources and capacities for state intervention (Cardoso and Faletto, 1979; Knight, 2017). Even the cases where liberal politics prevailed, deregulation and privatization were public policies effectuated by relations of power established by the state. This does not mean that the state is simply strong. There are countries in which the state was historically weak – that is, where it had little ability to impose itself on other powerful groups in society. Such is the case in Colombia, for example, where the central state always depended on the power play of regional elites in their relation to institutions. This is one of the reasons frequently given for the extreme fragmentation of the Colombian state and its limited repressive power, its inability to impose order, which has cleared a path for generalized violence as a way of resolving conflicts among elites vying for control of the central state (González, 2014).

Other states, by contrast, were strong. These included the state that resulted from the Mexican Revolution, beginning with the presidency of Lázaro Cárdenas, or the Chilean state backed by the institutional armed forces until Pinochet's coup, which paradoxically weakened the state by politicizing the military hierarchy. Or consider the Brazilian state, whose federal government was an essential mechanism for the construction of the nation on the basis of the corporate diversity of its elites, who had been vying for control over decentralized institutions in an effort to increase their negotiating power. Or consider, finally, the state in Argentina, beginning with Juan Domingo Perón, although this was a dangerously two-headed state divided by conflict between Peronists and the armed forces who always proclaimed themselves to be the guardians of the nation.

All that said, our purpose in this book is not to produce a comparative historical analysis of the relationship between states and powerful groups, but rather to underscore the persistence of the state's centrality and of conflicts over the state as the nucleus for social dynamics and strategies of development in almost all Latin American societies. Globalization, which profoundly changed regional and national economies throughout Latin America at the end of the last century, required an opening up of conflicts over the state, their giving way to a more diversified and complex system of actors, in which the obligatory integration into multinational networks of production, exchange, technology, and finance would lessen the importance of the traditional distinction between domestic and foreign economies. The state connected these economies, as had occurred in the Asia Pacific during its development. The degree of direct state intervention was, and is, highly variable, but in any case, the strategic direction of the process of global integration depended on what the state did or did not do, on the correlation of economic and social forces that competed and negotiated by way of the state.

The models of development that we have treated as successively predominant in the first two decades of the century, neoliberalism and neo-developmentalism, did not result from the business strategies of national or multinational companies, but rather from state policies, which articulated diverse interests in keeping with two models of integration into globalization. (This integration is something that was common to both models.) Gone were the vagaries of semi-autarchic national development as defined by the Economic Commission for Latin America and the Caribbean. The reality of globalization, a process initiated by the United States and the United Kingdom, also through state policies, and decisively reinforced by the support of China, left no more room for different forms of integration, with the local and the national variously forming part of the global. Clearly this sketch of the tendencies that shaped Latin America at the dawn of the twenty-first century is an oversimplification. If by neoliberalism we mean the domination of the market not only in the economy, but also in society and ideology, then we cannot say that Ricardo Lagos's Chile or Fernando Henrique Cardoso's Brazil were neoliberal in the strict sense. In his book on Chile, Castells documented how the social policies and human development in Chile, under pressure from the state, were essential for the creation of a basis for society, for institutional stability, and for human capital. On this basis, Chilean businesses could compete in the global economy, compensating for the one-dimensional, neoliberal strategy (privileging capital) pursued under Pinochet's dictatorship. Cardoso's presidency in Brazil, in addition to modernizing the country's infrastructure and overcoming protectionist restrictions, implemented substantial reforms in education, healthcare, and social cohesion, exemplified by the Comunidade Solidária (Community Solidarity), devised and led by the feminist leftist Ruth Cardoso, although this was a minor and not strictly speaking a state program. In other contexts, neoliberal policies were explicit, especially in Colombia, Mexico, Peru, Ecuador, or, above all, Carlos Menem's Argentina, which implemented a convertibility plan. The so-called "Washington Consensus" (really imposed by the International Monetary Fund) predominated in Latin American politics during the last decade of the twentieth century and in the first years of the twenty-first. The economic and social consequences of this model of development, ideologically defined as neoliberal, have been described in this book's previous chapters. They include: partial integration into globalization, at the cost of a substantial increase in inequality in all countries in the region and increases in poverty and social exclusion in most countries as well. This led to widespread social protests in nearly all of the region, and to decisive political changes that enshrined a new model: what we have called neo-developmentalism, a model that we also described above. Both models, deriving from a new link between society and the state under globalization, had a decisive influence on this relationship. The final, and relatively recent, result has been systemic state corruption, a source of institutional crisis with unpredictable consequences. We will see how and why this is the case.

Determinants of State Corruption

When we use the term "state corruption," we refer to the taking of political decisions (whether in governments, systems of public administration, or any other mechanism of governance) by public officials, that is those paid by taxpayers, for the benefit of specific people or organizations. Such decisions contravene established laws and put private interests before the general interest, in exchange for something of value, whether this takes the form of money or the ability to exercise influence in other contexts, be they financial or geopolitical. These decisions depend, in other words, either on trading or barter.

The increasing strategic importance of corruption in Latin American states seems to be the result of profound transformations in the economy, politics, and society. The forms of political corruption that have arisen are common to the neoliberal and neo-developmentalist models, although these models, both anchored in the state, have different effects on the intensity and the modes of corruption, and different consequences for the workings of the state. The substantial change in the economy comes from the necessary articulation between finance, production, the market, and technology and the global networks in which economic activities take place, whether directly or indirectly. Both informational extractivism and the criminal economy, to cite the two most dynamic sectors in Latin America in the twenty-first century, are based on advantageous forms of integration into global networks. This is true not only for industries in each country, but for the flows of capital, production, and goods and services that originate in foreign economic circuits. As we have indicated, the main connector between the foreign and the domestic is the state, which exercises its powers of regulation in all realms of the economy and its capacity to intervene as an economic actor, both through state industries and through the creation of demand in key public markets. The traditional, hegemonic influence of major multinational corporations has been displaced by multiple forms of investment, export, and import through global networks. Obtaining favorable treatment from the state is one of the new global economy's essential mechanisms – so much so that it is factored into investment proposals made by major companies. In some cases, this is a matter of transferring technology or access to global markets to state-held companies in exchange for a favorable connection between the global and the local. But often the simplest thing is paying a bribe to political organizations or people in the state administration with the ability to make decisions.

This skewed relationship affects the granting of licenses for import and export, as well as the permissions necessary for investing or repatriating capital. All of these are mechanisms that have always existed, together with corresponding forms of corruption. The difference is that the extent and acceleration of globalization and extreme competition in global networks exponentially increase the resources that are invested into efforts to subvert legal rules. And since everyone does this, the system as a whole functions on the basis of savage competition in terms of who gives the most and with the lowest risk of exposure.

The second major productive transformation is what Calderón has identified as "informational extractivism," which we analyzed in chapter 2. These agricultural, mining, and fuel-extracting activities make up the most dynamic sector in many countries, including Argentina, Brazil, Mexico, Bolivia, Peru, Ecuador, Uruguay, and Paraguay. They thus largely shape Latin America's integration into the global economy. It is obvious that, although the dynamism of this sector, including significant technological innovations, is the work of mostly private companies, the state plays a key strategic role throughout the sector. This is both because of the importance of major companies like Pemex, Petrobras, YPF, Codelco, Boliviana, and so on, and because of regulations and the granting of licenses for export and production by the state in its negotiations with companies and with governments throughout the world, in particular the Chinese government. There are numerous cases of mediation by intermediaries who have influenced these negotiations, including with favors from political leaders at the highest level, as in what is perhaps the most infamous case, the "White House" mansion built for the first lady of Mexico during Enrique Peña Nieto's presidency.

To be sure, bearing in mind the economic importance of the criminal economy in several countries – its importance, that is both for the production and illegal trafficking of drugs and for money laundering – the state's permissiveness can also be seen as a mechanism for regulating a certain kind of informational extractivism. It is informational because it is based on a sophisticated system of production (increasingly involving synthetic drugs and chemical precursors) as well as a system of transport. It draws on information about specific markets and requires digital transfers of capital as this capital makes its way to the stage of money laundering, integration into the global financial economy. And as we know, the criminal economy only functions thanks to its deep infiltration of the state and the political system, including courts and the police. This infiltration requires an immense investment of resources, used for corruption or to intimidate millions of public officials throughout the region.

The third major structural transformation is, as we saw in chapter 4, the explosion of cities in Latin America (the most urbanized region in the world, with around 80 percent of the population living in cities), especially with the formation of immense metropolitan areas, several of which now house more than ten million residents, or even up to twenty million if the real metropolitan areas of megacities, areas that exceed municipal borders, are counted. This urbanization has been wild and uncontrolled, or controlled only by real estate scouts

171

and speculators. Construction and real estate have become dominant industries, leading to a concentration of capital and building capacities that lead to some of the highest rates of profit. These activities are dependent on administrative regulations, in particular on city planning, often done with the best of intentions without the real ability to control its execution on the part of city and land-use planners. The power of developers, public works and transport companies, and engineers is such that they have not had real difficulty in corrupting those they needed to corrupt, whether they were private citizens, functionaries, or politicians, including even those at the highest levels of the state. The market for public works is so great, and the conditions of urbanization have been so sped up, that round this market sprawling business complexes have arisen. In Latin America these are much more important and influential than tech companies, as in the case of Odebrecht, the massive construction and engineering company that has been a key source of corruption in Brazil, Peru, and other countries. Markets for public works created by the process of urbanization are a main source of state and political corruption. In the context of the political process, there are two determining factors for the spread of corruption. First, the increasing fragmentation of partisan political expression, resulting from the crisis of legitimacy of the major traditional parties, leads to the formation of unstable alliances among multiple groups as well as the generalization of "presidentialist coalitions" (Cardoso et al., 2018). That is, presidential elections grant centralized power, but in order to govern, a president needs to rely on shifting parliamentary coalitions. One legal way to achieve this is through the exchange of political favors: a vote favorable for a business is traded for public investment in the territory that a given deputy represents. This is a widespread practice in all democracies, and it is not illegal although it may be bad politics. But on many occasions and in all of Latin America's political systems, it is followed directly by the personalized buying of votes in underhanded ways. These are longstanding practices. What is new is that the increasing fragmentation of political choices makes these practices systematic. One can only govern with difficulty if one does not buy the votes of elected representatives. And since all presidents and parties engage in this practice, they cover for each other, because they know that everyone has to make a virtue of necessity, and that these are hard times for presidents.

The second determining factor is more directly related to technological and organizational changes in the political process. We are referring to the model that we discussed in an earlier chapter and that Castells analyzed in his book *Communication Power* (2013). Let us recall that this entails the domination of political practice by mass-mediated politics. The personalization of politics, resulting from electoral marketing, makes the images of leaders transmitted by the media into the fundamental ingredient in political victories. What is not in the media does not exist. But the domination of mass-mediated politics means that political struggle must take the form of an effort to destroy the image of the adversary, through the revelation (or falsification) of this adversary's corrupt practices or his or her condemnable behavior more generally. It is the so-called politics of scandal that dominates all political systems. And since all parties do this, all parties also prepare for it. Experts in "opposition research" investigate rivals and gather damaging information that poisons electoral campaigns and the politics of governance. The main thing that citizens are informed of is politicians' lack of honesty. The problem is that this type of informational politics (which includes mass-mediated politics but is not reducible to this) is extremely expensive, requiring enormous economic resources. To obtain these resources, candidates have to promise favors in the future, sharing the spoils of victory with those who finance their campaigns. This sustains corruption, which in turn intensifies the politics of scandal, as long as there are sufficient resources to expose the other's corruption and minimize one's own. If we add to this the new dimensions of informational politics – including digital data banks used to prepare targeted ads during electoral campaigns, the manipulation of information on social networks, charismatic political consultants (a polite way to name those who manipulate democracy) – we can conclude that there is a growing gap between the resources necessary to reach power and the legal financing of campaigns and parties. The result is that nearly all parties and coalitions are financed illegally. And those who attain state power have to repay what they have received, with administrative decisions that favor their financial supporters. Illegal financing thus leads to a politics that has become lawlessness.

Finally, at the source of systemic corruption in the political system we also find transformations in society. We are referring first of all to the ideology of competitiveness among individual persons. The dissolution of traditional, communitarian, and familiar structures increased individualization in society, and everyone now works for him- or herself, is his or her only point of reference. This sometimes includes immediate families, more as sources of support than as models of behavior. The causes of this individualizing tendency can be found in the processes that structure society, including the fragmentation of the urban environment, the individualization of labor relations, the emergence of an online sociability that privileges personal connections on digital networks. Consider as well the crisis of moral points of reference caused by popular disenchantment with the Catholic Church and the declining legitimacy of political parties, or the fragmentation of the media or the fact that media organizations whose views do not coincide with the entrenched beliefs of given individuals are seen to lack credibility. This increasing social atomization is reinforced by two ideologies that powerfully shape patterns of behavior. We are referring, on the one hand, to the neoliberal ideology that legitimates the market and the logic of profit and personal accumulation above any collective value. In this sense, neoliberal hegemony can be seen as an ideology that transcends the neoliberal model in the realm of public policies. This leads to a certain delegitimization of statist models of development. On the other hand, we are referring to consumerism, which is the concrete translation of market domination into the language of society, but which adds an undeniable element of satisfaction, fulfilling personal aspirations to the degree that success in life is manifested in access to desirable goods and services, in an endless spiral.

Competitiveness in the service of consumerism: this pattern of behavior has one extraordinarily important consequence, namely everyday violence. Because there is a contradiction between the expansive desire to consume and the reality of the scarce resources available to the majority of the population, and since social inequality has increased, mechanisms of appropriation are put in place that lead to the expropriation – the violent expropriation – of resources from those who have them. The appropriators are often sheltered by police who, themselves poor in many cases, participate in the extraction of resources from others, using their capacity for intimidation and taking advantage of their association with the state. Everyday violence and its corollary, fear, are considered to be the main problems in all Latin American societies. Unable to rely on the state, people protect themselves, and social ties gradually dissolve. Other people become "the other," inhuman others to whom one can only relate defensively as one struggles for survival. In this social and cultural context, corruption, or rather the exchange of services outside the law, appears as the most reliable mechanism for satisfying everyone's interests. We mean everyone from large businesses evading regulation and taxation to neighbors who need electrical repairs or protection from the armed gangs that proliferate in the region's cities. The protection afforded by corrupt practices is vertical and often extends from the highest

174

levels of the state to the local or regional levels. Hence the normalization of corruption. The cultural construction of society, corruption is assumed to be present in all institutional structures. What varies is how much, whose corruption, and for whose benefit.

A Typology of Political Corruption

Sources of corruption take different forms when corruption appears in state practices:

(a) Payment for political and administrative decisions. We mean payment to political agents, whether they are parties, persons, or administrations, paid by businesses that seek to secure beneficial decisions or to establish a relationship of debt, where the debt is to be discharged when the business sees fit.

(b) The use by the state of resources owned by public industries under the state's control. We mean, for example, the financing of political activities of the governing party, or those of its allies in strategic collaborations.

(c) The use of public markets by the state, where these markets are made to favor certain businesses or service providers in exchange for the latter's financing of political actors, whether parties or persons.

(d) These practices are very widespread, and they extend from infrastructural projects to the purchasing of military equipment, a source of some of the most significant cases of corruption in the world and in Latin America.

(e) The buying of government concessions, whether legal or financial, on the part of foreign governments or foreign businesses protected by their governments.

(f) The buying of allowances or the complicity of state actors or institutions (including the judiciary in the broadest sense) in the activity of criminal networks, whether they are involved in drug trafficking, money laundering, extortion, or intimidation.

(g) The appointment of specific people, suggested by economic or social actors, to strategic roles by the highest-ranking state officials. This is a way of establishing a privileged relationship between the state and those actors.

(h) The buying of deputies' and senators' votes, whether by private interests or the executive.

(i) The intimidation of judges or imposition of court decisions

175

by state authorities. In particular, this takes place through the practice of facilitating judges' nominations to the highest levels of the judiciary. It can also happen, however, through personal threats made to independent judges and their families.

(j)   The buying, on the part of political actors, of favorable treatment by the media. This can happen both through contact with media corporations and through direct payments made to editors or journalists. Other practices include the granting of licenses for establishing media, in particular for radio and television.

(k)   On the other hand, direct threats to independent editors or journalists can also take place, when their critiques displease the powers that be. That is, both the media and the judiciary operate in a world of shadows, where in their decisive role in guiding affairs of state they are subject to a system of incentives or disincentives that effectively restricts their independence from political power and economic interests.

(l)   The mechanisms of corruption operate in all structures of the state, from the national to the regional and, even more so, the local. Nothing and no one escapes this structure. Although corruption may not be an inevitable practice in politics, it is present in one form or another throughout the landscape of administration and public affairs. The mechanisms that operate in each context depend on the organization and the history of the state as well as on its relation to the global context, where macro-processes of corruption operate through money launder-ing in global financial markets. Many honest politicians and administrators resist the pressures that they are under or the suggestions that they receive, and this periodically allows for the maintenance by the state of a certain autonomy, an independ-ence from the shadows that surround it. But this does not clear away the shadows, because they constantly arise in the type of society that has been built in Latin America, and in the world in general.

Neoliberalism, Neo-developmentalism, and the Politics of Corruption

The roots of systemic corruption can be found in the transformations of Latin American societies, including those that we have previously analyzed. Consequently, these forms of corruption do not depend on the models of development that have been both successive and overlapping and have characterized political economy in the early twenty-first century. Nevertheless, aspects of each model have been reflected in different and specific forms of state corruption. In what is called neoliberalism, the deregulation and privatization of businesses were the sources of many kinds of corruption. The partial dismantling of the public sector benefitted national and multinational business groups, who gave loans, both legal and illegal, to the political actors from whose decisions they stood to benefit. On the other hand, neoliberal ideology legitimated these privatizations, equating the market with efficiency and favoring an antistatist culture centered on the identification of the public sector with bureaucracy. In addition, neoliberalism placed the individual at the center of social action and turned competitiveness between persons, businesses, and countries into the yardstick by which to judge success in both personal and business terms. This gave the market the power to decide on the allocation of resources in all sectors. This was true even in those sectors, like health, education, security, and environmental protection, in which there are primary human values at stake that cannot be protected by the market in a context of extreme social inequality. In this context, practices of corruption found a breeding ground and a certain kind of legitimation in the competition that makes the primitive accumulation of property into the most important thing for persons and companies, no matter the means employed. Thus the neoliberal mode's main contribution to increased corruption was the legitimation it offered.

Having said that, this legitimation was limited to the social sectors that directly benefited from the dynamism of the market, from the region's integration into global networks, and from the private appropriation of public services. These were essentially social sectors characterized by their high levels of education and their upper-middle-class origins. By contrast, for the majority of the working class, neoliberal ideology effectively collided with their experience. Supposed individual freedoms became strategies for survival. The partial loss of social coverage by the state was especially resented as an injustice, given the view of a society in which the strongest wrote their own rules and were above the law. Thus a forceful social and political opposition to state neoliberalism arose, with a critique that centered on the unregulated corruption of groups and individuals with access to power. From this opposition, various national-popular movements emerged, together with a politics that sought to defend the public sector through a dual project: defending the nation as a cultural community, and advocating social policies that would prioritize the most disadvantaged.

177

At the socioeconomic level, the neo-developmentalist model depended on Latin America's integration into the global economy, led to increased growth, and brought about a redistribution of resources that improved the conditions of the poor. But paradoxically, at the political level it resulted in delegitimization of the state, which in many ways originated in state corruption. It is difficult to empirically determine which model of development was more corrupt. But what we can assume is that under neo-developmentalism, corruption was more systemic, was more visible, and especially gave rise to serious political crises. At first, it seems only logical that, in the absence of explicit and durable policies for institutionally correcting corruption, state corruption would increase to the degree that the state substantially increased its role in the economy. Accumulated capital, especially in public industries associated with informational extractivism, gave governments, and left parties in power, a store of resources that allowed them to devise a strategy for maintaining power. It also let them deepen the social change that they were projecting. On the one hand, this meant buying the cooperation of other political forces, whether legally or illegally, through an expanded from of "presidentialist coalition." On the other, it meant capturing resources for their own parties (and taking personal advantage of them, in some cases), in order to finance their political projects and confront the powerful interests that were mobilizing to oppose their efforts at reform (agricultural interests in Argentina, financial and industrial elites in Brazil, multinational corporations in Bolivia, a traditional oligarchy in Ecuador). And finally, when their politics of redistribution came up against fiscal limits and growth gave way to recession, they sought to finance social programs using funds from public companies, bypassing a hostile congress. This was precisely the issue that led, in Brazil, to the impeachment of Dilma Rousseff, although the ultimate cause of her removal from office was this corrupt congress's hostility to the constitutional reform that she was proposing as a way to end collusion between regional chiefs and representatives of the financial elite, who feared losing their power.

The paradox, however, is that the counter-reforms that have taken place in Latin America, even those supported by the traditional right and US-backed interest groups in Brazil, Ecuador, and Argentina, have been successful because they have resulted from the mobilization of new middle classes created in part by neo-developmentalism, a source of growth and employment for a decade. Moreover, political rights and rights to freedom of expression that were advocated by reformist political elites, both neoliberal and neo-developmentalist,

178

convinced citizens that they had rights and encouraged their aspirations to better lives, their effort to overcome reliance on public assistance, on which they depended before exiting poverty. Thus an old middle class, supported by neoliberalism, joined a new middle class without a concrete model, one that proclaimed itself against the dominant form of statism, betting instead on a life independent of politics. In this context, the issue of state corruption became central, because this corruption sustained the power of a state that supported its politicians through the secret use of public resources. The paradox in Brazil was that state corruption revealed by the affair known as Lava Jato (or Car Wash) was attributed to the PT (Workers' Party) administration, when it was known that the resources of Petrobras and other public companies were used by all political parties in all Brazilian governments.

In Brazil, in the movement opposing corruption, the demands of a new middle class seeking democratic regulation and registering their moral disapproval of those who spoke precisely in the name of justice converged with the old middle class, which sought to defend its privileges and even began to nourish nostalgia for the dictatorship. But in fact the return to military rule had been ruled out by the professionalization of the armed forces that took place during Cardoso's presidency and that of Lula. In Argentina, the traditional corruption of Peronism again became the target of middle-class opposition, which weakened the other great reformist movement in Latin America, Kirchnerism. Little by little, the Bolivarian or neo-developmentalist regimes in the region lost popular support, degenerating in some cases (like those of Venezuela and Nicaragua) into regimes reliant on repression. The exception was Bolivia, where Evo Morales secured economic growth, modernization, the redistribution of profits, dignity for indigenous workers, and the maintenance of freedoms, with less corruption than was traditional in Bolivia, or with forms of corruption that have not yet been proven. Strong opposition from the Bolivian middle class, though it also appealed to the issue of corruption, was based on ethnic prejudice, a response to the increased political presence of indigenous people and especially the presence of *cholas*, or indigenous women, in centers of power. This affront showed the depths of ethnic prejudice even in university structures, although we should also keep in mind the hostility in some indigenous sectors, especially in urban communities and especially in El Alto, who are critical of the governing party's authoritarianism and of the emergent elites. In Ecuador, the national-popular coalition survived an electoral, anti-corruption assault led by business sectors in Guayaquil, although

179

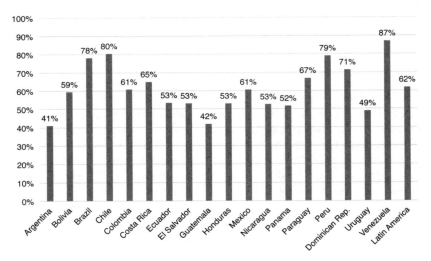

Figure 11.1: Perceptions of Increases in Corruption, in Relation to the Previous Year. Latin America, 2016 (%)

Note: Total number of responses indicating corruption had "increased a lot" and those indicating it had "increased some"

it lost its charismatic leader (Rafael Correa), precisely because he was accused of personal corruption. In any case, this was a Pyrrhic victory. Lenin Moreno, elected with Correa's support, changed the strategic orientation of the reformist movement, distancing himself from any identification with Chavismo, an association or label that marginalized other Bolivarian projects.

As we can see in figure 11.1, according to data from Latinobarómetro, 62 percent of Latin Americans perceived an increase in corruption from 2015 to 2016. The highest percentages were in Venezuela, Chile, Brazil, and Peru. In these four countries, more than 78 percent of residents believed that corruption had increased. Lower percentages were noted in Argentina and Guatemala, with 41 percent and 42 percent of residents, respectively, perceiving an increase in corruption.

Corruption as a Structural Factor

At the level of methodology, this book does not engage in detailed case studies of individual countries, because our hypothesis is that, over and above the region's social and cultural diversity, there are structural elements that define Latin America. One of these is state corruption, present in almost all regimes and governments. In a certain way, the phenomenon transcends specific models of development. And it is the autonomy of state corruption with respect to these models that we would like to illustrate by considering two countries whose economic dynamism is guided by neoliberal patterns, but where systemic corruption has not affected rates of growth: Peru and Colombia.

Twenty-first-century Peru exemplifies the autonomy of economics and politics. Peruvian politics is characterized by the corruption of all presidents and presidencies that have succeeded one another since the end of the last century. In each case, they led to criminal charges against all presidents, who were imprisoned or went into exile: Alberto Fujimori, Alan García, Alejandro Toledo, Ollanta Humala, and Pedro Pablo Kuczynski. And in all of these cases there was forceful popular mobilization centered on a critique of corruption. Nevertheless, this continuous political instability, closely related to systemic corruption, has not affected sustained rates of growth in the Peruvian economy. These are the highest in the region, under the control of a mining and financial oligarchy, which has worked to tighten connections between Peru and international networks of investment and export. This has led, without ideological fuss, to the corruption of all of the presidents who have led the country's government (Ballon, 2018).

Something similar has happened in Colombia. Here, less successfully than in Peru, a disconnect has come about: on the one hand, there is a profound crisis in the political system, which remains mired in a brutal war against a narco-insurgency and finds itself attacked by narco-paramilitaries and supporters of the United States; on the other hand, there is stable economic growth overseen by the Colombian business class, heirs to the traditional oligarchy, which has been streamlined just in time to prosper under conditions of globalization.

The analytic goal of these brief discussions of Peru and Colombia is to show that when the state is weak, as in these cases, and oligarchies are strong, corruption is caused by the initiatives of the dominant economic groups, whatever the political orientation of the state. No matter the state's discourse, networks of power continue to function on their own. From the extreme neoliberalism of Fujimori to the national-popular and indigenist threat posed by Ollanta Humala, all Peruvian governments ended up as instruments in the direct service of economic power, in a strategy for using and discarding presidents, undermining the legitimacy of democracy. In the same way, conservatives and liberals in Colombia maintained consistent economic and social policies and were still mired in corruption, although in the

Colombian case the context of civil war, which threatened to cause the disintegration of the state itself, meant there was no room for criminal proceedings against presidents.

There are two common factors that would seem to be decisive in the Peruvian and Colombian cases. On the one hand, they are the two main producers of drugs in the region (Mexico serves above all as a center for distribution), with economic effects that are difficult to quantify in terms of capital. On the other hand, both Peru and Colombia are countries where active oppositions kept the state in check. In Peru, the Sendero Luminoso (Shining Path) was exterminated by Fujimori, whose legitimacy was based on his success in this effort. And in Colombia, "Uribismo," whose political legacy persists despite Álvaro Uribe's complicity in human rights violations, received support from part of the population as well as from the United States. This was on account of its brutal confrontation with guerrillas, which finally led to a state of relative peace after the insurgents' military defeat, which gave way to the political realism of Juan Manuel Santos, the president who succeeded Uribe. In the cases of both Peru and Colombia, the weakness of the state was countered by the decisive influence of the army, which was armed and trained by the United States, favored for its success in the fight against guerrillas, and strengthened by the formation of paramilitary groups working in its service. It was the alliance between business oligarchies and the armed forces that allowed for the maintenance of economic stability and control over the state. This made the political system into an appendage in the pay of these oligarchies.

In other words, state corruption adopts diverse methods, responding to the different sociopolitical dynamics of individual countries. This can even mean becoming functional in those cases where the de facto powers assume direct control, even without needing to stage military coups – that is, through the successive removal and replacement of political leaders, who are vulnerable because their ascent to power generally depends on their corruption by economic powers. The latter, incidentally, directly financed the military hierarchy, bypassing public funds. This brief summary of interactions between the state, economic power, and the workings of society is another argument for understanding the centrality of corruption. The strategic power of corruption can be seen, in both neoliberalism and neo-developmentalism, in another shift in the social structure characterized by the shrinking of the political system as an agent of the state. The fusion of economic and military power generates a corrupt state that is outside legal institutions.

182

Narcos and the State

The importance of the criminal economy in Latin America, analyzed in chapter 3, can also be seen in one of the most decisive forms of state corruption. Although reference is often made to the narco-state, we believe that it is more appropriate to differentiate among the many different relationships there are between drug trafficking and the state. These differ in their intensities and involve different kinds of infiltration of state institutions. The state is not absorbed into the criminal economy; instead, drug trafficking acts economically and socially to exercise a substantial influence on the politics of the state. This influence varies in space and time, leading to specific forms of state infiltration. In any case, we cannot understand the state in twenty-first-century Latin America without referring to the relationship between states and drug traffickers, defined as collective actors (Miguez et al., 2018).

There are two main factors at the root of this relationship. On the one hand, the action or inaction of state institutions is intrinsic to the workings of drug trafficking. Without the cooperation or collusion of these institutions, the industry could not cultivate, process, transport, or distribute illegal products in all countries; nor could it launder the money resulting from the drug trade. Nor could it exercise coercive means – that is, employ armies of hitmen as well as providers of information and purveyors of intimidation, without whom the industry could not enforce respect for its rules. These rules include the resolution of conflicts among gangs through extremely violent means. The systemic infiltration of the state is a fundamental prerequisite for the functioning of the drug economy and the criminal activities organized around it. This means the corruption, intimidation, or elimination of security forces, state functionaries, customs and transit officials, banks and financial institutions, judges, politicians, parties, mayors, governors, parliamentarians, presidents, and other government officials. Each site of infiltration guards an area of activity, and together these mechanisms create an assemblage, driven by a coordinated logic founded in the last instance on practices of extreme and irreversible violence. State corruption is consubstantial with the expansion of the criminal economy.

The second factor to consider is the extraordinary accumulation of capital that takes place in drug trafficking. This is accumulation that is extraordinary both for its volume and for its velocity. Some sources value drug trafficking at 8 percent of the total of world trade and estimate that it accounts for 5 percent of global GDP. This would be a relative importance greater than the value of the electronics and automobile industries combined. The availability of such vast resources, the ability to use them without legal limits, offers immense power to the major crime syndicates. Precisely for this reason, during the last decades of the twentieth century, there was a tendency toward the formation of oligopolistic cartels. There was also fierce competition among cartels, who enlisted various parts of the state, which they could put at their service in this violent competition. This resulted in an accumulation of power and capital in the two major economies most thoroughly infiltrated by drug traffickers: first in Colombia, then in Mexico. Bolivia and Peru joined the global network formed by this industry, but in a subordinate position as producers of raw material. With the exception of Costa Rica, smaller countries in Central America and the Caribbean were in many cases dominated by drug traffickers or by the money laundering economy. Only in these cases is the term "narco-state" appropriate.

But as the power of the *narcos* grew and the ability of the state to exercise its authority diminished, relationships between the two gradually changed. In fact, when the drug traffickers felt sufficiently powerful, especially in Colombia, they sought to legalize themselves and integrate themselves fully into the economy, as a business sector and political actor with institutional status. In addition, they created a social base in the regions and cities that they dominated, like Colonia 13 in Medellín. Even in 2018, in fact, it is common to find fresh flowers placed at Pablo Escobar's grave in Medellín. But the project failed. The deputy-elect Pablo Escobar was expelled by the Colombian Parliament. And the negotiation that took place between the cartel based in Cali and President Belisario Betancur – who met with members of the cartel in Panama and received an offer from them to pay all of Colombia's foreign debt – was blocked by the United States. This was not so much for moral reasons, but rather because the infiltration of cartels by the DEA and the CIA became a useful tool for covert action in an always booming Latin America. And when, under pressure from the United States, Colombia began extraditions to that country (contravening Colombian law), Escobar, leading a group known as "The Extraditables," declared a frontal war on the state that led to bloodshed and the destruction of cities, lasting until Escobar's prosecution and death in 1993. Although the cartel in Cali attempted to engage in more traditional forms of corruption, like the financing of President Ernesto Samper's campaign, it was also left leaderless by the intervention of the DEA. Gilberto Rodríguez Orejuela was extradited to the United States.

But this was not the end of the story. On the one hand this was because the major cartels became networks with multiple centers of activity, more difficult to repress and more adept and infiltrating the state in capillary ways. On the other hand, geopolitics and drug trafficking become increasingly interconnected. The Fuerzas Armadas Revolucionarias de Colombia (FARC, or Revolutionary Armed Forces of Colombia) recognized the possibility of financing its long revolutionary march by entering a market in which they no longer had to compete with Colombian cartels. Here they could take charge of the networks connecting Colombia with the rest of the world by way of the Mexican cartels that were then in the process of being formed. But the Colombian state under President Uribe and the DEA decided to combat insurgent drug trafficking by backing the drug trafficking of paramilitary groups that had been formed, armed, and financed by agents of the United States under the protection of the Colombian army. In this way, violence became widespread, as did insecurity and criminality in all its forms, especially in the forms of kidnapping and extortion. This persisted until President Santos, working together with Cuba and the Pope and with the acquiescence of the Obama administration, reached a peace agreement that opened new perspectives, though these remained fragile because the de facto powers retained control.

A similar process took place in Mexico, but at a scale that was even greater and through forms that offer significant analytical lessons on the workings of the state. With Colombian cartels under pressure, Mexican distribution networks, benefitting from Mexico's land border with the United States, rapidly accumulated capital during the 1990s and ultimately displaced the Colombians as key actors, relegating them to the role of suppliers, as we noted in a previous chapter. This was the epoch of cartels from Sinaloa, Ciudad Juárez (with the legendary Amado Carrillo), the Gulf, and Tamaulipas. And later came El Chapo Guzmán, also from Sinaloa. The cartels alternated between intermittent wars fought for control of local markets and export routes, on the one hand, and, on the other, periodic peace agreements when losses of life were excessive. The Mexican state entered the competition, with some of its structures opening themselves up to the corruption of the cartels, while in other cases they used the cartels' hitmen to resolve their own political contradictions. One extreme instance, analyzed by Castell in his book *The Power of Identity* (1997), was the 1994 assassination of then presidential candidate Luis Donaldo Colosio by the Sinaloa cartel, with the likely collusion of some sectors of the PRI. This party's Secretary General, José Francisco Ruiz Massieu was also assassinated, perhaps to cover over the traces of this collusion. President Ernesto Zedillo was not implicated in this unprecedented intervention by the cartels in the highest levels of Mexican politics. (The assassinations occurred during the end of the government of administration of President Carlos Salinas de Gortari, and Zedillo took office on December 1, 1994.) But his party was implicated, and this marked a fundamental change in the relationship between the *narcos* and the state. Emboldened and facing less competition from Colombia, the cartels, and especially the Sinaloa cartel, used their economic power to corrupt the state at all levels, including the office of the anti-drug czar, Jesús Gutiérrez Rebollo, who offered protection to Carrillo, who was arrested in 1997 and condemned to 40 years in prison. He did not serve this time, however, because he died of cancer in prison in 2013. Still, he and his family always claimed that in fact he was obeying orders from his superiors, aides to the president who were in the pay of drug traffickers.

The PRI lost power in 2000, and the conservative presidency of Vicente Fox saw the implementation of a new strategy, secretly agreed on with the Sinaloa cartel. According to the terms of this agreement, repression concentrated on the other cartels, while the state would maintain a privileged relationship with the Sinaloa cartel, in an arrangement approved by the DEA. The other cartels reacted violently. Paradoxically they demanded that the state remain impartial in the distribution of repression. In an effort to enforce this, they unleashed violence in their territories. New cartels, like the Zetas, emerged in the Gulf, made up of military veterans and specialized hitmen, who further heightened the confrontations with the army and with rival cartels.

The next phase in the relationship with the state was led by President Felipe Calderón, elected in 2006 on the promise of eradicating the *narcos* by force and advised by George W. Bush and José María Aznar, promoters of the "war on terror." This was apparently the most intense effort to solve the problem of drug trafficking by force. The military budget increased by 100 percent, and troop salaries were raised by 120 percent. Special units were formed, especially in the navy, the least corrupt branch of the Mexican military and the one with the closest relationship to the United States. The army grew in size to 270,000 soldiers, or one in every 541 residents, a higher proportion than in China. The war that was thus unleashed was one of the most violent conflicts in Latin America, since the *narcos* responded in kind, intimidating the population with extreme cruelty, assassinating journalists, judges, and politicians. For their part, the security forces were responsible for numerous human rights violations, according to denunciations filed with national and international organizations. The result? Some 135,000 dead and 25,000 disappeared, for nothing. To be sure, drug lords were assassinated or extradited to the United States, and the bloodiest cartels, like the Zetas, were harshly beaten, although they did not disappear but rather transformed themselves. The criminal industry continued to flourish, the atrocities continued, and at the end of Calderón's six-year term, the conflict had gotten worse, and the Mexican state drifted toward uncontrolled violence. Hence the PRI's return to power under Enrique Peña Nieto in 2012.

This signaled a revival in the party's old ways: it opened the doors to corrupt negotiations, while, as had happened in Colombia, the cartels went up in smoke, to the benefit of numerous local and regional criminal organizations spread throughout Mexico's territory. This was particularly true in Guerrero, in Michoacán where La Familia was based, in Jalisco, which saw the emergence of the extremely violent gang known as Jalisco Nueva Generación (led by El Mencho), and in Quintana Roo, where Mexican tourism, concentrated in this state, was threatened. For the first time, Mexico City was seriously affected by the presence of gangs, which no longer limited themselves to drug trafficking. Instead, they entered all markets: extortion, kidnapping, and fuel and automobile robbery.

State corruption also extended its territory and spread to different institutional spheres with this new model of criminality. Governors, mayors, and local police officers began to mix with more than 200 major criminal organizations, whose power was distributed throughout Mexico. The 2013 killing of students from a teacher training school in Ayotzinapa, Guerrero, which involved the local municipal government (led by the Partido de la Revolución Democrática [PRD, or Party of the Democratic Revolution], no less) and a cover-up by the federal government, brought the indignation in Mexican society to a boiling point. Violent crime had become an everyday and ubiquitous fact of life throughout the country.

The year 2017 was the most violent in Mexico's history, with more than 31,000 people murdered. This is why President Andrés Manuel López Obrador, elected in July 2018 in a groundswell of social support, offered an amnesty limited to low-ranking *narcos* and the withdrawal of the armed forces in exchange for peace. He rejected any interference from the DEA, which had only served to escalate the conflict. The most significant thing about this offer – whose fate remains to be seen as we write these pages, since it depends on congress and the cooperation of the security forces – is its emphasis on the re-moralization of Mexican society, in an effort to achieve an internal peace, saying "enough's enough" after the spiral of destruction in which Mexico has been involved since the erratic and thoroughly corrupt relationship between the state and the drug traffickers began. In a country of symbols, it is notable that the name chosen by President López Obrador for his new party seeks to set the direction of Mexican politics straight: Morena, or the Movimiento de Regeneración Nacional (Movement for National Regeneration). This is effectively not only a matter of governing, but one of regenerating the social and ethical fabric of society that has refused to die. But the name of the party obviously connotes the Virgen Morena as well, one of the few sources of solace and trust on which millions of Mexicans can still rely.

Thus the relation between the *narcos* and the state depends largely on the destruction or the reconstruction of the ties between society and the state. In societies in which a predatory and excluding state has taken shape, one enveloped in empty, demagogical rhetoric that has sustained cynicism and popular despair, the vultures of organized crime offered an exit for young people sick of being humiliated and of the lack of opportunities in their lives, as well as those for whom death was not a problem. The problem was the life they suffered through every day. In this way, relationships to *narcos*, an indication of the decomposition of society, depend on transformations of the state: a state that, in many ways, lives on corruption and is embroiled in an internal struggle against its own corruption.

The Revolutionary State and Corruption

If by "revolution," we mean the institutional transformation of relations of power in the state, then we could imagine a regeneration of the rules of governance that would begin with a revolutionary effort to defend those oppressed by and excluded from society.

At least, this is what Castells thought when, in 1980–1, he led a program at the University of California, Berkeley, with the aim of advising the Sandinista government in Nicaragua, which had recently emerged from a revolution, on the construction of a new system of municipal, democratic, and participatory governance. This was a program sponsored by then-Vice President Sergio Ramírez and praised by President Daniel Ortega in a televised speech to the nation. Both Ramírez and Castells broke with Ortega many years ago, after noting the process of political degeneration in Sandinismo that would lead to the bloody repression of the civil, democratic movement begun on April 18, 2018. But the analytical question posed by this new revolution, "betrayed" in its ideals, is why Sandinismo was subverted and what mechanisms have allowed it to stay in power since 2006, even after elections lost by Ortega.

In an article written in June 2018, Ramírez refers to Ortega's rule as a dictatorship, one that follows the sinister, autocratic, and violent pattern that characterizes the whole history of Nicaragua (Correa, 2018). This is a pattern that people thought they had overcome with the revolutionary ousting of the Samoza dynasty by Sandinista guerrillas and their subsequent victory against the "Contras" backed by Reagan. This movement forcefully reemerged during the first decade of the twenty-first century.

In large part, the institutional organization of state corruption, its practice by the government, seems to have been the key means by which the Sandinistas remained in power in a context of economic crisis and in a country that had been supported by Bolivarian Venezuela. In fact, Ortega's victory in 2006 was made possible by a constitutional reform agreed to by the corrupt liberal President Arnaldo Alemán, in exchange for immunity. This reform made it possible to elect a president in the first round of voting provided the candidate obtained 35 percent of votes cast. This was the highest level of popular support Ortega had reached. Once it was thus installed in government, Sandinismo made corruption systematic, colluding with key businesses, creating clientelist networks in all strategic sectors of the state, starting with the armed forces, and extending its reach into paramilitary groups formed by the most militant factions of the Frente Sandinista.

As in all systems based on authoritarianism without concessions, incentives for the beneficiaries of corruption, or those who were hooked, was combined with intimidation of the opposition, especially journalists and activists defending human rights. The development of a new middle class and the strengthening of civil society with connections to the world, with the support of the influential Episcopal Conference, led to the formation of a determined movement, especially of young people, and to the destabilization of the regime. The movement staged its most visible demonstration in a massive civil disobedience in Masaya, the very city at the center of the Sandinista revolution against Somoza.

But even so, Ortega has been president for 21 years, counting various mandates: this longest period of any president in Nicaragua's history. The installation of a parallel system of rules, controlled by the party and oblivious to the demands of citizens, is the privileged way to maintain control over the state behind the facade of a democratic system.

Although the process of political change in Hugo Chávez's Venezuela is much more complex and marked by different phases, here too we find a way of retaining power in the midst of economic chaos and political delegitimation: a practice of systemic corruption that managed to draw in the armed forces, and that divided the administration and the population into two groups: the beneficiaries or those who received the perks and those who suffered under an arbitrary system. In the case of Venezuela, however, we have to distinguish clearly between the different phases of the revolutionary process, some of which coincide with Chávez's government, others with the government of Nicolás Maduro after Chávez's death. At the origin of Chavismo, we find a popular reaction against one of the most corrupt democracies in Latin America, exemplified by President Carlos Andrés Pérez and his Acción Democrática (Democratic Action) party, and especially the repression in February 1989, in the context of structural adjustment programs, implemented with the support of the middle and upper classes. Chávez's military nationalism and his cadre of patriotic officials were stopped in their effort to stage a coup, but they ignited the revolutionary imagination in the majority of the country's poor. It is crucial to remember that Chávez won seven elections and referendums, in votes that, at the time, showed no significant evidence of fraud. This is the legitimate origin of Bolivarianism, which, aided by a boom in oil prices, proceeded to underwrite political projects similar to those undertaken throughout Latin America, forging connections with Cuba and implementing generous social policies without an economic basis to sustain them. Thus, when the global conjuncture changed, without the charismatic presence of Chávez (who couldn't be replaced), the legitimacy of the regime gradually frayed, and middle-class opposition was radicalized.

The Bolivarian state's patrimonialism was reduced to clientelist networks as its resources diminished, so that only the use of force – supported by the poor, who retained the historical memory of the pseudo-democracy that had preceded Chavismo – could allow the state to hold onto a margin of negotiating power, in order to effect an agreed-upon transition to recognized democratic institutions.

Again, deliberate corruption, focused on obtaining political support, was a way of retaining power rather than a matter of personal enjoyment or leveraging among leaders, although to be sure these leaders did not hesitate to enrich themselves in the midst of the people's suffering. In this sense, they did what those who have governed Venezuela have always done.

After this brief description of significant political processes in Nicaragua and Venezuela, we can identify a new type of corruption: corruption organized by the state as a way of coopting political and institutional actors (beginning with the armed forces) in order to remain in power through para-legal maneuvers that benefit the dominant party in electoral showdowns or judicial decisions that can provide cover for its arbitrary actions. This is a sectoralized and politicized form of corruption that causes confusion in public administration because it no longer follows an instrumental logic, instead becoming a set of specific forms of control exercised at the margins of institutions. The economy suffers, as does the legitimacy of institutions, as does social cohesion. Society is divided into factions that confront one another against a backdrop of violence.

There is an additional factor that plays a powerful role in corrupting revolutionary and counter-revolutionary processes: the influence of foreign intelligence agencies, in particular those of the United States and Cuba, which manipulate social actors and media in keeping with their geopolitical strategies. Corruption then becomes a weapon that can be used in a war of all against all, in an all-out battle that tears at societies. Inverting the classic affirmation of Carl von Clausewitz, who claimed that war was politics by other means, we can say that this is war by means of politics. The politics of corruption.

Can a State *Not* Be Corrupt?

If we suggest that state corruption is a systematic feature of Latin American societies in the twenty-first century, then, from an analytic point of view, it is necessary to consider those countries where, empirically, systematic corruption does not appear in the same way as in the countries we have been discussing. And it is necessary to explain why this is the case. We are thinking specifically of Chile, Costa Rica, and Uruguay, countries that, according to Transparency International, have low levels of corruption compared to others worldwide, as can be seen in figure 11.2, which shows various Latin American countries' rankings in the Corruption Perceptions Index, during the period from

191

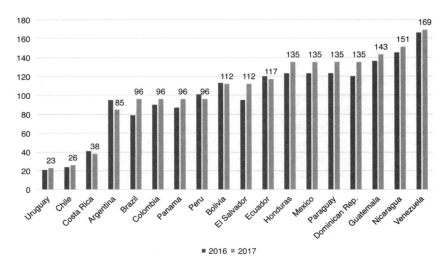

Figure 11.2: Changes in the Rankings in the Corruption Perceptions Index, Latin America, 2016–2017

2009 to 2017, when New Zealand, Finland, and Denmark were at the top of the list, that is, perceived to be least corrupt. Let us consider some factors that might account for the exceptional status of these Latin American countries, in order to determine whether there is a factor that might let us identify another type of state, not in normative terms but in terms of the situation we observe there.

In the case of Chile, it is necessary to remember that Pinochet's dictatorship was, among other things, a special case: a semi-predatory state, where perks and public resources were seized by the dictator and distributed to those in his circle of close advisors. It suffices to recall his foreign bank accounts and his 14 false passports, part of his preparation to flee the country. But within this purely parasitical and repressive state, an entrepreneurial bourgeoisie developed, a class that knew how to take advantage, in capitalist terms, of the exceptional conditions created by the dictatorship, which did away with social rights and environmental protections. Still, beginning in 1990, the governments of the Concertación Democrática brought these corrupt practices under control, implementing institutional reforms in the judiciary and professionalizing public administration. Chile was even innovative in allowing bidding on government purchases in an open and transparent web, where various offers were made. The administrations of Patricio Aylwin and Ricardo Lagos managed to drastically reduce corruption. We could call this the "democratic effect." That is, the reconstruction of democracy, with support from the majority in society, became a priority for the agents of political change, who even limited competition between different parties through a democratic agreement (the Concertación). This situation changed as it was institutionalized and normalized. In our empirical analysis of the transformation of the Chilean model of development (Calderón and Castells, 2014), we characterize democratic Chile as an efficient model of growth on the basis of a version of neoliberalism. We called this "neoliberalism with a human face." That is, it continued to guarantee the primacy of the market as a mechanism of development, centered on exports. But it also introduced social rights, led to increased salaries agreed on with unions, and, especially, fostered the creation of a network of protections in education, healthcare, and pensions (although relying on partially privatized services). The student movement, centered on the demand for equality in teaching, brought about a social shift that gave greater importance to the state. But in this very context, corruption began to expand (as in the case of La Sociedad Química y Minera de Chile or SOQUIMICH) in political parties, both on the right and in the Concertación. This corruption reached the family of President Michelle Bachelet, despite her unimpeachable honesty. The right's return to power, represented by Sebastián Piñera, a successful, ideologically neoliberal businessman supported by ultra-conservative Catholics, opened the state's doors to all manner of influences. What happened? Our hypothesis is that ideology seeps through the walls of the state. And it is difficult to be economically neoliberal and socially consumerist and keep these forces at bay. The corruption in many parties, especially on the right but also on the center-left, continued in the attenuated form of business and media influences on key sectors of the state, especially its management of the economy. Chile is no longer an exception when it comes to corruption, although there have been resistance movements in society, movements with historical memory, represented by increasingly visible social movements originating in the student movement. These have also found their cause in the struggle against corruption.

Costa Rica's model of development is in and of itself exceptional with respect to all known patterns: a sort of tropical social democracy, historically represented by the Partido de Liberación Nacional (PLN, National Liberation Party), rooted in a structural pacifism that managed to eliminate the armed forces in 1948. This was a historical decision taken by President José María Figueres after the country's civil war. Costa Rica, a society of modest farmers since its origins and one without extractive riches that would have whet the appetites of multinational corporations, knew to keep its distance from the violence in Central America, playing a neutral role and maintaining a strategic alliance with the United States. Building on good education and healthcare systems, the country created a model of modern development centered on electronics, eco-tourism, organic agriculture, and specialized exports (especially of fresh cut flowers), while also retaining its traditional coffee sector. This has sufficed to satisfy the needs of this small country, which values its peace and its democracy above all else.

Nevertheless, global connections led to cases of corruption at the highest levels of the state (as in the case of France Telecom), controlled by an independent and active judiciary that did not hesitate to imprison the former president Miguel Ángel Rodríguez. In fact, the destabilization of the political system came from the opposition of new middle classes who were critical of the PLN's traditional bureaucracy, and especially from a group of religious fundamentalists who formed a curious alliance between evangelicals and the Catholic Church. This alliance nearly won the presidency in 2018. In any case, references to corruption were intermittent and of secondary importance for the opposition. The key factor in citizens' discontent, which led to two presidential victories for a new party (the Partido de Acción Ciudadana, or Citizens' Action Party), was insecurity caused by the infiltration of criminal networks from other countries. We can therefore speak of Costa Rican exceptionalism, in that systemic state corruption has not arisen there. The country's exceptionality comes from its political history; the consolidation of its democracy through the elimination of the danger of military coups; the strengthening of its independent judiciary; and the absence of economic groups, whether national or international, with enough power to subjugate the state. But there is another factor: the low level of inequality, combined with high rates of education, both structurally linked to a profound belief in democracy. In this sense, Costa Rica can offer a formula for limiting state corruption: long-standing policies that promote equality, legitimacy, and the stability of democratic institutions, all built on the foundation of an elimination of the risk of military coups.

The other possible exception is Uruguay, long considered the "Switzerland of Latin America" until the brutal military dictatorship that, working with Argentina's dictatorship, took the revolutionary Tupamaro movement as a pretext for terrorizing the country. But the overcoming of this dark period in Uruguay's history perhaps suggests that a new democratic impulse has transformed Uruguay, especially since the calm, charismatic presidency of José Mujica (the local Mandela), into a relatively coherent society, one with a state in which corruption is reduced and a model of development all its own. This model is based on an agricultural form of informational extractivism, but it includes a welfare state that offers strong social support. Key to the health of this democracy are a population with high levels of education and a robust democratic consciousness. Any effort to corrupt the state at a grand scale would have to face an active movement against those corrupted and the corruptors.

Peace, democracy, education, decreased social inequality, a welfare state, and antimilitarism: these would seem to be the antidotes to state corruption in Latin America. They are present in the two small countries that seem relatively immune to the phenomena that characterize the state in almost the whole rest of the region. The question is whether this formula for anticorruption is scalable.

Conclusion: The Consequences of State Corruption

The first and most important consequence of state corruption is the destruction of the bond of trust between those who govern and the governed. Democratic legitimacy depends on this bond. And this cuts across ideological positions. It is not a matter of right against left, or dictatorship against democracy. Simply put, the majority of citizens distrust any ideological formation that is in power. There is thus a retreat into individualism, into strategies of free-for-all that give up on the idea of the common good. Because the common has been appropriated by a succession of actors who are not recognized as legitimate by the rest. Because they obtain power through the destruction of their opponents for their own benefit. Thus the destruction of trust also leads to the breakage of national community; it separates the state from the nation and opens an era of immediate domination by global networks, characterized by individual strategies of competition in these networks.

The second feature that is becoming dominant is the consecration of a politics of scandal, which has become the formula for political conflict. Conflicts are no longer resolved through institutions but rather in the skewed public space formed by the media and social networks, which are often manipulated. Mass-mediated politics consists in the destruction of the image of one's political opponent, the exposure of his or her corruption. Who is more corrupt and who is to

195

be believed?: these, rather than any programs or ideologies, become the criteria for political choices.

In this context, the judicialization of politics becomes the ultimate means of resolving conflicts. Because beyond the acknowledgment of judicial decision, there is only the pure and simple violence of direct confrontation. But if we do not believe in the angelic nature of the judiciary and we accept personal bias, then the naming of justices and the formation of judicial and constitutional panels becomes a real means of exercising control over the state apparatus. Which, in a certain way, brings us back to our point of departure, because the possibility of judicial corruption blocks the way to any exit from state corruption at all.

— 12 —

IN THE *KAMANCHAKA*

In the recent political history of Latin America, despite enormous efforts and equally great sacrifices, societies and social actors have been unable to resolve crucial questions related to democracy. And here we are referring not only to the general problems with institutions, representation, and citizens' participation that are common to many contemporary societies, problems that have been underscored by Touraine and Castells in their respective books on democracy (Touraine, 1994; Castells et al., 2017). We are also referring to the persistence of hard limits to the development of democracy. These include the persistence of an egocentric logic and culture among powerful elites who have not only increased their own wealth, but have also increased human misery. We also have in mind the persistence of corrupt, clientelist, and bureaucratic practices in the state and society, whatever the political orientation of the regime in power. It turns out to be so difficult to follow the law … Another hard limit to the development of democracy in the region results from a chronic lack of justice and genuine liberty, especially for the dispossessed. And finally, we have in mind hard limits that result from maintenance, and at times the growth, especially in moments of crisis, of hidden and parallel forms of power: intelligence agencies, various lobbies, and opaque financial systems. All of these factors forcefully limit democracy in Latin America, and they are more evident in the context of today's multidimensional global crisis. They are also more evident in light of the new, regressive political conjunctures or regressions in democracy that have followed from the emergence of conservative, ultranationalist movements with broad social support in the region.

On October 28, 2018, Jair Bolsonaro was elected president of Brazil by a sizeable majority. This marked the culmination of a political crisis in Latin America's largest country, a crisis that had begun in 2013 with massive youth demonstrations against corruption and in defense of rights. The crisis continued with the election of the most right-wing congress in Brazil's history, and with Dilma Rousseff's removal from office by this same congress, half of whose deputies were implicated in corruption by the justice department. But the election of Captain Bolsonaro also had a more profound significance, because throughout his 27-year-long political career, after retiring from the army, he refused to hide his preference for the military dictatorship against which millions of Brazilian citizens had struggled. Nor did he hide his sexist, racist, homophobic, fascist, and antidemocratic opinions, or the fact that he was in favor of torture and military control over society. On the contrary, he expressed these opinions in the coarsest and most brutal ways, so that there could be no doubt about his holding them. That a majority of Brazilians, among them many young people, communicating with each other on WhatsApp, would vote for this person was an indication of a mental and political transformation in Brazil, one that had undermined the legitimacy of the democracy that so many had longed for during the decades of dictatorship. And that major national and foreign corporations would greet Bolsonaro's election with enthusiasm was also an indication of the weakness of their democratic commitments, as opposed to their economic interests. Because what Bolsonaro promised under the banner of authoritarianism was simply the promotion of the neoliberal model: the privatization of the public sector and the liberalization of markets. Or rather, a return to the so-called Washington Consensus, which had already failed throughout Latin America in the 1990s.

What Bolsonaro promised with his nationalist, militarist ideology was a return to dictatorial neoliberalism in an idealized form, *à la* Pinochet, a return to a past form of neoliberalism that has stopped working economically in every part of the world, as Castells showed in his books *Rupture: The Crisis of Liberal Democracy* (2019) and *Europe's Crises* (2018). This imagined return is aligned with Donald Trump's ideology and with the redefinition of the United States' interest in Latin America. Here an illusion prevails: the fantasy of returning to what was in fact a terrible past that did not even work for the ideologues of the end of history. It is worth emphasizing, however, that unlike the Latin American dictatorships of the 1970s and 1980s, which hid the atrocities and the genocides that they were committing, Bolsonaro touted his openly. Of course, this nightmare, which has become a reality thanks to democracy, is inseparable from the de-structuring of the state and from cases of structural corruption in Brazil including Lava Jato (or Operation Car Wash) and especially Odebrecht. The latter scandal involved various countries in the region in the financing of political parties and implicated figures from across almost the whole ideological spectrum.

Although they are led by figures who are different from the stereotypical Bolsonaro, politically conservative movements are emerging in most countries in the region, returning power to a more retrograde right wing and economic control to national oligarchs and global markets, as in Argentina and Chile. In Argentina, despite considerable progress made in the struggle for human rights, the limits of previous governments' Kirchnerism are inseparable from the state's inability to resolve basic questions related to its constitution. These include questions about the acts of terrorism that targeted the Israeli Embassy and the Asociación Mutual Israelita Argentina (AIMA, or Argentine Israelite Mutual Association) in the 1990s, and other questions about historical and structural forms of corruption among many of the country's elites and much of its political class and the inefficiency of a justice system that is inherently slow and susceptible to manipulation. The result is a confused hodgepodge, where corruption, conspiracies by intelligence agencies, and judicial spectacles promoted by the media generate even more confusion and anguish. In this way, even a country as creative as Argentina sees its potential burn to the ground.

In Peru, politics has become judicialized, and state corruption of the kind associated with Odebrecht, for example, and with the limits of neoliberalism exacerbates the breakdown of democracy in the region. The drawn-out and dramatic end of Fujimorismo has not given way to a political replacement. In fact, four successive presidents have ended up in prison or in exile.

In Chile, the crisis of one model of development and one political system that had been successful for 20 years, driven by the Concertación, culminated in a return to neoliberalism, supported by ultraconservatives like those in the Unión Democratica Independiente (UDI, or Independent Democratic Union), and by Senator José Antonio Kast, who is deeply identified with Bolsonaro.

In Colombia, although President Juan Manuel Santos, successor to Álvaro Uribe, who protected paramilitaries, managed to sign a peace treaty with the rebel Fuerzas Armadas Revolucionarias de Colombia (FARC, or Revolutionary Armed Forces of Colombia) and Ejército de Liberación Nacional (ELN, or National Liberation Army) after decades of civil war, the population's wounds remain open, to the point that the majority of citizens voted against the treaty. They wanted neither peace nor forgiveness, but instead war and death, served with a combination of vengeance and a sense of justice.

Among the progressive movements in the south, we can point to the social and cultural changes brought by neo-developmental and indigenist movements in Bolivia, but these have taken place in a context of heightened political polarization, accusations of corruption and state authoritarianism, and an institutional crisis that involved both the judiciary and the National Electoral Court. The revolutionary movements in Venezuela and Nicaragua have degenerated into authoritarian governments that, for a time, resisted with bloodshed and fire both internal opposition and foreign conspiracies, but have now been plunged into economic chaos, poverty, and famine. The roads of Latin America have been filled with refugees, who at times find themselves rejected and discriminated against by their Latin American brothers and sisters. While an almost biblical exodus has led thousands from Honduras to try to reach the promised land in the north, they have found that the doors have been closed by a disproportionate military deployment. Perhaps only Costa Rica and Uruguay can continue to sail against the wind.

In Mexico, in a limit situation of social and institutional disintegration, a shock to the system came from the election of Andrés Manuel López Obrador (known as AMLO), a political veteran who had spent a long time working to counter the effects of institutional decay. In this sense, we share the hope held by many Mexican people for a profound political change, although we are also conscious, as is AMLO more than anyone, of the difficulties and dangers that he will have to confront in his effort to renew the country.

The crisis in the region was much more than a collapse in the process of sociopolitical change after the successive failures of neoliberalism and neo-developmentalism. It was related to the breakdown in trust in institutions and a breakdown in trust between people. It was, and is, a crisis of coexistence, a crisis that follows from the perception of the "other," any other, as a potential threat. On the walls of El Alto, on the periphery of La Paz, we read, "Ladrón pillado, ladrón quemado" [A thief caught is a thief burned]. And so it was in a good number of cases. So it was in the lynching of thieves and murderers of children in Chichicastenango, a beautiful city in Guatemala, and in numerous other places in the region's geography of fear.

This fear is sustained by the reality of rampant criminality, enabled in part by the collusion or the passivity of police. So in Mexico, in 2018, 10,000 calls for ransom were recorded every day, and it was found that the majority of the calls came from cellular phones in just seven prisons. This clearly proved that citizens were vulnerable, the victims of corrupt functionaries in all realms of the state. 2018 was ultimately the most violent year in Mexico's history, both in terms of homicides and in terms of disappearances. Those who sought to oppose this epidemic of violence were its first victims. In particular, the journalists who investigated and denounced the crimes risked their lives, and for taking this risk, they lost their lives, in fact. Consider Sergio Martínez González, director of the online seminar Enfoque, murdered in Tuxtla Gutiérrez, on the border with Guatemala, on October 3, 2018. There was nothing special about this journalist; he was one of many, and less visible than many others. For this reason, we mention him, in order to pay homage to an unknown journalist.

In Rio de Janeiro, those who murdered Marielle Franco, the city councilor, on March 15, 2018, have never been found. Marielle was a charismatic Afro-Brazilian leader, a defender of the *favelados*, or those living in Rio's slums, and a critic of police and military intervention. Hence, we suspect, her death sentence.

The criminal economy extended into numerous realms, competing and commanding through the work of various gangs of hitmen, who teem in the neighborhoods of the region's megacities. The cartels, targets of politically profitable repression, gave way after their collapse to a structure of violence distributed across hundreds of groups, thousands throughout Latin America, and these are ever more violent. This is what in Mexico they call "the cockroach effect."

In the ruins of all political projects and of a democracy with little credibility, fragmented societies are all that is left. In these societies, people can only count on themselves, and sometimes on their families. The Catholic Church, traditionally a source of spiritual support for much of the population in the region, has been beset by scandals and is marked by arrogance. This does not include, however, the many religious men and women whose daily devotional practice involves a commitment to the poor and the most disadvantaged. At a time when the Church has been in crisis, many evangelical congregations have prospered, congregations that in many cases are ultraconservative and "do business" with the desperation of the most disadvantaged people, who find a refuge in their churches. But from the rubble of institutions, new projects and new experiences can emerge. Still, these projects, these emergent efforts at reconstruction, take place under extremely difficult conditions, conditions of darkness and uncertainty. In fact, searching for a word that, at the end of our analysis, might begin to capture Latin America's current experience, we venture the following: *kamanchaka*.

Kamanchaka is an Aymara word used to describe the dense fog that occasionally envelops mining encampments and valleys in the Andes. But a *kamanchaka* is not a fog like any other. It is dark (this is what the Aymara term means: darkness); it totally blocks vision and penetrates the lungs. It oppresses and distresses. It is associated with myths and legends that describe disorientation, the loss of direction, the absence of visible paths. This is perhaps also a way to describe the situation in which Latin America has been living since the first two decades of the third millennium. Clearly, human beings always end up finding paths, even if we do not know where we are going. But in order to search for these paths, we have to begin from where we are, or rather without knowing where we are or how we can exit the fog. We have to proceed with historical patience and an awareness of the crisis, until we see a spark that shines with the color of hope.

IN PLACE OF A CONCLUSION: THE COLOR OF HOPE

Despite the *kamanchaka* that is the result of recent Latin American history, we can also recognize the force of today's social actors, their ability to produce a new society capable of struggling and renewing life. There are two social dynamics in particular that are worth highlighting in this context of institutional and experiential crisis: the creative dynamics visible especially in the world of work, and the resistance of sociocultural movements. A particularly hopeful sign in the world of work, especially the world of informal workers, is the existence of a double code that, on the one hand, allows them to play with and to reinvent productive roles in their communities, unions, neighborhoods, workshops, stores, and especially families as they develop practices, abilities, and strategies for production, reproduction, and self-esteem that then allow them reassert their human dignity, every day. But consider, on the other hand, their capacity for resistance, organization, and social creation in different, crucial political moments in the region's history.

One characteristic of the struggle for democracy has stood out since this struggle's beginnings. It is worth highlighting this here, bearing in mind the range of temporalities and politics in the region: one way or another, and despite their conflicts and differing political and ideological orientations, social movements have placed the issues of human rights and human dignity at the center of their work. They have sought to act autonomously, responding to the challenge of reaching emancipatory and egalitarian horizons and realizing the creative capacity to imagine changed lives and forms of coexistence among different peoples.

From this perspective, the movements for human rights from the pre-democratic period stand out, as in the case of the miners' wives in Bolivia in the 1970s, or the famous Mothers and Grandmothers of the Plaza de Mayo in Buenos Aires. With their ethical examples, these movements created a humanistic culture that was critical of power. Similarly, a wide range of new movements emerged throughout the region not only to demand democracy but to call for a new form of life. They sought to build new political and cultural practices on the basis of foundational principles: the value of human life, justice, and especially the critique of power, whatever its ideological orientation. These were clearly not only new ways of doing politics, but also new ways of making society. They did not pursue political power, but rather sought new forms of sociability anchored in everyday life. The examples of several of the leaders of these movements are fundamental. In this connection, it is worth remembering Domitila Chungara, the leader of the miners' wives in Bolivia, who insisted on speaking out in the midst of repression and who staged hunger strikes that showed that the only response to the *kamanchaka* is resistance, combined with patience. Her role in the fall of the dictatorship of Hugo Banzer and the introduction of democracy in Bolivia was central.

These movements lost their force during the long neoliberal period, but they left an inheritance that has been crucial for the new movements that were reignited at the end of the twentieth century. The beginning of the twenty-first century was a historical turning point that allowed for a long progressive period, with various manifestations, in much of the region. These various movements, though dispersed and not always in contact with one another, pointed to the necessity of connecting citizens' deliberative participation with democratic institutions, especially at the territorial level. The experience of "participatory budgeting" in Porto Alegre and its reproduction in various Brazilian cities and in other countries in the region, including Peru, Colombia, and Argentina, was important. The World Social Forum in Porto Alegre was also a point of reference that was not only regional but global. It allowed for debates throughout Latin America among different social and political leaders. In this respect, the role that Brazil played in the workers' movement and in the experience of peasant struggles fought by the "landless" was especially significant. But the fundamental thing remains the inclusion and participation of these actors and movements in neo-developmentalist projects in various countries, where what stood out was the connection between these movements and charismatic leaders, who organized political projects that led to concentrations of power, as we see almost everywhere in the region today. In these decisive moments, a sort of "autonomous citizen" emerged, one whose political decisions were based on analytic reflection and the capacity to bring together different choices in the construction of individual autonomy. For this reason, crossover votes increased. But we should not forget that a significant part of society found authoritarian choices legitimate or simply did not vote. For example, in 2002, a study sponsored by the United Nations Development Programme, "La democracia en América Latina," 54.7 percent of citizens said that they would support an authoritarian government if it could resolve economic problems (UNDP, 2004). And in Chile's presidential election in 2017, only 50 percent of the population voted, and the other 50 percent was largely made up of young people. This suggests that there is an increasing apathy or indifference to the political system, a tendency that has been observable since the beginning of the century. That is to say, the current *kamanchaka* has its roots in the past.

During the second decade of the present century, under neo-developmentalist as well as liberal regimes, in a context of change and multidimensional global crisis, new sociocultural movements were born again. Among them, the women's and gender movements stand out, as do ethnocultural movements including the movements led by people of indigenous and African descent. So, too, do environmental and youth movements, with the latter advocating support for education and ethics in politics. All of these movements are closely linked to the informational changes that have taken place in the last 20 years. They are new, emergent actors in the information age, and their action also depends on the culture, the experience, and the habitus of past struggles. In other words, for them one challenge involves the resignification of human rights struggles, and of other past struggles for ethical societies and politics. These will need to be resignified in the context of a new society of networks and a new techno-economy of information and communication. What's more, these networks and this economy are already a constitutive part of the new movements.

Current women's movements act in the midst of a crisis in the legitimacy of the patriarchy and the structure of the nuclear family. They are strengthened by the proactive role that they play in the world of information. Among young people of different ages and social classes, we can see a capacity for acting, a capacity for transforming goals into realities. Such capacities are greater for women than for men, and women's participation grows, if only incrementally, every day. Many women finally see themselves as the leaders of their own destinies, often responding to femicides: the taking of a life is a limit.

Countless women reject the world that is offered to them, questioning the hypocrisy and the dated values and obsolete ideologies of their ancestors and even their contemporaries. This change in cultural power in Latin American societies is surely one of the most powerful transformations that the region has experienced in recent years, even while it participates in various global feminist networks. It is only just beginning.

Movements led by people of indigenous and African descent are long-standing in the region's history, but now they are being redefined by claims to identity and political autonomy. The construction of the Plurinational State in Bolivia, which seeks to give institutional form to cultural identities and regional diversities in a system of institutionalized coexistence, is a revealing example of one such recent process of construction.

Similarly, environmental movements, often identified with indigenous peoples, represent communal and personal responses to the effects of the new informational extractivism. These movements are glocal, radiating outward from their territories to connect actions and communications globally. One advantage they have is the perception of their legitimacy and support in national and international public opinion. For instance, Mapuche leaders in Vaca Muerta in Argentina – who are opposing one of the most significant projects for the extraction of oil and gas in the world – are connected to regional and international networks. Many of these movements, although they are more reactive than proactive, have drawn attention to values and perspectives that center on the earth and animal life, including human relationships to nature. The women coffee producers in Colombia, who combine creative forms of work with environmental sustainability and high-quality products, represent another novel case of this.

Finally, young people today oscillate politically between a desire to participate, especially at a local level, in the building of solutions to problems that afflict society, and a countervailing sense of overwhelming pessimism and hyper-individualization. Youth movements were and are crucial mainly because of their ability to use information to move through the modern world, making demands related to the strategic values of education, science, and technology in development, and questioning political and corporate corruption. In these movements, we find a search for a new ethics capable of governing both politics and development.

The question is whether these movements have the capacity to grow and to create alternatives in the midst of *kamanchaka* and crisis, in a context of global changes, and in the face of an enormously destructive power that rules so much of the world.

We do not know. For now, these movements build a future out of a difficult and complex present.

ABOUT THE AUTHORS

Fernando Calderón, in 2018, is the Simón Bolívar Chair in Latin American Studies at the University of Cambridge. He is also director of the Program on Innovation, Development, and Multiculturalism at the Universidad Nacional de San Martín, Buenos Aires. He has taught at the Universidad de Chile and the Universidad Católica de Valparaíso, as well as at the Universidad de San Andrés in La Paz and the Universidad de San Simón in Cochabamba; in the Facultad Latinoamericana de Ciencias Sociales; and at the University of Chicago, the University of Texas-Austin, Cornell University, and the University of California, Berkeley. He has been an invited speaker and professor at several Latin American universities and in many other parts of the world. He has also been the Executive Secretary of the Consejo Latinoamericano de Ciencias Sociales (CLACSO), Advisor on Social Policy for the Economic Commission for Latin America and the Caribbean, and Special Regional Advisor on Human Development and Governance for the United Nations Development Agency in Latin America. He has coordinated and advised more than ten reports on human development at the national, regional, and global levels, and directed the Proyecto de Análisis Político y Prospectiva para América latina (PAPEP), for which he led studies on political change in Latin America. Recently, he was professor in the Facultad Latinoamericana de Ciencias Sociales (FLACSO) in Argentina and at the Universidad de Córdoba, the Universitat Oberta de Catalunya, and the Universidad Alberto Hurtado in Santiago de Chile.

Calderón has been an invited researcher at the Institute for Global Studies at the Maison de Sciences de l'Homme, Paris, and in the School of Communication at the University of Southern California.

He has published 24 books on issues related to social movements, politics, culture, and development and edited 35 collections on these issues.

Manuel Castells, in 2018, is Professor Emeritus of Sociology and Urban Planning at the University of California, Berkeley, as well as a professor of sociology at the Universitat Oberta de Catalunya and professor of communications at the University of Southern California. He has taught and completed research at the Facultad Latinoamericana de Ciencias Sociales, Chile, and at the Catholic Universities of Chile, Campinas, and Brasilia, at the Universidad Central de Venezuela, the Universidad de Puerto Rico, the Universidad de San Simón de Cochabamba, and the Universidad Iberoamericana de Santo Domingo as well as at the Universidad Nacional Auotónoma de México, the Universidad Autónoma Metropolitana in Mexico, the Universidad de Guadalajara, the Universidad Nacional de San Martín in Buenos Aires, and the Universidad de Córdoba. He has published 30 books on issues related to information technology, development, urbanism, politics, and social movements.

NOTES

Notes to Chapter 1

1 For more detail, see BID (2016).
2 https://elpais.com/especiales/2016/guerra-narcotrafico-mexico/

Notes to Chapter 2

1 The main source for the history that we recount in this section is the study edited by F. Calderón, *Extractivismo informacional y territorialidades en Argentina. Un estudio comparativo sobre el litio en Olaroz, el gas y el petróleo en Vaca Muerta y la soja en Casares*. A previous version was presented at Asociacion Latinoamericana de Sociologia (ALAS) XXXI Congreso. Panel: "America Latina en la era de la Informacion y Multiculturalismo," Montevideo, 2017. This section is based on case studies on the production of lithium, soy, and unconventional hydrocarbons. These studies are: "El Extractivismo Agrícola Informacional en la Argentina: el caso de Los Grobo y las disputas territoriales socioambientales en la era de la Información," by Juan Wahren; "Extractivismo informacional, territorio y desarrollo: el caso de YPF S.A. en Vaca Muerta," by Ignacio Cretini; and "Minería del litio en el Salar de Olaroz," by Debora Pragier and Juan Pablo Deluca.
2 For more detail, see the section "Long Life, Expandable & Sustainable Resource" at: https://salesdejujuy.com/projects/
3 It is worth mentioning, however, that some of these communities have managed to acquire visibility for their demands through collaboration with other actors, including the Multisectorial contra el Fracking (made up of students, the members of the Asamblea por Agua, and workers from Zanon, among others), during protests that took place in 2013 against an agreement between YPF SA and Chevron (Cretini, 2018).
4 On the one hand, the members of the CTA and indigenous communities report on different oil pollution sites. On the other hand, representatives of the corporation and of departments within the university contend that there is no surface water pollution in the area, and probably no groundwater pollution either (Cretini, 2018).

Notes to Chapter 3

1 For more details on drug trafficking in Latin America, see Escobar (2014).
2 For more details, see https://elpais.com/especiales/2016/guerra-narcotrafico-mexico/#tab-1
3 https://www.infobae.com/sociedad/policiales/2018/01/09/con-la-caida-de-los-monos-dos-familias-narco-se-disputan-el-poder-en-rosario-a-sangre-y-fuego/

Notes to Chapter 4

1 See also the data presented in the website that accompanies this book (available at www.fondodeculturaeconomica.com/apendices/014607R, as well as on the Polity page for *The New Latin America*.
2 See, for example, Svampa (2001) and (2004) for analyses of the emergence of private neighborhoods and country clubs in Argentina.
3 Latin America is exposed to a range of natural dangers, including those stemming from earthquakes, volcanos, storms, extreme temperatures, droughts, floods, and landslides, among others, many regularly worsened by the phenomenon known as the El Niño-Southern Oscillation. It is likely that the global tendency toward greater climate variability will exacerbate many of these dangers. In fact, many of the region's major cities are located near or above seismic faults. Population growth and rapid urbanization cause many cities to expand onto plains susceptible to flooding or hillsides where landslides occur. The growth of informal settlements, unregulated urban expansion, unsafe construction practices, environmental degradation, and poor basic infrastructure all further worsen social and economic vulnerability in various countries, especially for those who are poorest and already most vulnerable. In a World Bank study of natural disasters, seven of the fifteen most vulnerable countries in the world were in Latin America or the Caribbean (Jordán et al., 2017: 262).
4 In the 2018 Mercer Quality of Living Survey, no Latin American or Caribbean city was among the 20 highest-ranked in the world. The highest ranked city in South America is Montevideo (77), followed by Buenos Aires and Santiago, ranked 91 and 92, respectively (Mercer, 2018).
5 According to the Small Arms Survey, in 2016 Brazil, Mexico, and Venezuela were among the ten countries with the highest rates of violent death in the world (McEvoy and Hideg, 2017: 18). In the same study, we find that between 2015 and 2016 deaths per 100,000 residents caused by firearms increased in Brazil and Venezuela (McEvoy and Hideg, 2017: 50), and homicides caused by firearms increased 30 percent and 29 percent in Chile and Uruguay from 2005 to 2011 and from 2011 to 2016, respectively (McEvoy and Hideg, 2017: 51).
6 For an analysis on the status of this imaginary, Escobar Díaz (2014).

Notes to Chapter 5

1 This section is based on UNDP (2009) and on Calderón and Szmukler (2014).
2 Between 2006 and 2016, young Latin Americans' perceptions of the main problems affecting their countries changed. In 2006, the most frequently

mentioned worry was unemployment; in 2016, people surveyed between the ages of 16 and 25 most frequently mentioned delinquency and public safety (Latinobarómetro, 2018).

3 For an interactive map of the movements of global migrants, one that is constantly being updated, see https://www.iom.int/world-migration

Notes to Chapter 7

1 For more details on this subject, see Mallimaci (2008).
2 For more detail, see Morello (2010).

Notes to Chapter 8

1 "Thirty kilometers from Cuzco, in a place called Paccari Tampu (or 'place of procreation'), you could see a hill called Tampu Tocco (or 'the house with the windows'), with its many openings.

"According to this account, the *ayllus* that formed the Inca Empire emerged from these openings. After the god Viracocha gave shape to the world, Manco Cápac, who at this time was called Ayar Manco, appeared through one of the openings, together with his brothers, Ayar Auca, Ayar Cachi, and Ayar Uchú, and their four wives, Mama Ocllo, Mama Huaco, Mama Cora, and Mama Raua" (https://pueblosoriginarios.com/sur/andina/inca/ayar.html, 2018).

2 We have relied on studies by Marcos Yvon Le Bot, José Bengoa, and Xavier Albó in our effort to understand these intercultural dynamics. On the Colombian case, see Escobar (2018).

3 See the *Pronunciamiento conjunto que el Gobierno Federal y el Ejército Zapatista de Liberación Nacional enviarán a las instancias de debate y decisión nacional*, San Andrés Accords (February 16, 1996).

4 For further details, see Rosenstone (1990).

5 Chile is divided into 14 regions. Each one is assigned both a name and a Roman numeral, with numerals arranged from north to south.

6 According to the *Mapa de la Violencia 2014*, "while among white people [the rate of homicide] fell by 24.8%, among black people it rose by 387%. Since the national rate of homicide remained stable during this period, we can conclude that the logic of socially produced violence became more selective. Translated into numbers, this means that during the period from 2002 to 2012, 72% more black people were killed than white people" (Waiselfisz, 2014).

7 For this information, see IPEA (2015).

8 For more detail, see IPEA (2015), Jaccoud (2008), and Olbemo (2012).

9 http://diarioalfil.com.ar/2014/06/16/las-madres-de-mayo-brasilenas-independientes/

Notes to Chapter 9

1 This phrase refers to a "concept formulated by the American sociologist William Isaac Thomas (1863–1967), who stated that 'facts' do not have a

uniform existence apart from the persons who observe and interpret them. Rather, the 'real' facts are the ways in which different people come into and define situations. Famously, as he and his research assistant and wife Dorothy Swaine Thomas (1899–1977) put it in 1928, 'If men define situations as real, they are real in their consequences.' Such a 'subjective' definition of the situation by a social actor, group, or subculture is what Merton came to call a self-fulfilling prophecy (as in cases of 'mind over matter'). It is at the heart of symbolic interactionism." See the entry for Thomas's theorem in *A Dictionary of Media and Communication*.

2 For a more detailed analysis of multimedia conglomerates in Latin America, we refer readers to the data presented on the website that accompanies this book.

3 In this connection, see Rachel Boynton's *Our Brand Is Crisis* at www.teledocu mentales.com/our-brand-is-crisis-subtitulado. Boynton's film is about Gonzalo Sánchez de Lozada's 2002 presidential campaign in Bolivia.

4 For further information, see Nogueira (2013).

5 See Morales *et al.* (2017).

Notes to Chapter 10

1 Ideological and political radicalization and confrontations between friends and enemies have very negative effects on governance and democratic coexist-ence. It is therefore crucial to protect democratic spaces and conflicts and to protect political and ideological coexistence.

2 This section is taken from Calderón and Szmukler (2014).

3 During the period between 2002 and 2010, many countries in the region doubled their internet use, from 19 percent to 39 percent (Latinobarómetro, 2010). More recent data from 2016 show that on average 60 percent of residents of selected Latin American countries use the internet. This is an increase of 25 percentage points from 2010. In 2016, there were around 118 mobile phone subscriptions for every 100 residents (International Telecommunication Union, 2018). See also chapter 5 in this book.

4 An analysis of the movement can be found in Monteverde et al. (2013).

5 For a detailed guide to how both sets of medications should be used, see World Health Organization (2014: 28–33).

6 See https://legislativo.parlamento.gub.uy/temporales/leytemp5723191.htm

7 In Argentina, Misoprostol was marketed under the name Oxaprost; in Peru and Colombia, it was marketed under the name Cyotec, among others. Although abortion is not legal in either of these countries, Misoprostol can be obtained because it was developed as a gastric protector. However, the drug's side effects for women include uterine contractions. For more on the availabil-ity of Misoprostol, see https://www.womenonwaves.org/en/map/country

8 Ochoa et al. (2017).
http://www.telam.com.ar/notas/201410/81514-culmino-el-29-encuentro-naci onal-de-mujeres-con-fuerte-reclamo-por-la-legalizacion-del-aborto.html
http://www.bbc.com/mundo/noticias/2011/01/110112_mexico_juarez_susana _chavez_an.shtml
http://www.lanacion.com.ar/1799162-niunamenos-tras-la-manifestacion-cre an-una-unidad-de-registro-de-femicidios,http://www.lanacion.com.ar/184968

8-fabiana-tunez-presidira-el-consejo-nacional-de-mujereshttp://www.unidiver
sidad.com.ar/el-mundo-clamo-ni-una-menos
http://www.sociales.uba.ar/wp-content/blogs.dir/219/files/2010/11/encuesta-n
i-una-menos-COPES-INFORME-FINAL-enero-2016.pdf
http://bastadesexismo.blogspot.com.ar/2015/06/niunamenos-la-hipocresia-de-
una.html
http://www.lanacion.com.ar/1848532-realizan-la-primera-encuesta-sobre-viol
encia-de-genero-en-capital-federal
http://entremujeres.clarin.com/genero/NiUnaMenos-tuitazo-violencia_0_1582
641837.html
http://www.clarin.com/extrashow/fama/famosos-unieron-campana_0_158864
1231.html
https://www.pagina12.com.ar/diario/elpais/1-300967-2016-06-04.html
http://www.lanacion.com.ar/1945528-multitudinaria-marcha-del-encuentro-n
acional-de-mujeres-en-rosario
https://www.pagina12.com.ar/diario/elpais/subnotas/311435-79335-2016-10-
10.html
http://www.lanacion.com.ar/1948651-vestidas-de-negro-las-mujeres-pararon-
durante-una-hora
http://www.lanacion.com.ar/1948677-la-protesta-contra-los-femicidios-se-co
nvirtio-en-un-clamor-nacional
http://www.radioagricultura.cl/2016/10/19/video-el-mensaje-de-michelle-bach
elet-por-la-marcha-ni-una-menos/
https://www.pagina12.com.ar/diario/ultimas/20-312165-2016-10-19.html
https://www.pagina12.com.ar/diario/sociedad/3-312291-2016-10-21.html
http://www.lanacion.com.ar/1948746-highton-de-nolasco-los-jueces-no-pue
den-dejar-a-todo-el-mundo-preso-de-por-vida
9 For information on protests and conflicts related to the environment, organized by country, see https://ejatlas.org/

REFERENCES

Introduction

Calderón, F. (ed.). (2003). *¿Es sostenible la globalización en América Latina? Debates con Manuel Castells, 2 Vols.* Santiago de Chile: Programa de las Naciones Unidas para el Desarrollo Bolivia-Fondo de Cultura Económica.

Calderón, F. (ed.). (2018). *Navegar contra el viento. América Latina en la era de la información.* San Martín: Universidad de San Martín.

Chapter 1

Araníbar, A., Canedo, F., and Vicente, M. (2013). "Perú: la hora de la inclusión." In Araníbar, A. and Rodríguez, B. (eds.). *América Latina, ¿del neoliberalismo al neodesarrollismo? Cuaderno de Prospectiva Política 3.* Buenos Aires: Siglo XXI.

BID (2016). *Síntesis del programa Bolsa Família en Brasil.* Banco Interamericano de Desarrollo. Available at https://publications.iadb.org/bitstream/handle/113 19/7548/Sintesis-del-programa-Bolsa-Familia-en-Brasil.pdf?sequence=1&is Allowed=y

Calderón, F. (ed.). (2008). *Escenarios políticos en América Latina. Cuaderno de Gobernabilidad Democrática 2.* Buenos Aires: Siglo XXI.

Calderón, F. (ed.). (2012). *La protesta social en América Latina. Cuaderno de prospectiva política 1.* Buenos Aires: Siglo XXI.

Calderón, F., and Moreno, D. (2017 [2013]). Carisma, sociedad y política. In Calderón, F., *Antología esencial. Tomo I.* Buenos Aires: CLACSO.

Cardoso, F. H., and Faletto, E. (1979). *Dependency and Development in Latin America.* Translated by Marjory Mattingly Uquidi. Berkeley: University of California Press.

Castells, M. (2005). *Globalización, desarrollo y democracia: Chile en el contexto mundial.* Santiago de Chile: Fondo de Cultura Económica.

Castells, M., and Himanen, P. (eds.). (2014). *Reconceptualizing Development in the Global Information Age.* New York: Oxford University Press.

Cohen, M., Lupu, N., and Zechmeister, E. J. (eds.). (2017). *The Political Culture of Democracy in The Americas 2016-2017: A Comparative Study of Democracy and Governance.* USAID-LAPOP. Available at https://www. vanderbilt.edu/lapop/ab2016/AB2016-17_Comparative_Report_English_V2_ FINAL_090117_W.pdf

Diario el País México (2016). *Año 11 de la guerra contra el narco*. Available at https://elpais.com/especiales/2016/guerra-narcotrafico-mexico/#tab-1
Economic Commission for Latin America and the Caribbean (ECLAC). (2017). *Panorama Social de América Latina 2016*. Santiago de Chile: United Nations.
ECLAC (2018a). CEPALSTAT. *Statistics and Indicators*. Available at https://estadisticas.cepal.org/cepalstat/WEB_CEPALSTAT/estadisticasIndicadores.asp?idioma=i
ECLAC (2018b). *Panorama Social de América Latina 2017*. Santiago de Chile: United Nations.
Fajnzylber, F. (1990). *Unavoidable Industrial Restructuring in Latin America*. Durham, NC: Duke University Press.
Latinobarómetro (2010). *Informe Latinobarómetro 2010*. http://www.latinobarometro.org/documentos/LATBD_INFORME_LATINOBAROMETRO_2010.pdf
Latinobarómetro (2018). *Análisis online*. http://www.latinobarometro.org/latOnline.jsp
United Nations Development Programme (UNDP) (2004). *La democracia en América Latina. Hacia una democracia de ciudadanas y ciudadanos*. Buenos Aires: Aguilar, Altea, Taurus, Alfaguara.
United Nations Development Programme (UNDP) (2016). *Human Development Report 2006: Human Development for Everyone*. New York: UNDP.
UNDP Chile (1998). *Las paradojas de la modernización. Informe de Desarrollo humano en Chile 1998*. Santiago de Chile: UNDP. World Bank (2018). *DataBank*. Available at http://databank.worldbank.org/data/home.aspx

Chapter 2
Almaraz Paz, S. (1967). *El poder y la caída: el estaño en la historia de Bolivia*. La Paz: Los amigos del libro.
Calderón, F. (ed.). (2018). *Navegar contra el viento. América Latina en la era de la información*. San Martín: Universidad de San Martín.
Cretini, I. (2018). "Transformaciones socioeconómica en torno a la extracción de hidrocarburos no convencioanales. El caso de YPF SA en Vaca Muerta". *Identidades N°14*. Available at https://iidentidadess.files.wordpress.com/2018/08/02-identidades-14-8-2018.pdf
Di Tella, T., Di Brams, L., Reynaud, J.-D., and Touraine, A. (1966). *Huachipato et Lota. Étude sur la conscience ouvrière dans deux entreprises chiliennes*. París: Centre National de la Recherche Scientifique de París.
García Márquez, G. (1976). *The Autumn of the Patriarch*. Trans. Gregory Rabassa. New York: HarperCollins.
Giuliani, A. M., Fernández, N., Hollmann, M. A., and Ricotta, N. (2016). "La Explotación de Vaca Muerta y el Impacto Socioeconómico en la Provincia de Neuquén. El Caso de Añelo. Efectos de la Reforma de la Ley Nacional de Hidrocarburos (2014)." *Ciencias Administrativas*, 7. https://revistas.unlp.edu.ar/CADM/article/view/2069
Gras, C., and Hernández, V. (eds.). (2013). *El agro como negocio. Producción, sociedad y territorios en la globalización*. Buenos Aires: Editorial Biblos.
Guerrero, L. (2015). "El rey de la soja." *Revista Gatopardo*, 15 October. Available at https://gatopardo.com/reportajes/el-rey-de-la-soja/
Murra. J. V. (2017 [1969]). *Reciprocity and Redistribution in Andean Civilizations: The 1969 Lewis Henry Morgan Lectures*. London: HAU.

Ortiz, F. (1995). *Cuban Counterpoint: Tobacco and Sugar.* Trans. Harriet de Onís. Durham, NC: Duke University Press.

Pragier, D., and Deluca, J. P. (forthcoming). "Minería del litio en el Salar de Olaroz. In Calderón, F. (ed.). *Extractivismo informacional y territorialidades en Argentina. Un estudio comparativo sobre el litio en Olaroz, el gas y el petróleo en Vaca Muerta y la soja en Casares.* San Martín: Programa de innovación, desarrollo y multiculturalismo, Universidad de San Martín.

Svampa, M., and Viale, J. (2014). *Maldesarrollo. La Argentina del extractivismo y el despojo.* Buenos Aires: Katz Editores.

Ugarte, M. (2010 [1922]). *La patria grande.* Madrid: Editorial Internacional (Reprinted by Capital Intelectual S.A.). Available at http://www.elforjista.com/Manuel%20Ugarte%20-%20La%20Patria%20Grande.pdf

United Nations Development Programme (UNDP) (2006). *Human Development Report 2006: Beyond Scarcity: Power, Poverty and the Global Water Crisis.* New York: Palgrave Macmillan.

United Nations Development Programme (UNDP) (2007). *Human Development Report 2007-8: Fighting Climate Change: Human Solidarity in a Divided World.* New York: Palgrave Macmillan.

Wahren, J. (2011). "Territorios insurgentes. La dimensión territorial de los movimientos sociales en América Latina." *IX Jornadas de sociología. Facultad de Ciencias Sociales, Universidad de Buenos Aires.* http://cdsa.aacademica.org/000-034/665.pdf

Wahren, J. (forthcoming). "El Extractivismo Agrícola Informacional en la Argentina: el caso de Los Grobo y las disputas territoriales socioambientales en la era de la información". In Calderón, F. (ed.). *Extractivismo informacional y territorialidades en Argentina. Un estudio comparativo sobre el litio en Olaroz, el gas y el petróleo en Vaca Muerta y la soja en Casares.* San Martín: Programa de innovación, desarrollo y multiculturalismo, Universidad de San Martín.

Chapter 3

"Año 11 de la guerra contra el narco." *El País*.https://elpais.com/especiales/2016/guerra-narcotrafico-mexico/#tab-1

Bureau for International Narcotics and Law Enforcement Affairs (2018). *International Narcotics Control Strategy Report. Vol. I. Drug and Chemical Control.* Washington, DC: United States Department of State. Available at http://www.state.gov/documents/organization/278759.pdf

"Con la caída de Los Monos, dos familias narco se disputan el poder en Rosario a sangre y fuego." (2018). *Infobae*, January 9. Available at https://www.infobae.com/sociedad/policiales/2018/01/09/con-la-caida-de-los-monos-dos-familias-narco-se-disputan-el-poder-en-rosario-a-sangre-y-fuego/

Escobar, D. (2014). *Una ruta de trabajo para abordar la economía y dinámica criminal en América Latina. XIII Jornadas de Investigación de la Facultad de Ciencias Sociales, Universidad de la República.* Montevideo, September 15–17. Available at http://cienciassociales.edu.uy/wp-content/uploads/2014/09/Ponencia-Una-ruta-de-trabajo-para-abordar-la-econom%C3%ADa-y-din%C3%A1mica-criminal-en-Am%C3%A9-Escobar-diaz.pdf

García Márquez, G. (1997). *News of a Kidnapping.* Trans. Edith Grossman. New York: Vintage.

Haken, J. (2011). *Transnational Crime in the Developing World.* Global Financial

Integrity. Available at https://www.gfintegrity.org/wp-content/uploads/2014/05/gfi_transnational_crime_high-res.pdf

INEGI (2018). *Tasa de defunciones por homicidio por cada 100 mil habitantes (Casos por cada 100 mil habitantes)*. Available at http://www.beta.inegi.org.mx/app/buscador/default.html?q=homicidios#tabMCcollapse-Indicadores

Jaitman, L. (ed.). (2017). *Los costos del crimen y la violencia. Nueva evidencia y hallazgos en América Latina y el Caribe*. Washington, DC: Banco Interamericano de Desarrollo (BID). Available at https://publications.iadb.org/bitstream/handle/11319/8133/Los-costos-del-crimen-y-de-la-violencia-nueva-evidencia-y-hallazgos-en-America-Latina-y-el-Caribe.pdf

Latinobarómetro (2018). *Análisis online*. Available at http://www.latinobarometro.org/latOnline.jsp

National Center on Drug Abuse (2018). *Overdose Death Rates*. Available at https://www.drugabuse.gov/related-topics/trends-statistics/overdose-death-rates

Organization of American States (2014). *The OAS Drug Report: 16 Months of Debate and Consensus*. Washington, DC: Organization of American States. Available at https://www.oas.org/docs/publications/layoutpubgagdrogas-eng-29-9.pdf

Pedrazzini, Y., and Sánchez, M. (1992). *Malandros, bandas y niños de la calle: cultura de urgencia en las metrópolis latinoamericanas*. Caracas, Venezuela: Vadell Hermanos Editores.

Sherman, M. (2018). "How it Hurts: Culture, Markets, and Pain in the U.S. Opioid Epidemic." PhD thesis, University of Southern California, Annenberg School for Communication and Journalism

Sullivan, J. (2015). "Mexico's Drug War: Cartels, Gangs, Sovereignty and the Network State." PhD thesis, Open University of Catalonia.

United Nations Office on Drugs and Crime (UNODC) (2013). *Global Study on Homicide. Trends, Context, Data*. Vienna: UNODC. Available at https://www.unodc.org/documents/gsh/pdfs/2014_GLOBAL_HOMICIDE_BOOK_web.pdf

UNODC (2018). *UNODC Statistics Online*. Available at https://dataunodc.un.org/crime

Chapter 4

Economic Commission for Latin America and the Caribbean (ECLAC) (2016a). Horizontes 2030. "La igualdad en el centro del desarrollo sostenible." *Trigésimo sexto período de sesiones. Ciudad de México 23 a 27 de mayo de 2016*. Santiago de Chile: ECLAC. Available at http://repositorio.cepal.org/bitstream/handle/11362/40159/4/S1600653_es.pdf

ECLAC (2016b). *La nueva revolución digital. De la Internet del consumo a la Internet de la producción*. Santiago de Chile: ECLAC. Available at http://repositorio.cepal.org/bitstream/handle/11362/38604/4/S1600780_es.pdf

ECLAC (2018). CEPALSTAT. *Statistics and Indicators*. Available at https://estadisticas.cepal.org/cepalstat/WEB_CEPALSTAT/estadisticasIndicadores.asp?idioma=i

Escobar Díaz, D. (2014). "Banco de datos sobre la economía y dinámica criminal en América Latina." In *Programa Innovación, Desarrollo y Multiculturalismo*. San Martín: Universidad de San Martín.

Glenny, M. (2008). *McMafia: Crime Without Frontiers*. London: Bodley Head.

218

Guerrero, I, López-Calva, L. F., and Walton, M. (2006). "The Inequality Trap and its Links to Low Growth in Mexico." Working Paper No. 298. Stanford Center for International Development. Stanford University. Available at https://globalpoverty.stanford.edu/sites/default/files/publications/298wp.pdf

Jordán, R., Riffo, L., and Prado, A. (eds.). (2017). *Desarrollo sostenible, urbanización y desigualdad en América Latina y el Caribe*. Santiago de Chile: ECLAC.

Latinobarómetro (2018). *Análisis online*. Available at http://www.latinobaro metro.org/latOnline.jsp

McEvoy, C., and Hideg, G. (2017). *Global Violent Deaths 2017. Time to Decide*. Geneva: Small Arms Survey, Graduate Institute of International and Development Studies. Available at http://www.smallarmssurvey.org/fileadmin/docs/U-Reports/SAS-Report-GVD2017.pdf

Mercer (2018). *Vienna Tops Mercer's 20th Quality of Living Ranking. Ranking Press Release* (March 2). Available at https://www.mercer.com/newsroom/2018-quality-of-living-survey.html

Muggah, R., and Aguirre Tobón, K. (2018). Citizen Security in Latin America: Facts and Figures. In Igarapé Institute. Strategic Paper 33, April 2018. Río de Janeiro: Instituto Igarapé. Available at https://igarape.org.br/wp-content/uploads/2018/04/Citizen-Security-in-Latin-America-Facts-and-Figures.pdf

Saviano, R. (2016). *ZeroZeroZero: Look at Cocaine and All You See is the Powder. Look Through Cocaine and You See the World*. Trans. Virginia Jewiss. New York: Penguin.

Svampa, M. (2001). *Los que ganaron. La vida en los countries y barrios privados*. Ciudad de Buenos Aires: Biblos.

Svampa, M. (2004). *La brecha urbana. Countries y barrios privados en Argentina*. Ciudad de Buenos Aires: Capital Intelectual.

United Nations Development Programme (2009). *Informe sobre Desarrollo Humano para Mercosur 2009–2010. Innovar para incluir: Los jóvenes y el desarrollo humano*. Buenos Aires: Libros del Zorzal. Available at http://www.latinamerica.undp.org/content/dam/rblac/docs/Research%20and%20Publications/RHDR_Mercosur_2009_ES.pdf

UN Habitat (2016). *World Cities Report 2016: Urbanization and Development: Emerging Futures*. Nairobi: United Nations Human Settlements Programme. Available at http://wcr.unhabitat.org/?wcr_process_download=1&download_id=117118

World Bank (2018). *DataBank*. Available at http://databank.worldbank.org/data/home.aspx

World Health Organization (2018). *Air Quality and Health*. Press Release (May 2). Available at http://www.who.int/es/news-room/fact-sheets/detail/ambient-(outdoor)-air-quality-and-health

Chapter 5

Calderón, F. (ed.). (2012). *La protesta social en América Latina. Cuaderno de prospectiva política 1*. Buenos Aires: Siglo XXI.

Calderón, F., and dos Santos, R. (1995). *Sociedades sin atajos*. Buenos Aires: Ediciones Paidós.

Calderón, F. and Szmukler, A. (2014). "Los Jóvenes en Chile, México y Brasil. Disculpe las molestias estamos cambiando el país." *Vanguardia Dossier*, 50, 89–93.

Economic Commission for Latin America and the Caribbean (ECLAC) (2016).

La nueva revolución digital. De la Internet del consumo a la Internet de la producción. Santiago de Chile: ECLAC. Available at http://repositorio.cepal. org/bitstream/handle/11362/38604/4/S1600780_es.pdf

Economic Commission for Latin America and the Caribbean (ECLAC) (2018). *Estado de la banda ancha en América Latina y el Caribe 2017.* Santiago de Chile: ECLAC. Available at http://repositorio.cepal.org/bitstream/handle/ 11362/43365/1/S1800083_es.pdf

ECLAC-UNESCO (1992). *Educación y conocimiento: eje de la transformación productiva con equidad.* Santiago de Chile: ECLAC and UNESCO. Available at https://repositorio.cepal.org/bitstream/handle/11362/2130/S9250755_es.pdf

International Telecommunication Union (ITU) (2018). *ICT Statistics Home Page-Country ICT Data.* Available at https://www.itu.int/en/ITU-D/Statistics/ Pages/stat/default.aspx

Latinobarómetro (2018). *Análisis* online. Available at http://www.latinobaro metro.org/latOnline.jsp

Rivoir, A. (2013). *Plan Ceibal e inclusión social. Perspectivas interdisciplinarias.* Montevideo: Universidad de la República/Plan Ceibal.

Szmukler, A. (2015). *Bolivianos en la diáspora. Representaciones y prácticas comunicativas en el ciberespacio.* Ciudad de Buenos Aires: Editorial Teseo.

United Nations (UN) (2017). *International Migration Report 2017. Highlights.* New York: Department of Economic and Social Affairs-United Nations Secretariat. Available at http://www.un.org/en/development/desa/population/ migration/publications/migrationreport/docs/MigrationReport2017_Highlig hts.pdf

United Nations Development Programme (UNDP) (2009). *Informe sobre Desarrollo Humano para Mercosur 2009–2010. Innovar para incluir: Los jóvenes y el desarrollo humano.* Buenos Aires: Libros del Zorzal. Available at http://www.latinamerica.undp.org/content/dam/rblac/docs/Research%20and %20Publications/RHDR_Mercosur_2009_ES.pdf

Chapter 6

Arriagada, I. (2004). "Transformaciones sociales y demográficas de las familias latinoamericanas." *Papeles de Población* 10.40: 71–95.

Bott, S., Guedes, A., Goodwin, M., and Adams Mendoza, J. (2014). *Violence against Women in Latin America and the Caribbean: A Comparative Analysis of Population-Based Data from 12 Countries.* Washington, DC: Pan-American Health Organization and Centers for Disease Control and Prevention. Available at https://www.paho.org/hq/dmdocuments/2014/Violence1.24-WE B-25-febrero-2014.pdf

Cabella, W. (1998). "La evolución del divorcio en Uruguay, 1950–1995," *Notas de Población*, XXVI 67/68, 209–45.

ECLAC (2018). CEPALSTAT. *Statistics and Indicators.* Available at https:// estadisticas.cepal.org/cepalstat/WEB_CEPALSTAT/estadisticasIndicadores.as p?idioma= i.

Gammage, S. (1998). "La dimensión de género en la pobreza, la desigualdad y la reforma macroeconómica en América Latina." In Ganuza, E., Taylor, L., and Morley, S., *Política macroeconómica y pobreza en América Latina y el Caribe.* Madrid: Mundi-Prensa Libros. Available at https://repositorio.cepal.org/bit- stream/handle/11362/31164/S301441G211_es.pdf?sequence=1&isAllowed=y

Geldstein, R. (1999). *Los roles de género en la crisis: mujeres como principal sostén económico del hogar.* Buenos Aires: Centro de Estudios de Población.

Gutiérrez, E., and Osorio, P. (2008). "Modernización y transformaciones de las familias como procesos del condicionamiento social de dos generaciones." *Última Década* 29: 103–35.

Valdés, T., and Valdés, X. (eds.). (2005). *Familia y Vida Privada ¿Transformaciones, tensiones, resistencias y nuevos sentidos?* Santiago de Chile: Facultad Latinoamericana de Ciencias Sociales.

Chapter 7

Albó, X., and Layme, F. (1984). Introduction. In Bertonio, L. *Vocabulario de la Lengua Aymara.* Cochabamba: Centro de Estudios de la Realidad Económica y Social de Cochabamba, Instituto Francés de Estudios Andinos de Lima, and Museo Nacional de Etnografía y Folklore.

Bertonio, L. (1984). *Vocabulario de la Lengua Aymara.* Cochabamba: Centro de Estudios de la Realidad Económica y Social de Cochabamba, Instituto Francés de Estudios Andinos de Lima, and Museo Nacional de Etnografía y Folklore.

Chinchilla, P. (ed.). (2010). *Los jesuitas formadores de ciudadanos. La educación dentro y fuera de sus colegios, siglos XVI–XXI.* Mexico City: Universidad Iberoamericana.

Droz, J. (1972). "Les Republiques des Guaranies: Les utopies socialistes a la aube des temps modernes." In Droz, J. (ed.). *Histoire générale du socialisme.* Vol. 1. Paris: Presses Universitaires de France.

Inglehart, R., Haerpfer, C., Moreno, A., Welzel, C., Kizilova, K., Diez-Medrano, J., Lagos, M., Norris, P., Ponarin, E., Puranen, B., et al. (eds.). (2014). *World Values Survey: Round Six Country-Pooled Datafile.* Madrid: JD Systems Institute. Available at http://www.worldvaluessurvey.org/WVS DocumentationWV6.jsp

Latinobarómetro (2018). *El Papa Francisco y la religión en América Latina. Latinobarómetro 1995–2017.* Santiago de Chile: Corporación Latinobarómetro. Available at https://www.cooperativa.cl/noticias/site/artic/20180112/asocfile/20180112124342/f00006494_religion_chile_america_lat ina_2017.pdf

Mallimaci, F. (ed.). (2008). *Modernidad religión y memoria.* Buenos Aires: Ediciones Colihue Universidad.

Maoz, Z., and Henderson, E. A. (2013). "The World Religion Dataset, 1945–2010: Logic, Estimates, and Trends." *International Interactions*, 39: 265–291.

Morello, G. SJ (2010). "Ciudadanos católicos en la ciudad postsecular." In Chinchilla, P. (ed.). *Los jesuitas formadores de ciudadanos. La educación dentro y fuera de sus colegios, siglos XVI–XXI.* Mexico City: Universidad Iberoamericana.

Strotmann, N. (2007). *¿Y, después de Aparecida, qué?* Available at http://oclacc.org/redes/teologia/files/2008/04/strotmann-norberto-9-4-07-y-despues-de-ap arecida-que_artculo_de_preparacin.pdf

Worldwide Independent Network of Market Research (WIN)/Gallup International (2012). *Global Index of Religiosity and Atheism.* Available at https://web.archive.org/web/20131021065544/http://www.wingia.com/web/files/news/14/file/14.pdf

WIN/Gallup International (2015). "Losing Our Religion? Two Thirds of People Still Claim to Be Religious." Available at https://www.west-info.eu/world-map

-of-the-most-religious-countries/win-gallup-international-losing-our-religion
-two-thirds-of-people-still-claim-to-be-religious-2015/
Worldwide Independent Network of Market Research (WIN)/Gallup
International (2017). "Religion Prevails in the World." Available at https://
web.archive.org/web/20171114113506/http://www.wingia.com/web/files/new
s/370/file/370.pdf

Chapter 8
Bengoa, J. (2009). "¿Una segunda etapa de la Emergencia Indígena en América
Latina?" *Cuadernos de Antropología Social*, 29: Available at http://www.
redalyc.org/articulo.oa?id=180913914001
Calderón, F. (2007). "Politischer Wandel und neue soziokulturelle Ordnung".
In: *Bolivien: Ein Land zum Entwickeln?. Nueva Sociedad 209*. Buenos Aires:
Nueva Sociedad.
Calderón, F., Hopenhayn, M., and Ottone, E. (1996). *Esa esquiva modernidad.
Desarrollo, ciudadanía y cultura en América Latina y el Caribe*. Caracas:
Nueva Sociedad.
Calderón, F., and Jelin, E. (1987). "Clases sociales y movimientos sociales en
América Latina. Perspectivas y realidades." *Proposiciones*, 14. Santiago de
Chile: Ediciones SUR.
Cantoni, W. (1978). "Relaciones del mapuche con la sociedad nacional chil-
ena." In UNESCO (ed.). *Raza y Clase en la Sociedad Postcolonial*. Madrid:
UNESCO.
Castedo, L. (1966). "Algunas constantes de la arquitectura barroca andina."
*Boletín del Centro de Investigaciones Histórico Estéticas de la Universidad
Central de Venezuela*, 4. Caracas: Facultad de Arquitectura y Urbanismo.
Castells, M. (2010). *The Information Age: Economy, Society, and Culture,
Volume II: The Power of Identity*, 2nd edn. Oxford: Wiley-Blackwell.
Denevan, W. (ed.). (1976). *The Native Population of the Americas in 1492*.
Madison, WI: University of Wisconsin Press.
Droz, J (1972). *La historia générale du socialisme: Tome 1*. Paris: Press
Universitaire de France.
Escobar, D. (2018). La modernización conservadora de Colombia: tensiones y
nuevas perspectivas. In F. Calderón (ed.). *Navegar contra el viento. América
Latina en la era de la información*. San Martín: UNSAM Edita.
Fuentes, C. (1992). *El espejo enterrado*. Mexico City: Fondo de Cultura
Económica.
Instituto Brasileiro de Geografia e Estatística (IBGE) (2014). *Síntese de indica-
dores sociais: umaanálise das condições de vida da população brasileira 2014*.
Río de Janeiro: IBGE. Available at https://biblioteca.ibge.gov.br/visualizacao/
livros/liv91983.pdf
Instituto de Pesquisa Econômica Aplicada. (IPEA) (2015). *Políticas sociais:
acompanhamento e análise*. Brasilia: IPEA. Available at http://www.ipea.gov.
br/portal/images/stories/PDFs/politicas_sociais/bps_23_14072015.pdf
Jaccoud L. (2008). "Racismo e Republica: o debate sobre o branqueamento e a
discriminacao racial no Brasil." In Theodoro, M. (ed.). *As políticas públicas e
a desigualdade racial no Brasil: 120 anosapós a abolição*. Brasilia: IPEA.
Latin American and Caribbean Demographic Centre (CELADE) (2010).
*Observatorio Demográfico de América Latina | Demographic Observatory of
Latin America*. CELADE.

Latin American and Caribbean Demographic Centre (CELADE) (2018). *Sistema de Indicadores Sociodemográficos de Poblaciones y Pueblos Indígenas (SISPPI)*. CELADE. Available at https://redatam.org/redbin/RpWebEngine. exe/Portal?BASE=SISPPI

Le Bot, M. Y. (1997). *El sueño zapatista*. Barcelona: Anagrama.

Mayorga, F. (2018). "Bolivia: paradojas y desafíos del neodesarrollismo indígena". In Calderón, F. (ed.). *Navegar contra el viento: América Latina en la era de la información*. San Martín: UNSAM Edita.

Murra. J. V. (2017 [1969]). *Reciprocity and Redistribution in Andean Civilizations: The 1969 Lewis Henry Morgan Lectures*. London: HAU.

Olbemo, J. (2012). *La discriminación en el mercadolaboral en Brasil*. Stockholm: Institutionen för spanska, portugisiska och latinamerika studier, Stockholms Universitet. Available at http://www.diva-portal.org/smash/get/diva2:533937/ FULLTEXT01.pdf

Reed, J. (2016). *Ten Days that Shook the World*. New York: Penguin.

Ríos, F. (2012). "O protesto negro no Brasil contemporâneo (1978–2010)." *Lua Nova: Revista de Cultura e Política*, 85, 41–79.

Rosenstone, R. A. (1990). *Romantic Revolutionary: Biography of John Reed*. Cambridge, MA: Harvard University Press.

Touraine, A. (1988). *La Parole et le sang: Politique et société en Amérique latine*. Paris: Editions Odile Jacob.

Tricot, T. (2009). "El nuevo movimiento mapuche: hacia la (re)construcción del mundo y país mapuche." *POLIS, Revista de la Universidad Bolivariana*, 8 (24).

United Nations (UN) (2017). *International Migration Report 2017. Highlights*. New York: Department of Economic and Social Affairs-United Nations Secretariat. http://www.un.org/en/development/desa/population/migration/pu blications/migrationreport/docs/MigrationReport2017_Highlights.pdf

United Nations Development Programme (UNDP) (2006). *Desarrollo humano en Chile 2006. Las nuevas tecnologías ¿Un salto al futuro?* Santiago de Chile: UNDP. Available at http://desarrollohumano.cl/idh/download/informe-2006-COMPLETO.pdf

Waiselfisz, J. J. (2014). *Mapa da violencia 2014. Os jovens do Brasil*. Rio de Janeiro: Facultad Latinoamericana de Ciencias Sociales. Available at https://www.mapadaviolencia.org.br/pdf2014/Mapa2014_JovensBrasil_Preli minar.pdf

Zen, D. (2014). "Las madres de mayo brasileñas, independientes." *Diario Alfil*. June 16. Available at http://www.diarioalfil.com.ar/2014/06/16/las-madres-de-mayo-brasilenas-independientes/

Chapter 9

Araníbar, A., and Rodríguez, B. (eds.). *América Latina, ¿del neoliberalismo al neodesarrollismo? Cuaderno de Prospectiva Política 3*. Buenos Aires: Siglo XXI.

Calderón, F. (ed.). (2003). *¿Es sostenible la globalización en América Latina? Debates con Manuel Castells, 2 Vols*. Santiago de Chile: Fondo de Cultura Económica.

Calderón, F. (2012a). *América Latina y el Caribe: Tiempos de cambio. Nuevas consideraciones sociológicas sobre la democracia y el desarrollo*. Buenos Aires: Teseo, Facultad Latinoamericana de Ciencias Sociales.

Calderón, F. (ed.). (2012b). *La protesta social en América Latina. Cuaderno de prospectiva política 1. Buenos Aires*: Siglo XXI.

Calderón, F. (ed.). (2018). *Navegar contra el viento. América Latina en la era de la información*. San Martín: Universidad de San Martín.

Castells, M. (2012). *Redes de indignación y esperanza: los movimientos sociales en la era de internet*. Madrid: Alianza Editorial.

Castells, M. (2013). *Communication Power*. Oxford: Oxford University Press.

Castells, M. (2014). "El poder de las redes." *Vanguardia Dossier*, 50, 6–13.

Castells, M. et al. (2017). *Another Economy is Possible. Culture and Economy in a Time of Crisis*. Cambridge: Polity.

dos Santos, M. (1994). *¿Qué queda de la representación política?* Buenos Aires: Consejo Latinoamericano de Ciencias Sociales.

Economic Commission for Latin America and the Caribbean (ECLAC) (1990). *Educación y conocimiento, eje de la transformación productiva con equidad*. Santiago de Chile: ECLAC.

International Federation of Journalists (IFJ) (2017). *Concentración de Medios en América Latina: Su impacto en el derecho a la comunicación*. IFJ Latin America. Available at http://www.ifj.org/index.php?eID=dumpFile&t=f&f=76 88&token=e7188af599baab408315484a15fac437978bbeb2

LAPOP (2014) *Barómetro de las Américas 2014*. Latinamerican Public Opinion Project. Available at https://www.vanderbilt.edu/lapop/ab2014.php

Latinobarómetro (2015). *La confianza en América Latina: 20 años de opinión pública latinoamericana*. Available at http://www.latinobarometro.org/ LATDocs/F00005085-INFORME_LB_LA_CONFIANZA_1995_2015.pdf

Morales, E., Palmiciano, C., and Valera, C. (2017). "Anónimos: ¿un nuevo movimiento social?" M.A. Thesis in Human Rights and Democracy. San Martín: Universidad Nacional de San Martín.

Moscovici, S. (1993). Toward a Social Psychology of Science. *Journal for the Theory of Social Behaviour*, 23 (4), 343–74.

Nogueira, M. A. (2013). *As Ruas e a Democracia. Ensaios Sobre o Brasil Contemporâneo*. Rio de Janeiro: Contraponto.

Thompson, J. (1995). *Media and Modernity: A Social Theory of the Media*. Cambridge: Polity.

Touraine, A. (1994). *Qu'est-ce que la démocratie?* Paris: Fayard.

United Nations Development Programme (UNDP) (2003). *Informe sobre Desarrollo Humano 1993. Los Objetivos de Desarrollo del Milenio: un pacto entre las naciones para eliminar la pobreza*. Madrid: Ediciones Mundi-Prensa.

Chapter 10

Adimark GfK (2011). *Encuesta: evaluación gestión del gobierno. Informe mensual agosto 2011*. Available at https://www.adimark.cl/es/estudios/document os/08_ev_gob_agos_2011.pdf

Aramayo, A. (2018). "Análisis de conflictividad del Tipnis y potencialidades de paz." *Cuaderno de investigación*, 1.1. La Paz: UNIR.

Bebbington, A. (2011). "Social Conflict and Emergent Institutions: Hypotheses from Piura, Peru." In Bebbington, A. (ed.) *Social Conflict, Economic Development, and Extractive Industry: Evidence from South America*. London: Routledge, pp. 67–88.

Calderón, F. (ed.). (1985). *Los movimientos sociales ante la crisis*. Buenos Aires: Consejo Latinoamericano de Ciencia Sociales (CLACSO).

Calderón, F. (ed.). (2009). *Movimientos Socioculturales en América Latina. Cuaderno de Gobernabilidad Democrática 4*. Buenos Aires: Siglo XXI.

Calderón, F. (ed.). (2012). *La protesta social en América Latina. Cuaderno de prospectiva política 1*. Buenos Aires: Siglo XXI.

Calderón, F. and Szmukler, A. (2014). "Los Jóvenes en Chile, México y Brasil. Disculpe las molestias estamos cambiando el país." *Vanguardia Dossier*, 50, 89–93.

Castells, M. (2012). *Redes de indignación y esperanza: los movimientos sociales en la era de internet*. Madrid: Alianza Editorial.

Castells, M. (2015). *Networks of Outrage and Hope: Social Movements in the Internet Age*, 2nd edn. Cambridge: Polity.

Fundación Tierra (2018). *Cuestión Agraria*, 4. Available at http://ftierra.org/index.php/publicacion/revistas/176-cuestion-agraria-n-4-tipnis

Humphreys Bebbington, D. (2011). "State-Indigenous Tensions over Hydrocarbon Expansion in the Bolivian Chaco." In Bebbington, A. (ed.) *Social Conflict, Economic Development, and Extractive Industry: Evidence from South America*. London: Routledge, pp. 134–52.

International Telecommunication Union (ITU) (2018). *ICT Statistics Home Page*. Available at https://www.itu.int/en/ITU-D/Statistics/Pages/default.aspx

Latinobarómetro (2010). *Informe Latinobarómetro 2010*. Santiago de Chile. Available at http://www.latinobarometro.org/documentos/LATBD_INFORME_LATINOBAROMETRO_2010.pdf

Latinobarómetro (2017). *Informe Latinobarómetro 2017*. Santiago de Chile. Available at http://www.latinobarometro.org/LATDocs/F00006433-InfLatinobarometro2017.pdf

Monteverde, A., Carrillo, R., and Esteve del Valle, M. (2013). "#YoSoy132: ¿Un nuevo paradigma en la política mexicana?" Washington, DC: Latin American Studies Association Conference, May.

Nogueira, M. A. (2013). *As Ruas e A Democracia. Ensaios sobre o Brasil contemporáneo*. Brasilia: Fundacao Astrojildo Pereira.

Ochoa, M., Ducrot Anguita, P., and Vallarino, R. (2017). "Ni una menos." Work completed for the seminar *Movimientos socioculturales en América Latina*. M.A. Program in Human Rights and Democratization. San Martín: Universidad Nacional de San Martín.

Palermo, V., Aboud, L., and Musseri, A. (2009). "El gobernador pasó en helicóptero. La Asamblea Ciudadana Ambiental de Gualeguaychú en el conflicto por las papeleras." In Calderón, F. (ed.). *Movimientos Socioculturales en América Latina. Cuaderno de Gobernabilidad Democrática 4*. Buenos Aires: Siglo XXI.

Rival, L. (2011). "Planning Development Futures in the Ecuadorian Amazon: the expanding oil frontier and the Yasuní-ITT Initiative. In: Bebbington, A. (ed.) *Social Conflict, Economic Development, and Extractive Industry: Evidence from South America*. London: Routledge.

Rolnik, R. (ed.). (2013). *Cidades Rebeldes. Passe livre e as manifestacoes que tomaram as ruas do Brasil*. Sao Paulo: Boitempo-Carta Maior.

United Nations Development Programme (UNDP) (2007). *Human Development Report 2007/8. Fighting Climate Change: Human Solidarity in a Divided World*. New York: Palgrave Macmillan.

UNDP (2009). *Informe sobre Desarrollo Humano para Mercosur 2009–2010*.

Innovar para incluir: Los jóvenes y el desarrollo humano. Buenos Aires: Libros del Zorzal. Available at http://www.latinamerica.undp.org/content/dam/rblac/docs/Research%20and%20Publications/RHDR_Mercosur_2009_ES.pdf

World Bank (2018). *DataBank*. http://databank.worldbank.org/data/home.aspx

World Health Organization (2014). *Manual de práctica clínica para un aborto seguro*. Geneva: World Health Organization. Available at http://apps.who.int/iris/bitstream/handle/10665/134747/9789243548715_spa.pdf;jsessionid=BA75EA0EA2896A789881435B45A81D32?sequence=1

World Health Organization (2017). "Worldwide, an Estimated 25 Million Unsafe Abortions Occur Each Year." Press Release. Available at http://www.who.int/news-room/detail/28-09-2017-worldwide-an-estimated-25-million-unsafe-abortions-occur-each-year

Chapter 11

Ballon, E. (2018). *Perú: en la telaraña de la incertidumbre*. Lima, DESCO.

Calderón, F. (ed.). (2003). *¿Es sostenible la globalización en América Latina?*, Santiago de Chile: Fondo de Cultura Económica.

Calderón, F., and Castells, M. (2014). "Development, Democracy, and Social Change in Chile." In Castells, M., and Himanen, P. (eds). *Reconceptualizing Development in the Global Information Age*. New York: Oxford University Press, pp. 175–204.

Cárdenas, G., García, S., Salas, A., and Nieto, L. (2016). *Análisis de la corrupción y la gobernanza en América Latina*, Instituto L.R. Klein, Universidad Autónoma de Madrid.

Cardoso, F. H., and Faletto, E. (1979). *Dependency and Development in Latin America*. Trans. Marjory Mattingly Uquidi. Berkeley: University of California Press.

Cardoso, F. H., Darcy De Oliveira, M., and Fausto, S. (2018). *La crisis política en Brasil*. São Paulo: Companhia Das Letras.

Castells, M. (1997). *The Power of Identity*. Oxford: Blackwell Publishing.

Castells, M. (2005). *Globalización, desarrollo y democracia: Chile en el contexto mundial*. Santiago de Chile: Fondo de Cultura Económica

Castells, M (2010). *The Information Age: Economy, Society, and Culture, Volume II: The Power of Identity*, 2nd edn. Oxford: Wiley-Blackwell.

Castells, M. (2013). *Communication Power*. Oxford: Oxford University Press.

Castells, M. (ed.). (2018). *Europe's Crises*. Cambridge: Polity.

Castells, M. (2019). *Rupture: The Crisis of Liberal Democracy*. Trans. Rosie Marteau. Cambridge: Polity.

Correa, S. (2018). Entrevista con Sergio Ramírez. *Diario El Tiempo de Colombia*, 2 June. Available at https://www.eltiempo.com/mundo/latinoamerica/entrevista-con-el-escritor-sergio-ramirez-sobre-el-sandinismo-en-nicaragua-y-la-salida-de-ortega-225758

Gonzalez, F. (2014). *Poder y violencia en Colombia*, Bogotá: Odeacap-Cinep-Cociencias.

InfoLEG (2018). Ley No. 23.928 de Convertibilidad del Austral. Información Legislativa. Ministerio de Justicia y Derechos Humanos de Argentina. Available at http://servicios.infoleg.gob.ar/infolegInternet/anexos/0-4999/328/texact.htm

Knight, A. (2017). "El Estado en América Latina desde la independencia." *Economía y Política*. 1.1: 7–30.

Latinobarómetro (2018). *Análisis online.* Available at http://www.latinobarom etro.org/latOnline.jsp

Los cuadernos de las coimas: uno por uno, todos los registros del chofer Oscar Centeno. Reportaje especial de *La Nación.* Available at https://www.lanacion. com.ar/2159363-cuadernos

Miguez, D., Misse, M., and Isla, A. (eds.) (2018). *Estado y crimen organizado en América Latina.* Santander: La Vorágine.

Ravelo, R. (2018). *Los Incomodos 2. Los Gobernadores que amenazan el futuro político del PRI.* Mexico City: Temas de Hoy.

Transparency International (2018). "Comparación IPC 2009–2017." Available at https://transparencia.org.es/wp-content/uploads/2018/02/comparacion_ipc-2009-2017.pdf

Chapter 12

Castells, M. (ed.). (2018). *Europe's Crises.* Cambridge: Polity.

Castells, M. (2019). *Rupture: The Crisis of Liberal Democracy.* Cambridge: Polity.

Castells, M. et al. (2017). *Another Economy is Possible. Culture and Economy in a Time of Crisis.* Cambridge: Polity.

Touraine, A. (1994). *Qu'est-ce que la démocratie?* Paris: Fayard.

United Nations Development Programme (UNDP) (2004). *La democracia en América Latina.* New York: UND2P.

FIGURE SOURCES

1.1: Authors' own calculations, based on data in ECLAC, 2017

1.3: Authors' own calculations, based on data from Latinobarómetro

3.1: Authors' own calculations, based on data from UNODC (https://dataunodc.un.org/crime/intentional-homicide-victims)

3.2: Authors' own calculations based on data obtained from the National Institute on Drug Abuse.

3.3: Authors' own calculations based on data from Latinobarómetro

3.4: Jaitman (2017: 29).

4.1: Authors' calculations, based on data from the UN Habitat World Cities Report, 2016

4.2: Authors' calculations, based on data from the World Bank (2018) https://data.worldbank.org/indicator/SP.URB.TOTL.IN.ZS

4.3: Jordán et al. (2017)

4.4: Authors' own calculation, based on the World Health Organization's Global Urban Ambient Air Pollution Database: http://www.who.int/phe/health_topics/outdoorair/databases/who-aap-database-may2016.xlsx?ua=1

5.1: ECLAC (2018) *State of Broadband in Latin America and the Caribbean, 2017*

5.2: Authors' own calculations, based on data from Latinobarómetro (2018)

5.3: Report on Human Development for Mercosur, by the United

Nations Development Programme, 2009–2010: *Innovar para incluir: Los jóvenes y el desarrollo humano* (2009)

5.4: United Nations Department of Economic and Social Affairs (2018)

6.1: Authors' own findings based on data from ECLAC (2018)

6.2: Authors' own calculations, based on data from Arriagada (2004)

7.1: Maoz and Henderson (2013), http://www.correlatesofwar.org/data-sets/world-religion-data/world-religion-data-v1-1

8.1: Del Popolo (2017)

8.2: Instituto Brasileiro de Geografia e Estatística (IBGE)-Síntese de Indicadores Sociais (2014)

8.3: Instituto Brasileiro de Geografía e Estatística (IBGE)-Síntese de Indicadores Sociais (2014)

9.1: Authors' own calculations, based on tata from *Digital in 2018: We Are Social* (2018)

9.2: *La confianza en América Latina, 1995–2015* (Corporación Latinobarómetro, 2015)

10.1: Authors' own calculations, based on data from *Cuaderno 1 prospectiva política – La protesta social en América Latina*

10.2: Authors' own calculations based on data from *Cuaderno 1 prospectiva política – La protesta social en América Latina*

11.1: Authors' own calculations based on data from Latinobarómetro (2018)

11.2: Authors' own calculations, based on data from Transparency International (2018)

INDEX